Life As an Air Force Wife

by

Anita Hamilton

ISBN: 1-4107-4608-9 (e-book)
ISBN: 1-4107-4607-0 (Paperback)
ISBN: 1-4107-4606-2 (Dust Jacket)

This book is printed on acid free paper.

1stBooks – rev. 06/25/03

Dedicated to the memory of

Isaac Madison Hamilton
Lt Col USAF (Ret)
1928-1997

Ike and His Beloved F-51 Mustang

Table of Contents

Chapter 1 – How I Became an Air Force Wife.................................... 1

Chapter 2 – Basic Pilot Training..................................... 14

Chapter 3 – Advanced Pilot Training 23

Chapter 4 – Combat Crew Training.................................. 29

Chapter 5 – Going Overseas 33

Chapter 6 - The "Police Action" in Korea 36

Chapter 7 – Back Home Again – Part 1................................ 49

Chapter 8 - Operation "Tiger" 52

Chapter 9 - The Long, Long Trailer.................................. 54

Chapter 10 - AFROTC-FSU – Part 1..................................... 60

Chapter 11 - The Son of Promise....................................... 64

Chapter 12 - AFROTC – FSU – Part 2 71

Chapter 13 - Shaw AFB, SC.................................... 75

Chapter 14 - Squadron Officers School – Part 1.............................. 78

Chapter 15 - The Voodoo and Operation "Mobile Zebra" 82

Chapter 16 - Shaw AFB – Part 2 91

Chapter 17 - Survival Training, Stead AFB, Nevada 94

Chapter 18 - Phalsbourg AB, France - Part 1 97

Chapter 19 – The Port Call 99

Chapter 20 - Phalsbourg AB, France - Part 2 104

Chapter 21 – World Travelers 120

Chapter 22 - Shifting Gears 127

Chapter 23 – The *Mademoiselle* from Toul-Rosières.................... 131

Chapter 24 - The Land of the Big BX 147

Chapter 25 - The Boondoggle.. 155

Chapter 26 - Operation *"Kinderlift"* 161

Chapter 27 - Back Home Again, Part 2 166

Chapter 28 - USAF Academy, Colorado – Part 1 177

Chapter 29 – The ZI Field Trip... 195

Chapter 30 – USAF Academy – Part 2.. 200

Chapter 31 – Squadron Officer School – Part 2 208

Chapter 32 - Valparaiso, FL, and Udorn AB, Thailand.................. 237

Epilogue.. 255

Appendix.. 260

About the Author 265

Chapter 1 – How I Became an Air Force Wife

Although I didn't realize it at the time, I was on the way to becoming an Air Force wife when, in September of 1948, my husband of eight months walked into our Vet Village apartment at Southwestern Louisiana Institute in Lafayette and surprised me with the declaration, "Well, I joined the R. O. T. C."

"What?!" I exclaimed. "Why in the world?"

"Well, for one thing, they're going to pay me $27.90 a month. They are just forming the detachment and don't have any upper classmen. They were looking for veterans to be their upper classmen."

Well, that was a horse of a different color! $27.90 a month seemed like a small fortune to me, as we were going to have to live on the monthly $105 Ike would be receiving through the G. I. Bill because of the fourteen months he had spent enlisted in the Navy at the end of WWII. He had remained in the Naval Reserves until 1948; but, although it was to help him out for pay purposes when he retired, he was receiving nothing from that at the moment. So, though I wasn't overly thrilled, I uncharacteristically shut up.

Ike Hamilton already had a lot of experience under his young belt. Since his birthday was in February, he had begun the first grade as soon as he turned six at the beginning of the second semester of school in his hometown of Lake Charles. Then somewhere along the line, he had gone to Summer School and picked up the other half-year. Since, in our day, Louisiana didn't have but eleven years of school, he had graduated from High School at the ripe old age of sixteen. He had had two years in college, a year in the Navy, a year in the Merchant Marines; and now, barely out of his teens, was a married man.

The Air Force had had a venerable history as the Army Air Corps in two wars but had only become a separate branch of the U. S.

Armed Forces in 1947. The AFROTC detachment at SLI was just forming in the fall semester of 1948. Since it was a small school (about 2,700 students at the time), the detachment was small, too, the assigned AF personnel consisting of Major Richard T. W. Rivers, the Professor of Air Science and Tactics (PAST); Major Harley Cox, Executive Officer; Capt. Stanworth Verdier, Commandant of Cadets; Warrant Officer Earl Flannagan; Lt. Paul Robinson, Public Information Officer, and three enlisted men. They still wore, as did the cadets, the US Army uniforms *à la* WWII, that is, "Ike" jackets (the OD cropped jackets affected by General "Ike" Eisenhower) and Army Pinks. When about a year later Lieutenant Paul Robinson came out on the field in his new Air Force blues (with a waistline-less blouse), we thought that uniform was the funniest looking thing we had ever seen.

This Wing of USAFROTC was to have two squadrons that first year, three the next. So the veterans applying for the upperclassman positions had to try out for them. I'm not sure what all the criteria were, but I know that one of them was their ability to give close-order drill commands in a voice that would carry well. Ike's soft, mellifluous voice notwithstanding, he was able to shout out the commands, projecting his voice so as to be heard at a distance. His experience as a Platoon Commander in Navy Boot Camp stood him in good stead, also; so he was chosen as Commander of "A" Squadron with the rank of Cadet Lieutenant Colonel, with Major "Bill" Bacle as his Adjutant. Earl Barnett (not a veteran), who had sailed on a Standard Oil Tanker with Ike the year before, was given the rank of Corporal and became Squadron A's Guidon Bearer. James "Bruce" Broussard was chosen as the Wing Commander and given the rank of Cadet Col., with Lt. Col. Bill Dempsey as his Exec, and Major Jim Ardoin as Wing Adjutant. Squadron "B" was headed up by Lt. Col. F. G. LaRose, with Major R. J. Rice as his adjutant.

Three, and later four, female "sponsors" were voted in, one for the Wing and one for each of the squadrons. When Emily Scariano, the girl elected sponsor of Squadron A, left school at the end of the first year, I was elected to take her place and given the rank of Honorary Lt. Col. So, I, too, had my wool "Ike" jacket and "pink" skirt and learned to march (in the Louisiana heat) along with the guys. The sponsors were supposed to have marched in the President's parade when the first cadets were graduated; but at the last minute, somebody thought better of the idea; and we didn't get to march.

George Larrieu was also an ROTC friend of ours there. He was leader of one of the two flights in Sq. "A"; and was, in addition, an excellent amateur photographer, taking all the pictures of the cadet officers and us sponsor-gals. He even made <u>me</u> look glamorous in my uniform.

Ike and Anita Hamilton in Their AFROTC Uniforms
(Photos by George Larrieu)

We had George take some portrait shots of us in our wedding clothes about a year after our marriage, mainly because we didn't have any wedding pictures. He wasn't pleased with them, so didn't charge us for them; but we loved them, and I still cherish them. Ike later ran into him at Hickam AB, Hawaii, where he was base Information Officer.

Newlyweds Ike and Anita Hamilton (Photo by George Larrieu)

Since Ike had never really been what you would call a scholar, this idea of studying to make decent grades in college was something new to him, occasioned by his having taken on Family Responsibilities. Oh, he wasn't dumb at all—just unmotivated and lazy when it came to attending class, getting assignments in, studying for tests, and even staying awake in class. Fatherless from age 11, Ike had been the only child left at home. His sisters, Floyd (after their father) and Lydia Blanche, had already finished college and were out working on their own. The oldest, his brother, Randall, had sixteen years on him and was already away at LSU when little Madison (as the family called Ike) came along. Randall had graduated as a Civil Engineer and served in the Pacific in WWII. Ike's father, Floyd Hamilton, had also been a Civil Engineer; and in addition to teaching and serving on the School Board in several Southwestern Louisiana towns, had built many of the highways in Louisiana.

4

So, when the time came for Ike to go to college, he had no idea what he wanted his major to be. His mother assumed he would follow in his father's and brother's footsteps and become an Engineer. But he said, "That's not for me." I'm not sure why he didn't want to do that; but I suspect it was because he didn't want to have to measure up to standards he wasn't sure he could maintain. I'm surprised he didn't major in Music, since he loved classical music and played the violin very well. Later he told me that he didn't think he was good enough to be concert stage quality and didn't want a music career under any other circumstances. But he had no idea what major to choose. So his mother, Madeline, ("Mom" to everyone), made that decision for him—he would become a Businessman, majoring in Commerce. Period. So off to LSU he went.

It was a struggle for Mom just to keep him there since she hadn't been left very well off when widowed in 1939. She worked in a dentist's office and borrowed money to send Ike to college. He also had to work—if you can call the job he was given "work." He maintained the Listening Room in the Music Building. The 78 RPM records of the day were very delicate and had to be handled with great care. So when music students were given listening assignments, he was the only one who was allowed to handle the records. He got a music education just playing their assignments for them; and, in addition, when no one else was in the room, he could listen to any of the thousands of records in that library. He was in Hog Heaven.

Ike soon learned that he had not been cut out to be an Accountant. He later said, "I hated putting little numbers into little boxes." So, immature kid that he was, and away from home for the first time, he starting sloughing off in his schoolwork while enjoying his other great love—Track. At Lake Charles High School, he had garnered quite a few honors for himself in Distance Running—first Cross Country, then the Two Mile and, later on, the Mile. Since his feet were hard to fit for track shoes (11-1/2 AA), he ran barefooted on the grass tracks. Unwittingly, he was thereby contributing to the future back problems he was to suffer, as he became flat-footed.

At LSU Ike joined Coach Bernie Moore's track team (this time with proper shoes and arch supports) and became a valuable member of the team, running first the Mile and later the Half-Mile and even later, the Quarter-Mile and 220-yard dash. He even lettered that year. Naturally, there were frequent away meets, for which he would have to miss Friday and Saturday classes, even sometimes Thursday ones. Since he wasn't diligent about making up his schoolwork, his grades predictably fell. At the end of his first year at LSU (1944-45), he didn't even bother to go in to take his finals; so that semester was totally down the tubes. Since you can't go back to a State school in Louisiana for a year after flunking out, and since WWII, although winding down, was still going on, he decided it was time to join the war effort.

~~~

I'm not sure whether Mom had to sign the papers for him to join up (he was still only 17) or whether he used the Emancipation Papers he had gotten her to sign sometime after he left home. It always seemed ironic to me since, either way, she had to sign her name; so how emancipated was that? At any rate, on June 6th, 1945, he scrooched up his toes enough not to reveal to the doctors his flat-footed condition and passed the Navy physical, his actual entry date into active service being 27 June. He was sent to San Diego for boot camp, graduating from Basic Training on 8 September, and on 20 February 1946, from Cook and Bakers School. Ike and his new-found California buddy, Rod Ibers, had signed up for that school mainly because the working hours were shorter—bake a few hours in the cool of the early morning, have several hours off during the day, and work another couple of hours in the evening. After they arrived at their assignment at the Naval Station in Seattle, Washington, they even moonlighted working for a retired Army Colonel who lived out on Bainbridge Island in Puget Sound. They did everything from cleaning out his chicken coops to serving as butlers and waiters at his parties, making good wages and having the use of his outboard motorboat in their spare time.
~~~

Ike with Buddy Rod Ibers in the Navy

With WWII having ended, Ike and Rod mustered out of the Navy together on August 15th, 1946. Ike had saved up enough money to buy himself quite a few 78 RPM records and his Pride and Joy: a Philco tabletop radio-phonograph combination. Saving their Mustering-Out pay, they hitchhiked down to Rod's home in the Los Angeles area; then Ike hitchhiked on home to Lake Charles by himself. In those days it was still safe and respectable to hitchhike. Anyone in uniform was quickly picked up. When not in uniform, Ike would dress in nice trousers, sport jacket, white shirt and tie, and carry a small suitcase, whether he needed it or not, because it was more respectable-looking to have a suitcase. Since he had that clean-cut, Joe College look, he never had any trouble getting rides.

~~~
~~~

September, 1946, and back to LSU. Same Song, Second Verse. What to major in? Would you believe Ike Hamilton signed up a <u>second</u> time for the College of Commerce? Why, I'll never know; but that's what he did. Back into track again, he lettered for the second time. This time his dilatory study habits were exacerbated by the fact that he soon acquired a girl friend. He and I met at the Baptist Student Center through mutual friends. That blond wavy hair and the beautiful purple track sweater with the gold winged track shoe on the front played no small part in my attraction to him. We started dating in November of 1946 in my freshman year at LSU. Needless to say, Ike didn't spend a lot of time on his lessons. So, to shorten the story somewhat, at the end of the 1946-47 school year, he failed to take his finals again and, for the second time, flunked out of LSU.

Anita Rivers and Ike Hamilton – First Big Date
January, 1947, Court of the Two Sisters, New Orleans

This time Ike wound up sailing on a Standard Oil tanker, which made runs from the Gulf Coast ports around the Florida peninsula up to East Coast ports and back. Those round trips took about two weeks each; and I would occasionally get to see him when the ship came into

Baton Rouge, my hometown. The summer of 1947, before he had left, we had become engaged. He was able to save quite a bit of money because he wasn't a carouser as were many of the seamen with whom he worked. When the ship would go into port in Boston or New York, he would always go to a play or a concert—anything to do with his beloved music. But whenever his ship went into any other port, he would work extra watches, being paid by his shipmates who liked to hit the bars and houses of prostitution.

~~~

One cold Friday in January, 1948, his ship, which was supposed to have gone to Houston or Lake Charles, unexpectedly came into Baton Rouge, where I lived. LSU was between semesters, and I had a temporary job working in the Department of Commerce and Industry in the Louisiana Capitol Building. When Ike called me up at work, I was naturally surprised and even more so when he said, "Let's get married!" We had been planning to get married in June; so this was early. But we were in love; so I said, "Okay!" So we scrambled around like crazy the next day getting ready for the wedding in the First Baptist Church parlor that night, January 31, 1948. I thought things went very well for a small family wedding. I had a new suit and hat; we had flowers and a nice home reception that Mother had smoothly put together. The only thing no one thought to do was have a photographer there!

Ike managed to sweet-talk the secretary at Standard Oil into leaving his name off the duty roster for the next ship going out but not to put it completely at the bottom of the waiting list. So we were together three whole weeks before the next ship came into Baton Rouge and he was called back to duty. I saw him a sum total of twice between then and August—once when the ship came into Baton Rouge and once when it went into Galveston and I was able to meet him there during my Spring Break. I suppose we were in training for the many TDY's he was to have when he went in the Air Force.

~~~

The only kind of married student housing available at Louisiana universities in 1948 was for veterans. When we had become engaged in 1947, Ike had put his name on both the LSU and the SLI lists. Because of the tremendous influx of veterans after the war was over, it sometimes took two years to get into housing at LSU, because the student body had mushroomed from 3,000 to 9,000. The closer it got to August, when we would have to make a decision about going back to school, the more worried we got, because we could never have afforded to live in any other kind of housing. But, seemingly miraculously, his name came up on the list at SLI just before the fall semester was to start; so that's how we wound up there. That was fine with us: it was almost the same distance from Lafayette to each of our hometowns, and the tuition was much less than at LSU.

I was by that time a junior Education major; and Ike had decided to major in Physical Ed and become a track coach. I was one of only two Vet Village wives who were students, as not many married girls finished college in those days. Ike and I were paupers; but my folks, happy that I wanted to continue my education, had graciously offered to finish paying for my degree; so I was still in school. Ike had turned over a new leaf and was actually studying—well, at least by comparison. We would eat supper, clean up the kitchen, settle down to study about 6:30 and then break at 9 p.m. We'd have a snack; he'd go to bed; and I'd stay up studying until I was through, sometimes as late as 2 a.m. But his grades came up rapidly, and he finished with about a B+ average for his last two years. It irked me; because he would pick our brains when he and Bruce Broussard and I would study together on Thursday nights for the History quizzes we had on Fridays. Bruce and I would take voluminous notes; Ike would nod off after about two sentences of notes. But then he would make as good grades on the quizzes as we did. Bruce and I each made an A- at the end of the semester, and Ike made a B+. I would have <u>really</u> been teed off if he'd made an A!

~~~
~~~

Ike soon discovered that if football wasn't your main sport, you might as well forget being a coach. Track coaches who were not ex-football players and also football coaches were Second Class Citizens. Besides, by the end of our first year at SLI, he had been enjoying himself so much in ROTC that you might as well say he was majoring in it. With uncharacteristic vision for the youthful non-scholar that he was, Ike had determined that there would probably be "wars and rumors of wars" for most of his adult life; so he might as well make a career of the military. That was a major turning point in our lives. At the end of the 1948-49 school year, Ike had only one more year of ROTC, I had one year left until graduation, and he had at least two years of college remaining. So he went to the Dean Doucet of the College of Education and told him,

"I want a degree. I don't care what it's in; I just want a degree so I can graduate with Anita in one year."

So Dean Doucet basically put all Ike's credits in a basket, jumbled them up, and came up with a schedule of classes that would allow Ike to graduate in one year with a major in Physical Education and a minor in Biology. He would not have the credentials needed to teach but would have the degree he wanted and in only four years of college. Talk about smelling like a rose!

~~~

For Ike's last year of ROTC a third squadron was added; and these assignments were made:

Group CO – Cadet Col James Broussard
Gp Exec Off – Cadet Lt Col James Ardoin
Sq A CO – Cadet Lt Col Isaac Hamilton
Sq B CO – Cadet Lt Col Francis LaRose
Sq C CO – Cadet Lt Col Wm. Dempsey
~~~

Military Ball: Frugé and Date; George Larrieu and Date; Ike
and Anita Hamilton; Bill and Clothilde Bacle

~~~

While at SLI, Ike was a member of Blue Key honorary fraternity,
played his violin in the orchestra (another $10 monthly income!), and
belonged also to Phi Mu Alpha, the honorary Music fraternity. He
was a charter member and the first president of The Military Society
of the Sabre, an Honor Fraternity, which later became part of the
Arnold Air Society, a national military fraternity for ROTC cadets. It
was the Claire Chennault chapter, named after Louisiana's native son,
famous as a Flying Tiger in China.

~~~

Major Richard T. W. Rivers, the PAST, had been a fighter pilot in
WWII, serving as CO of the 70th Fighter SQ on Guadalcanal. He
probably really enjoyed the moment when, not long before school was
out, he called Ike into his office and said,

"Hamilton, you're going to pilot training." That came as
somewhat of a shock because, unlike many young men who had
always dreamed of flying, Ike had never even given it a thought. He
was later to say that his only interest in the air as a child had been in
flying kites, not even to make model airplanes, much less think of a
career as a pilot.

"Yes, Sir!" he answered and saluted, and that was that. Only two people from that graduating class had been selected for pilot training: Ike and our friend Jim Ardoin.

So on May 25, 1950, we graduated together, I with a BA in Education, with a double major in Spanish and English, and Ike with a BS in Liberal Arts. What meant more to him than anything else was being named a Distinguished Military Graduate and among the first thirteen to receive commissions from the AFROTC detachment as Second Lieutenants in the United States Air Force.

Chapter 2 – Basic Pilot Training

Since Jim Ardoin had received the only Regular Commission to be allotted in the first graduating class of SLI's ROTC program, the others all received only Reserve Commissions. As a Regular Officer, Jim was sent directly to his first assignment, Randolph AFB, Texas, where he would await the first phase of pilot training starting in September; but Ike had to stew a few months while waiting to be called up. (Bruce Broussard went later to Pilot Training and got his wings in the T-33 at Bryan AFB, TX in the spring of 1952.)

Since Ike's GI Bill money had run out two months before graduation, we were penniless; so, after graduation, we had to go live with my folks until he received his orders to report on active duty. He was too honest not to tell prospective employers that he was about to be called up to active duty; so, predictably, they weren't beating his door down offering him jobs. He finally got a job as a taxi driver. I attribute to that job many of his bad driving habits that were to become such a thorn in my flesh and the source of the majority of any marital problems we were to have in later years.

While in Baton Rouge, we bought our first "modern" car—a 1949 two-door Chevrolet sedan, which had only 1000 miles on it so was practically new. Ike had had no car when we met, and he used to say that I was the only girl he ever dated who didn't seem to be hung up on a guy's having a car. We did our courting on foot and riding buses and bicycles. We continued riding those bikes for a year and a half after we got married, when we got our first car, a 1929 black four-door Model A Ford, which we named Susie. She was the same age I was: twenty. We would have loved dearly to keep her for a second means of transportation when we got the Chevy; but our finances wouldn't allow it. We really needed the $175 she brought in order to get the Chevy.

Hamiltons' first car "Susie," a 1929 Model A Ford
(Vet Village apartment in background)

~~~

At long last Ike's orders came through to report in on August 19th to Randolph AFB, Texas, in San Antonio, for Basic Pilot Training. But, just before time to report, and while we were visiting some relatives in Shreveport, he received word that he had been turned down by the Air Force, having failed the entry physical because of some cavities in his teeth. That was that. Still in shock, Ike had the presence of mind to ask whether he could have them repaired and re-take the physical. They consented; so right there in Shreveport, with a four-hour deadline, he went to a dentist hurriedly pressed into service by his aunt, had four cavities filled, re-took the physical, and was given the green light by the Air Force. That was a close call, which would have made all the difference in how we were to live the rest of our lives.

~~~

The Ardoins, Jim, Valerie and their little girl, were already in San Antonio; so that made the transition not quite so traumatic for this small-town girl who had never really been very far away from home. My travels had been limited to trips back to Arkansas to visit relatives, and short forays into the surrounding states, usually with my parents. For all I know, San Antonio might not have been all that much larger than Baton Rouge. But I was scared to death, and "the devil you know is better than the devil you don't know." I knew Baton Rouge backwards and forwards, but San Antonio, Texas, was The Great Unknown to me.

We arrived in San Antone fairly early in the day, having driven only from Baytown, Texas, where we had been visiting Earl Barnett, the former shipmate of Ike's and Guidon Bearer of ROTC Cadet Squadron A. We had been invited to stay with Jim and Val Ardoin as long as we needed to in order to get settled; but we wound up spending only one night with them. We got a city map and a newspaper as soon as we hit town; and before the day was over we had found an apartment. It was a cute little single dwelling, brand-new, made from what had been passed off to the building inspectors as a garage. As such, it had a rather peculiar floor plan: one entire side was a huge bedroom, while into the other side were crammed a tiny living room, dinette, kitchen and bath. It was adequate for us and seemed like the Waldorf-Astoria after the paper-thin walls of the old converted Navy barracks buildings that were called Vet Village back at school. Our landlords, Mr. and Mrs. Strange, were very nice and invited us over to watch our very first television. The Mambo was big about that time, and that's about all I remember watching on it.

I soon learned my way around town on my own and hit the streets job-hunting. But since I was cursed with the same problem Ike had had in Baton Rouge and couldn't assure anybody I'd be working for very long, nobody wanted to hire me, in spite of my college degree and my scintillating personality. I did manage to find a job as General Flunky at the Broadway National Bank, which at that time was in an old Victorian-style house. I was paid only $180/month, as I recall. But Ike was now making a 2/Lt's salary with flight pay. That with my $180, compared to what we'd been living on at SLI, was living High off the Hog. We soon got car pools going and Ike's first Air Force assignment was under way.

~~~

Shortly after our arrival in San Antonio, we looked up a church of Christ after having studied about it briefly with Ike's sister Floyd and her husband, James Williams. We had promised them we'd investigate it. After much soul-searching and three weeks of intensive study with Cecil Hill, the minister of one of the many congregations of the church there, we made the decision to convert to the Church of Christ, leaving the Baptist Church of our childhood. This was to influence heavily many things that happened later in our lives.

~~~

We hadn't been at Randolph over a couple of weeks when Ike's back gave way on him while he was working on a flowerbed in the yard. He managed to get to bed, rest a while and then went right back out to bend over and work in the flowerbed. The same thing happened two or three times. We were afraid for him to report in on Sick Call at the base because we didn't know how that would look on his military record. We thought that it was even possible that it could have caused him to wash out of Pilot Training. So he went to see a private doctor, a diagnostician, who never really came up with anything. That, added to his flat feet, was just the beginning of a steadily deteriorating lower back problem that would plague him the rest of his life.

~~~

Surely he did, but I don't recall Ike's ever having asked me what I thought of his going to Pilot Training or even of the idea of making a career of the Air Force. But I didn't put up a fuss. I had married him For Better or for Worse, and that was that. We were in this thing together. Since I had a quicker memory than he did, I usually had his check lists, flight procedures, map and navigational information memorized before he did, as I coached him on all of them and
~~~

participated in every little aspect of the training that he worked on at home. So I could probably have flown those trainers, too, if I hadn't suffered from motion sickness and been deathly afraid of flying.

Previously, Pilot Training had consisted of three phases: Primary, Basic and Advanced. That had been changed to two phases: seven months of Basic and five months of Advanced. However, sometime before May of 1952, they went back to the original three phases and extended the time to eighteen months. No "Ninety-Day Wonders" here!

The plane used for Basic Pilot Training in those days was the T-6, a holdover from WWII. I have trouble recalling those early days when he <u>almost</u> washed out. He was just a little slower than some in making his first solo flight. Since he was usually intimidated by others whom he considered better than himself, he had a mental block and came excruciatingly close to being unable to solo. But finally he did and had no more problems, going on to become an outstanding pilot for the rest of his career.

A T-6 on the Runway at Randolph AFB, TX

He told me about <u>everything</u> that happened to him, good or bad. If he had an emergency, I heard about it. We were partners, weren't we? At first, I was scared but tried not to be a drag on him. As he developed more confidence in himself, so did I. I gradually learned that if anyone could handle a flying emergency, Ike Hamilton could. Therefore, I wasn't a basket case like some of the other wives who went into hysterics every time their guys flew. Oh, sure, over the years, when he'd be flying, I'd sometimes think, "You know—I could be a widow tonight!" So I wasn't oblivious to the danger; but that was morbid thinking, and I just wouldn't let myself indulge in it. That attitude, plus my faith in God, saw me through twenty years of active duty flying on his part, including two combat tours.

Jim Ardoin didn't make it. I'm not sure why, because he had been outstanding in every way in ROTC, as evidenced by the fact that he was the one chosen out of all thirteen of the graduates to receive a Regular Commission. Some of it might have been because he had a wife and little girl and would think about what would become of them if anything happened to him. I also heard of many guys over the years that washed out because of airsickness. At any rate, he washed out in Basic Training. He was given a desk job and served out his commitment in an exemplary way but got out of the AF as soon as the four years were up; and the last I heard of him, he was a bank president back in his hometown in Louisiana. So, the saying, "You can't keep a good man down," proved to be true in Jim's case.

~~~

In those days, the two phases of Pilot Training were carried out on separate bases, but later were given at the same base. In 1951, there were three possibilities for Advanced Pilot Training: Multi-Engines or Bombers (Multis), Reciprocating Engines (Recips or Prop Jobs), and Jets. By the time the fledgling pilots got to put in their preferences (which the AF wasn't always able to honor), they usually had <u>very</u> strong 'druthers. Most of Ike's class, 51-Fox, got what they wanted. A few were royally disappointed. You can imagine how you would feel if you really wanted jets (they were the newest thing) and got
~~~

bombers, or *vice versa*. Ike really dreaded the possibility of getting Multi's and possibly being stuck in SAC for the rest of his career. Since a cult had built up around the WWII F-51 "Mustang," a Prop Job, Ike had developed a strong desire to fly it, knowing that he would be among the last to do so, as jets were becoming more and more commonplace. I don't know that I'd have been able to live with him if he hadn't gotten the Mustang; but, thank goodness, he did. On March 19th, after seven months at Randolph, he was to be assigned to Craig AFB in Selma, Alabama.

~~~

Selma was a very small town, and the guys had been told not to take their families with them because of a lack of adequate housing. Ike and I didn't go along with that. I still feel that many of the AF marriages that went bad did so because the AF didn't make better housing available in those days so that the men in training could have their families with them. We weren't about to be separated for five months, knowing that, as soon as he had received his wings and gone through Gunnery Training, he would be in the pipeline to Korea, where the "Conflict" had been going on since the summer of 1950.

The guys had completed all of their work by the last Friday afternoon of Basic, but for some unknown reason, they had been asked to report back on Monday morning. So we didn't do a thing but take off immediately on Friday afternoon for a quick trip to Selma. We took with us an AF enlisted man from church who had a girlfriend in Gadsden, Alabama. We were going to beat the crowd to Selma and get us an apartment in spite of what the AF recommended. We were used to driving around the clock on our hair-brained cross-country trips; so what were 800+ miles to seasoned veterans like us? Off we went, Ike insisting on driving most of the way (since neither I nor our friend drove fast enough to suit him), with me spelling him only when he was dropping from fatigue.

As Ike departed the base, his classmate Chuck Sankey asked him where he was going.
~~~

Ike called back to him, "To Selma to find an apartment."

Sankey yelled, "Well, find us one, too."

"Okay," Ike shouted back.

When he told me that, I started asking questions. How many rooms did the Sankeys need? I barely knew them, and Ike wasn't sure whether they had kids or not. Did they need a furnished or an unfurnished place? How much were they able to pay? "I don't know," was Ike's reply to every question I asked him. Oh, well. We'd get ourselves an apartment if we could and one for the Sankeys, if possible. We'd let them worry about the details. They deserved what they got for trusting housing arrangements to two guys.

We arrived totally fatigued in Selma, where we put our friend on a bus for Gadsden. He was to meet us Sunday morning back in Selma. Not finding a reasonably-priced motel and afraid to ask about prices at the only hotel, we spent what was left of that night more-or-less sleeping in the car.

Things came together for us the next day, thank goodness. On King Street, we found a nice one-bedroom, furnished apartment for ourselves ($80 per month) and took a risk in paying down on one for the Sankeys not far away. It was a 3-bedroom house that was partially furnished, with the third bedroom "Off Limits" (filled with the landlord's stored furniture). We all lucked out: The Sankeys were thrilled to death. They needed two bedrooms; they had some furniture but not everything they needed; so the landlord let them have some of his stored furniture to fill out what they needed. Smelling like a rose again!

Now for the trip back to San Antone. Our friend turned up on schedule but was completely useless as far as helping with the driving back home. He and his girl friend had stayed up all night Saturday; so he hadn't had any sleep for two days. Ike came down with some sort of stomach virus; so driving home was up to the Airman and me. I drove my tank of gas and then turned it over to him. I was just about to zonk out when he started regaling me with a story. Seems he had made a trip with a friend and was supposed to have shared the driving. On his shift, he had gone to sleep at the wheel, run off the road and barely missed a telephone pole! Suddenly, I was no longer sleepy! So I took the wheel back over and drove the entire way back to San Antonio while those two guys snored away!

We hit town just before 8 a.m. when Ike was supposed to report back in for "Final Instructions." The Final Instructions consisted of, "Well, Good Luck, men! Take care!"

Chapter 3 – Advanced Pilot Training

After one of our quickie trips to northern New York State to visit my brother Lane Rivers and his wife Pic, Ike reported in April, 1951, for the second phase of Pilot Training at Craig AFB, Selma, Alabama. Happy that we already had an apartment, we were ready to settle down. Ike began intensive training and I began sitting around and molding over.

At first I enjoyed getting to socialize with the other AF wives. I had done little of that sort of thing, staying busy studying during my four years of college and working in San Antonio. At Randolph, we student wives had been introduced into the scary (at least to me) social life of an Air Force Officer and his wife. They were still going by the rules of protocol laid down for generations in the Army: the Commanding Officer and his wife were At Home a certain night of the week; and the junior officers and their wives were expected to come calling within two weeks after reporting into the new base, leaving calling cards in the silver tray on the table just inside the front door. Neither of us smoked; so we didn't make the mistake we had been warned about: lighting up in the General's presence without asking, only to discover that he didn't smoke and there were no ashtrays. I attended the requisite teas and coffees tendered for us student wives but, beyond that, stuck to my excuse of having to work during the daytime. Although in the Air Force the teas, receptions and coffees were still *de rigeur*, I'm glad to say that the strictness of Army protocol didn't carry over entirely into the Air Force and gradually faded away, at least to a certain extent and on certain bases, during Ike's career.

At Craig, things were quite a bit more relaxed than they had been at Randolph. Ike joined the Officers' Club, of course; we always did wherever we were stationed even though we didn't drink, play golf or party a lot. After he finished his training days and we had PCS assignments, staying a little longer at each base, I joined the Officers' Wives Club and participated to a certain degree, going to luncheons, singing with their choir on one base, taking bridge lessons on another and guitar lessons on another. There were certain things we could conscientiously participate in, such as eating, swimming, etc. We even went to the semi-official cocktail parties but carried around a Coke in our hands. Some of our friends in the church of Christ chose not to belong to the O Club; but one officer we knew received a bad OER as a result of staying too aloof from the social life of the Air Force.

Not long after we got to Craig, Ike felt the need to replace our perfectly good 1949 Chevrolet. It wasn't quite "hot" or new enough for him. This won't come as a surprise to many people, but cars are a Guy Thing. For most women I know, a car is a means of transportation. Period. If you asked me what make of car a person has, I couldn't tell you. I just don't even notice it. A car for me is a way to get from Point A to Point B. But for a guy a car is almost like his woman. He loves to show her off and show how she obeys him. And for a fighter pilot, his car is like an extension of his plane. He's a Hot Jet Jockey even on the ground and drives his car that way. At least that's what Ike Hamilton always did. Once he got a steering wheel in his hand, he made up for the years of not having had a car when everybody else did!

At Craig, I got together with the student wives that I knew. But I quickly got bored, and even a little depressed, at hearing all about how many diapers they had washed that day and what cute things their toddlers had said and done. Ike and I, after 2-1/2 years of trying not to have children, were now trying but having no success. It took us four more years and an application to adopt before I finally got pregnant.

So I was glad when I passed the Civil Service Clerk-Steno Test and was given a GS-4 assignment on the base. The rest of the time we were there I worked, at first in an office that had to do with construction (I've forgotten the name of it) and later in one in which we made training manuals. Once I was asked to take shorthand during a Court Martial, as the regular court stenographer was sick. I was shaking in my boots, but they were really considerate of me; and I managed to muddle through it, having to ask them only once to repeat a phrase I'd missed. I was glad that I had taken my high school shorthand book with me to San Antonio and brushed up on it while there, phasing in gradually to taking more and more notes in shorthand from the head Cashier, one of my bosses at the bank.

~~~

Although the church in Selma was small and didn't seem to be as friendly and close-knit as the one we belonged to in San Antonio, we did make a few good friends there. The day we "went forward" and "placed membership," there was another couple about our age who were placing membership at the same time; and we were all four sitting on the front pew during the singing of the last hymn. We noticed that the guy sang tenor and the girl, soprano, which made us a quartet with my alto and Ike's bass. So we invited them over and had several fun evenings of hymn-singing—pretty tame stuff when you think of the reputation that pilots have for hard drinking and partying. We did have some good friends in Ike's Pilot Training class who have remained so over many years.

~~~

There were lots of antebellum plantations in the Selma area; and Ike and I had an old book telling about them. Every Saturday we struck out to go visit one of those beautiful old homes. Some of the owners were unaware that they were in that book and hadn't had visitors like us for years but proudly showed us around anyway. Once we took with us one of Ike's classmates and his wife. It hadn't even registered on us that they were Yankees; but we were given the cold shoulder when trying to show them some of the plantation homes. One owner was frank and told us that they had shown the place to some reporters from the North who wanted to write an article about it. It had turned out that they had written an extremely inflammatory article about how the South was still harboring bad feelings over their losses in the Civil War. The author had made a big deal about such things as the old slave quarters on the plantation. You can see why the people were reluctant to open up their homes to more Yankees.

Craig wasn't too far from the Gulf Coast; so folks went deep-sea fishing a lot. Once Ike was invited to go with some of the guys in his class. He asked them if he could bring me along. Can you imagine? What could they say but "Yes, of course"? I did not want to go at all because I had always easily gotten carsick, airsick, seasick—you name it. But he refused to go without me (How dumb can you get?); so finally I gave in and, of course, was the only woman along. I took a Dramamine at 5 a.m. when we were to leave, and I did okay as long as we were under way heading out toward the open Gulf; but the minute the boat stopped, anchored and started rocking, I got deathly sick, feeding the fish multiple times. When we'd move on to another spot, I'd briefly recuperate, only to get sick again when we'd stop. There was absolutely no place to lie down, but I was desperate. I went below into the hold where all there was was a pile of ropes. I collapsed on those ropes and finally dozed off and got a little respite. This went on for <u>twelve</u> hours! Needless to say, that was absolutely the last time I ever let Ike talk me into anything like that.

Ike Hamilton was a Dr. Jeckyl and Mr. Hyde. While basically shy and not very gregarious, he had a wild streak that would cause him to do unpredictable things which embarrassed me, and later our children. I think it was his way of getting the attention that he didn't know how to get any other way. I guess that wild streak is what made him such a good pilot and not just a quiet, violin-playing, church-going tee-totaler. He didn't have a lot of close friends in his pilot training class; but the ones he had were life-long ones. One of those was Pete Blackley. He and Jeannie became our closest friends at Craig, and we kept in touch for years afterwards.

One of everybody's favorite guys in the class was Jim Young, who was given the nickname of Mighty Joe Young, after the gorilla in the current movie of that name. I didn't know him all that well while in pilot training but got to know him and his wife Lani later. When I get to the chapter on Korea, I'll say more about Jim and also Floyd O'Neal.

<center>~~~</center>

The guys were loving the Mustang, Ike probably the most of all. It was a dream come true for him to be able to fly that historic plane made by North American. Their instructors were combat veterans who really knew the ropes. In spite of all that, it was a hard bird to fly and at least one classmate of Ike's, Pete Peterson, was killed in a plane crash there at Craig. Everybody knew that there would undoubtedly be more of that to come when they got to combat in Korea. In looking back over *Pitch Out*, Class 51-F's annual, I see that Ike has written the word "killed" under the pictures of "Papa" Brouillette, Bender, Chuck Sankey, and Fluhr.

~~~

I guess because of all of the stress and whatever was basically wrong with Ike's back in the first place, it started acting up again while we were at Craig. It was bothering him so badly that he backed his ears and went to the Flight Surgeon. Not finding anything obviously wrong with it and not knowing what else to do, the doctor taped up Ike's back from his shoulder blades to below his belt and completely around his body at the waistline. The adhesive tape started itching him while we were on a weekend trip to Baton Rouge. I had to pull the tape off as soon as we got to my parents' house. His back and waistline area were one huge red whelp. Mother and Daddy hadn't known we were coming and had gone to a movie; so we couldn't get into the house. Ike was having fits from the itching by that time; so I went to the corner drugstore, got some ointment for his back, stripped him down on the bench in the front yard and slathered it all over him; but it didn't help much. The next day we had to have the family doctor make a house call, and I worked on cleaning off the old ointment and putting on the new every two hours for two days. He had to call his Commanding Officer to tell him what had happened and that he'd be late getting back. So that is how we learned about his allergy to adhesive tape.

~~~

Finally, Graduation Day arrived! The students of the class of 51-Fox were getting their hard-earned wings. My parents, Ike's Mom, and his sister Floyd and her family all came for the occasion and took a picture of me pinning on his wings. We were all as proud as punch, naturally. He was the first graduate of the ROTC detachment at SLI to earn his wings. We couldn't help worrying, though, because we knew that all too soon, he would be joining the "Police Action" in Korea.

Anita pinning wings on Ike at graduation of class 51-Fox
from Advanced Pilot Training

Chapter 4 – Combat Crew Training

Ike was then assigned for eight weeks of Combat Crew Training, better known as Gunnery School, to Luke AFB, outside Phoenix, Arizona. He didn't have to report in right away so we took some leave and detoured by way of Mexico. We had made a couple of quickie trips across the border while stationed in San Antonio but had never gotten any deeper into the country than quaint little Saltillo. I was in hog heaven because I had studied all about the history of the *conquistadores* and was getting to practice my Spanish for the first time. We went to Mexico City, Puebla, Cuernavaca and Acapulco, doing early Christmas shopping while seeing the sights. This was the first of the many exotic places we got to see over the years, courtesy of Uncle Sam. The scared little hometown girl was fast becoming the World Traveler.

~~~

While at Craig, we had purchased our first in what was to become a long line of Toy Manchester-Terrier dogs in our family. He was ten weeks old when we got him, a precious little black and tan thing that weighed all of seven pounds when fully grown, had long legs and tail, and ears that stood straight up. He was the original Mr. Personality. Jeannie Blackley inspired his name when she first saw him and exclaimed, "Oh! You cute little monkey!" So he became Monkey Doodle, Monk for short.
~~~

Monk

We couldn't take Monk into Mexico with us because of a quarantine; so we left him with Mother and Daddy in Baton Rouge and asked them to ship him to us when we reported into Luke. Daddy built a nice little crate for him, fixed him up with plenty of food and water for the two-day trip, and checked him at the railway station. We went to the station in Phoenix the day he was due to arrive; but he wasn't there. Nor the next day either. By then we had gotten really worried and unhappy. The attitude of the employee in the depot didn't help either—he seemed so nonchalant about the whole thing, saying, "It's only a dog."

The third day when we went to check on Monk, the employee acted like we were really bothering him. I started crying, and Ike was getting more and more worked up while the guy was thoroughly enjoying the whole occasion. But then we heard loud yelping from Monk from behind some boxes, where the sadistic employee had hidden him. The guy just gave us a big grin. What had happened was that Monk had been taken off the train in error in El Paso, Texas, and had just sat there for two days. Can you believe it?! He was totally out of water and food, was filthy and smelled like an outhouse. Thank Goodness we had brought along towels because we had feared just that. Even so we all reeked before we got home because he was so glad to see us that he kept jumping all over us. We bathed him three or four times that night and the next day before he got to smelling like our sweet little Monk again.

~~~

Arizona is a beautiful state; and we took advantage of that and drove up to see the Painted Desert, Grand Canyon, and many of the other sights around there, including the snow in the Prescott area. I used to walk Monk in short sleeves during the sunny days; then we would sleep under blankets at night. While we were in Phoenix, the Chambers of Commerce of Phoenix, El Paso and Albuquerque had a contest to see in which city the sun would melt a huge block of ice the fastest. Phoenix was ahead; but then we had an unseasonable cold snap and Albuquerque won the contest.

We had found an adequate one-bedroom duplex in Phoenix, but it wasn't anywhere near anybody that we knew; so Ike could not carpool to Luke each day. If I wanted to have the car for some reason, I'd have to get up at 5 a.m. and take Ike to work, returning in the evening to get him. Since I am definitely not a morning person, I rarely did that. So for three months, I experienced the only time in my life when I was bored to death. Having always been in school or working, I hardly knew what to do with myself. So I slept until noon, took Monk for many walks, sewed some Christmas presents on my little Singer Featherweight portable machine, and read practically every book in the Luke AFB library. Ike would bring me at least a dozen books every day or so from the library. Some of the wives I knew from Craig were there also; but we were spread out all over Phoenix, which is a big city; so I rarely got to see them. I did go to one luncheon held at the O Club for the student wives of that class. I remember also visiting with some of the wives from Craig at the home of Jim and Lani Young. "Lani" is short for Leilani; she was a
~~~

Military Brat who had been born in Hawaii. I liked her a lot. More about them later.

~~~

Ike's training was getting more and more serious. The guys did all of their gunnery practice out over the nearby desert. They were not supposed to fly close to the ground; but I guess the lure of those cacti just asking to have their heads chopped off was too great. Some of the students got reprimanded for doing that; but, surprisingly, Ike was not one of them. I guess he either kept his nose clean or managed not to get caught.

~~~

Ike would come home from his long days of training totally exhausted. He would lie down on the couch; and before I could get supper on the table, he would be asleep. Once I was unable to get him up, and he slept all night on the couch without ever eating. I remember having an attack of selfishness once and insisting that we go out to a movie I wanted to see at a drive-in theater. I knew he was tired; but I was bored. He gave in and we went; but he immediately fell asleep and I felt so guilty that we went on home. I learned my lesson and didn't do that again.

There was a break at Christmas time; so we made one of our by now famous quickie cross-country trips back home to Louisiana. The timing mechanism went out on our '51 Chevy at 2 A. M. in the middle of nowhere; and we and our passenger had to spend the rest of that night "sleeping" sitting up in a freezing car. Getting help on Sunday wasn't very easy; but we lucked out and were back on the road before too long. But Ike had lost confidence in his car, which wasn't even six months old. I guess that was excuse enough for him to want to get a newer, better and bigger car just before leaving for Korea.

Chapter 5 – Going Overseas

We had decided that I would stay in Baton Rouge and work while Ike was overseas. So when he finished Gunnery School in early February, we went back to Louisiana, where he had one last visit with our families.

Looking into his crystal ball, as he put it, Ike predicted that, just as it had happened in WWII, the production of new cars would come to a halt because of the war effort, and no new cars would be made. He declared that he didn't want to go off to war having to worry about my being stuck with an undependable car. Translation—he wanted a newer, more powerful car! So we traded in our '51 Chevy (still not paid for) for a '52 Olds 88; and he got to drive it a little before shipping out. He took me and the car to the Oldsmobile place in Baton Rouge, introduced us to the manager of the service department there, and said he wanted them to take good care of us. He said, "My wife knows a lot about cars; so don't try to put anything over on her." Yeah, right. It's true that I had experience in recognizing tappet problems and the noises a General Motors car makes when it needs a valve job, because we had had to have valve jobs done on both our Chevys. It's no wonder, since Ike always drove with the accelerator floor-boarded in those lightweight cars that had not been made to withstand such long-term hard driving.

~~~

Finally his orders came. Wilson, Randall, Bartolich, Fluhr, Rollag, Jansen, Smyk and Stull of Class 51-Fox were all being assigned to the 12th FBSQ along with Ike. Lovelace, Gossett, McShane, Gray, Lenhart, Rives and Blackley were assigned to the 67th FBSQ on the same base. Ike was to report for processing to the Port of Embarkation, Camp Stoneman, California, by 4 p.m. on 13 February 1952. He had arranged to get an AF hop from Carswell AFB in Fort Worth, Texas, to Travis AFB, California (from which he was later to leave for Japan). So we drove the new Olds 88 up to Fort Worth and visited a couple of days with some friends there while
~~~

waiting for the hop. During that time we had said our farewells, gotten our crying done and come to peace with the idea of his going off to war. But when he showed up the morning of the hop and was told that the flight had been canceled, it didn't take us a split second to figure out that, if we drove straight through, we could get to Camp Stoneman in time for him to report in before the deadline. We had a few days' reprieve, and we snatched it.

So off we went on one of our hair-brained, cross-country dashes, not even bothering to call my folks and tell them what we were doing. We made the 1,750 miles in thirty hours with time to spare and looked for a motel so we could rest up. Since his reporting date was on a Friday, he figured that if he waited until just before 4 p.m. to report in, there would not be time to process him until the following Monday. We looked around and learned that there were only three motels in the area. The first two we tried had a No Pets policy. So at the third one, we didn't even ask but smuggled Monk in under my fur coat.

When Ike reported in, it turned out that his crystal ball had been right this time.

"See you Monday at 0800," they said to him as they checked off his name. So we had two extra days to go sightseeing around the beautiful San Francisco area and visit the Jim Ardoins, who were stationed at nearby Hamilton AFB. We even cooked a meal in one cabin-like place where we stayed, inviting Ned ("Neddy Bear") Stull over for pork chops, as he was processing through Stoneman the same time as Ike. We had a sort of bittersweet second honeymoon, which we wouldn't have traded for anything.

~~~

Ike flew as far as Hickam AB in a DC-4, which he described as having "plush seats and a stewardess." (Hmmmm??) He was bounced from his flight to Tokyo and "had" to spend a day in Hawaii, where he spent some time with Bill Dempsey and George Larrieu of SLI ROTC fame. George, our "wedding" photographer, was just
~~~

reporting in as the base photographer; so Bill showed him and Ike around the island.

~~~

When I called Mother she was hopping mad that I had driven out to California with Ike, and she wanted to fly out and drive back with me. (That's why I hadn't called her.) But I assured her that I'd be careful, I'd stay with Rod Ibers, Ike's old Navy buddy, and his wife Marian in L.A., and with Daddy's sister Lila in Houston, thus having to spend only one night in a motel on the way home; and I would call them every night. I was, after all, still their little girl, only 22 years old, and had only a 7-pound dog to protect me. The trip back was uneventful, unless you count the time that Monk nearly took a service station attendant's arm off for opening the car door and reaching in to sweep out the floor. After the afore-mentioned visits, I arrived home to Baton Rouge to wait for hubby to finish his combat tour.
~~~

Chapter 6 - The "Police Action" in Korea

People were getting killed right and left in Korea, had been ever since the hostilities had begun in June of 1950. But for some reason I never understood, neither our government nor the United Nations had officially "declared war;" so they were calling the war there a "Police Action" or "Conflict." In my opinion, if ever there were a "moral" war, it was that one, as Communist North Korea, equipped and backed in every way by Russia and even China, was slaughtering weak, totally defenseless South Korea and rapidly taking over their country. Now it's called "The Forgotten War" but has finally gotten some recognition with a monument in Washington, D. C. Ike reported for duty there in February 1952. The entire time he was in Korea, the so-called peace negotiations were going on in Panmunjam; but they were stalemated much of the time, and nothing came of them as long as he was there.

He was assigned to the 18th Fighter Bomber Wing, 12th Fighter Bomber Squadron (known as "The Foxy Few"), which was based, first at K-10 and later at K-46 outside Wonju, Korea, on the 37.5[th] Parallel, the 38th Parallel being the dividing line between North and South Korea. The 18th FBW, made up of The Foxy Few (12th), Red Scarf (67th), and 39th Squadrons, had moved from their longtime home at Clark AB, Philippines, (where the 18th had been part of the famous Flying Tigers) to Korea in 1950, one of the first AF units to answer the urgent call that came out from HQ FEAF. In November of 1950, they had been joined by the South African "2" Squadron with their full complement of Mustangs, thus making them the first real UN Air Wing. Although a WWII plane, the F-51 Mustang became the workhorse of the Korean Conflict, the F-86 Sabre not being introduced until the fall of 1952. The Mustang pilots transitioned into the Sabre in January and February of 1953, at a new base, Osan, the 12th being the first Mustang squadron to stand down. The Mustang's last day of operation in Korea was January 23, 1953, five months after Ike had already rotated home.

The pilots slept on cots in thatch-roofed "hootches," which were too hot in the summer months and too cold in the winter months. There were so many pilots in each hootch (about twelve, if I remember correctly) and so much noise that they were lucky to get any sleep. One hut-mate of Ike's, Bruton, trying to get some sleep, would say laconically, "Get to bed right now, get five hours sleep." That expression later was added to the Hamilton family's collection of adages. We had stocked Ike up with as many niceties as we could think of to keep him from being too homesick. I sent him monthly care packages, never failing to include three pounds of his beloved Community Coffee, drip grind, dark roast, straight from the factory in Baton Rouge. Raised in 'Cajun country, Ike was addicted to that thick-as-tar and black-as-night coffee and had taken several one-, two-, and three-cup Drip-O-Laters with him. He said that when the guys smelled his coffee, they would run in either one direction or the other—some (who like me, couldn't stomach that strong brew) away from it, and some (who had learned to love it as he did), toward it.

I was proud of myself for thinking of this: I made him some bright red boxer shorts and sent them to him. I thought he'd be tickled to death; but I had unwittingly made them the color of one of the <u>other</u> squadrons in the wing, the 67th "Red Scarves"! The Foxy Few's color was yellow; so he took a lot of ribbing from the other guys about those red shorts.

Most of the guys had grown handlebar moustaches and liked to compare them to see who was ahead on the number of twirls in the moustache. Ike was soon ahead. The only trouble was that he was balding quite rapidly; and people who'd see his pictures would usually say something like, "It's too bad he can't transplant that up onto his scalp." Anyway, I was going to be very glad to see him when he got home but wasn't too happy about the moustache. I told him that I didn't mind his having it as long as I didn't have to kiss him. He told people I had said he could bring it as far the West bank of the Mississippi but not the East.

~~~
~~~

Ike was a very prolific letter writer; so I had a running account of the war, at least from his viewpoint. As was his wont, he didn't spare me any of the gory details; so it was almost like I was there, too. The only problem was that the mail was erratic at best and it took from six to eight days to get a letter from him. No one I knew had television in those days; so the only news I ever got was from him or through the newspapers. He belonged to Love Flight (he was to become Flight Leader in June when he had flown 44 missions [sorties]) and would tell of his dealings with the other three men in the flight, some of whom he literally trusted with his life and others who were loose cannons. I suppose the closest he ever came to being killed was one time when his flight was landing after a mission. The pilot who landed right behind him, having forgotten to turn off his guns (the trigger of which was built into the stick), let off a round of shots that tore up the rear of Ike's plane. One shot hit about one inch from the fuel tank. I still have a little bag with scraps of metal from that incident. I wish I had kept his letters. But, moving around as much as we did and having to lighten the load as much as possible, I finally disposed of them, thinking, "I have him back; why do I need to keep these letters?" Bad judgment on my part, as they literally recorded history.

F-80 Shooting Stars and F-84 Thunderjets were used in Korea; but the F-51-D Mustang was flown from Ike's base. It was a recip and therefore could do a lot of jobs that the jets, precisely <u>because</u> of their greater speed, could not. But the Mustang was already obsolete when Ike got there; and they had to cannibalize their own planes to get parts when one would have mechanical difficulties. I think Ike must have been exaggerating when he told me that they lost more planes from engine failure than from the enemy. The writer of an article in the base newspaper, *The Truckbuster*, dated 17 March 1952 stated that the 12th Squadron had lost fewer pilots than had any other in the Group and had flown almost 2,000 sorties more than any other squadron. At that time the Foxy Few had flown over 10,000 sorties and supposedly had the lowest accident record. Although I was naturally not happy for him to be in combat and prayed daily for his safety, I didn't worry unduly because I knew he was in God's hands, that he was a good safe pilot, and that if anyone could handle an emergency, Ike Hamilton could. In fact, the more emergencies I heard about, the greater my confidence in his flying ability grew. He respected his plane and never let down his guard or got cocky. He would quote whoever had said, "That bird doesn't know you are the hottest pilot in the world; so each time you go up, you have to prove it to it all over again." Some other wise person had said, "There are old pilots, and there are bold pilots; but there are no old, bold pilots;" and he knew that to be true. So while he pushed his bird and himself to the limit, he was never reckless.

The Mustangs flew many different kinds of missions. Some were Interdiction missions: they bombed strategic bridges, power plants, hydro-electric plants, depots, factories, railroads, supplies, supply vehicles, ammunition dumps, warehouses, bunkers, artillery positions, troop installations, and the like. In late 1951, after the Communist troops had been run out of South Korea back up above the 38th Parallel, the U.N. forces put on an all-out push involving B-29 Superfortress bombings. F-80 Shooting Stars and F-84 Thunderjets, and possibly some other types of UN Fighter-Bombers were involved in the wave of follow-up after the bombings. One newspaper article called it "the greatest allied air blow of the Korean war." They bombarded Pyongyang for days and days and destroyed the supply stations and bases from which the Communists were trying their best to take over South Korea. The Mustangs contributed a lot to getting things there a little better under control. The pointed front ends of the Foxy Few's Mustangs were painted to look like sharks' teeth. I'm sure that the menacing sneer on those sharks' faces put even more fear into the enemy when they saw them coming at them.

Foxy Few Mustang at K-46, 1952

Others were ResCap missions—when a plane would get shot down in enemy territory, a helicopter would be sent in to rescue the pilot if he had been able to eject; and the Mustangs would fly cover for the chopper to fend off enemy planes to keep them from shooting down the helicopter, as well. I think ResCap missions were among Ike's "favorites" if that's the right word to use, although sometimes he had to tangle with Russian MIG-15s to keep them away.

Ike got over there right in the big middle of that operation and immediately was involved in it, flying his first combat sortie on 11 March 1952. There was usually heavy anti-aircraft fire to greet them in this type of mission; so they would fly as close to the ground as possible and at maximum speed so as to get in and out as quickly as they could before their presence was detected by the enemy. I suppose that, after all, those cacti in the Arizona desert had served a useful purpose in helping to train the pilots. To say that it was very dangerous would be a ludicrous understatement. As Ike used to put it, "It isn't conducive to longevity."

~~~

In late March, the stress of combat, the Gs pulled, the austere living conditions, or <u>something</u>—probably all of the above—caused his bad back to act up more than it usually did. He must have reported in on sick call one too many times, as they sent him to the Orthopedic Section of the USAF Hospital in Nagoya, Japan, to have his problem diagnosed. Although Lt. Anshutz, the Aviation Medical Examiner, had suggested that Ike just be evaluated as an outpatient, the doctors at Nagoya saw fit to admit him. Since no one had ever been able to find out what was wrong with his back, he knew that was going to be a losing battle; and he grew more and more frustrated as the days dragged on and he was missing out on flying his required number of missions. To cap the climax, the doctors at Nagoya decided that it was "Fear of Combat" that was causing him to complain about back pain! What a scald! I guess they had seen a lot of fake ailments thought up by people who really were afraid of combat; so they couldn't fathom a guy's really <u>wanting</u> to get back into combat. He was just intent on getting in his required number of missions ASAP so that he could come home; so he flew every time he possibly could.

During the month that Ike was in Nagoya, Jim Young, of 51-Fox, Ike's Pilot Training class at Craig, showed up in the hospital there, having been badly burned when his plane was shot down. By the grace of God, Jim had ejected and landed in a rice paddy. He credited the cold water in that rice paddy for saving his life. Although he was in shock when the rescue team got there, he was able to direct them in handling him with the least amount of stress to his already traumatized body. He had been burned over a large percentage of his body and was given up for dead several times. He told Ike about overhearing a conversation from the hallway outside his hospital room one night, in which a nurse, who had become quite emotionally involved in his case, was crying. Another nurse came along and asked her, "What's the matter?"

"The doctor said that Jim would not make it through the night," his nurse friend sobbed in answer, not knowing that Jim could hear her.
~~~

"Well, I'll show <u>him</u>!" Jim said to himself. And by sheer will power he did make it through that night. He still had a long way to go and many operations to undergo. He was told, "You'll never be put back on active duty again, Jim, because you'll never walk again." His answer was the same, "Well, I'll show <u>you</u>!"

And he forced himself to work through unbelievable pain; but he did, indeed, walk again. He gradually built up his strength by playing golf every day. At first he could endure only a few holes. Then he would do nine. Then he would do eighteen. He told us when we saw him several years later at Myrtle Beach AFB, SC, that he had worked up to playing 36 holes of golf every day. All the time he was undergoing operation after operation on his leg and skin graft after skin graft on his burned face, neck, arms, hands and legs. He applied to be put back on flying status again but was predictably told, "You'll never fly again." By now you've guessed what Jim said to that: "I'll show <u>you</u>!" So he went out and got a commercial pilot's license and racked up I don't know how many flying hours in light planes before hand-carrying to Washington his application for return to flight status and finally having it favorably acted upon. When we visited Jim and Lani at Myrtle Beach, we heard his story. He had had innumerable operations and still had more in store. He credited Lani for helping him shake the prescription drug addiction that he had acquired as a result of all the excruciating pain he had gone through. In the early 1960's we ran into Jim again in the Officers' Club at Ramstein AB, Germany, and learned that he had finally gotten his own command: he was Wing Commander at one of the bases in Europe. I'm told that he made at least Brigadier General before retiring. "Mighty Joe" Young is not much of a misnomer for this guy in my book.

~~~

Since the enemy was flying Russian-built MIG-15 jets, it took some really skillful flying to out-maneuver them in a Mustang. Several times Ike's flight was accosted by a flight of MIGs; and they had to use Escape and Evasion tactics to come out alive. The Mustangs were nowhere near as fast as the MIGs. The only way they
~~~

could avoid being hit was by adroit maneuvering, making as tight turns as possible and praying that the MIGs' fuel ran out before theirs did. It was, therefore, unrealistic to think of a Mustang's shooting down a MIG. The "aces" you heard about in the media during the Korean conflict were all jet pilots, as they were more evenly matched. A Mustang pilot in an altercation with a MIG was just trying to save his own skin (and possibly that of a downed pilot), not looking for glory.

One unusual mission that Ike flew gained him no little fame around "Dogpatch," as K-46 was familiarly called. One of the US jets had been hit, and the pilot had ejected to safety on the South Korean side. But for some reason the plane stayed in the air, spiraling around near the enemy border. Since the Controllers didn't want the plane to go down in enemy territory, Ike was sent out to shoot it down so that it would land in South Korea instead of the enemy-held territory to the North. So he successfully shot down one of our own planes.

Ike earned the Distinguished Flying Cross for displaying "extraordinary achievement" in a mission over Sinanjungri, Korea, on 25 June 1952, in which Love flight was performing ResCap for a downed F-4-U Corsair pilot. To quote the citation,

> Upon reaching the area, Lieutenant Hamilton sent the number 3 and number 4 members of his flight to higher altitude to act as relay and as top cover while he and the number 2 man made low passes determining the downed pilot's position. They then withdrew to escort the helicopter in to the downed Marine. Lt. Hamilton made numerous strafing passes in an effort to suppress the intense flak. Despite Lt. Hamilton's untiring efforts and skillful maneuvering, the helicopter was shot down after picking up the downed flyer on its third pass. During the entire 30 minutes that the flight was in the area, intense flak was thrown up at them. By his high personal courage and devotion to duty, Lt. Hamilton has brought great credit upon himself and the United States Air Force.

In August, not long before returning home, Ike received the following Commendation letter from his CO, Major Frank L. Orth:

> During the past four months period your performance as a combat pilot and assigned Flight Commander and Operations Officer has demonstrated qualities of superior technique, judgment, and leadership. As Flight, Squadron, and Group Leader, you have compiled an enviable record in aggressively seeking out and destroying enemy targets, all the while evincing a complete sense of responsibility for the safety of all pilots under your direction and control. Your accomplishments are especially noteworthy in view of the complexity of assigned missions, which include close ground support, interdiction, weather and night bombing and air combat against superior jet type enemy aircraft... It affords me personal pride and gratification to commend you for your overall performance of duties, reflecting great credit upon yourself and the Air Force in support of our country and the United Nations.

~~~

The tour of duty of each pilot there depended, not on a specific length of time, but on a certain number of missions flown. That number fluctuated wildly, depending on the supply and demand of both pilots and aircraft. Sometimes the maximum number of missions was 100, sometimes 85, and sometimes 50. It went back and forth many times during Ike's tour of duty there. At the end of the requisite number of flights, the pilots had to Stand Down, that is, stop flying missions, and, usually within a few days, would be put On Report. Once they were On Report, they could not be placed back into the pool to fly more missions, and just waited for their orders to Rotate, or be sent Stateside.

~~~

Several months into his tour, Ike went on R & R to the Fujiya Rest Hotel in Japan, a luxury hotel the American officers were allowed to use at very low rates. He was taking luxurious baths ("Angel Bath,"

"Roman Aquarium Bath," "Dream Pool," and "Bath of Eternal Youth" were some of those featured), eating steaks, sightseeing, buying Noritake china in the BXs, and, in general, living high off the hog. <u>Then</u> he learned that the policy allowing Americans to pay with Script had been rescinded; and he would now have to pay in dollars. Consternation in the camp! He didn't have enough dollars to pay his hotel bill. That's when I got my one and only transoceanic call from him—asking me to wire him some money ASAP!

~~~

On 19 May 1952, the same day Ike flew his 26th combat mission, the Claire Chennault chapter of Arnold Air Society that Ike had helped start at SLI held their banquet and invited Ret. Gen. Chennault himself to be the speaker. Since Ike was the first graduate of the SLI ROTC Detachment to get his wings and serve in combat, and since he was unable to attend, I was invited to come and to sit at the head table. So I drove over to Lafayette from Baton Rouge for the occasion. Gen. Chennault had married a Chinese lady and they had five children and were then living in North Louisiana. One of the children had the chicken pox; so his wife had not been able to come. But he brought with him Miss Loretta Chan, his sister-in-law, a beautiful young Chinese lady, a university student visiting from California at the time. She sat between me and the General; and I enjoyed talking with her. I was introduced as Ike's wife and felt highly honored.
~~~

Nancy Robinson, Anita Hamilton, Loretta Chan
Lafayette, Louisiana, 19 May 1952

Another buddy of ours from Craig was Floyd O'Neil, a happy-go-lucky guy and one of my favorite people. While in Korea he was shot down and taken Prisoner of War. Ike had told me that upon arrival at K-46, they had been instructed not to be martyrs but to tell the enemy anything they wanted to know because the planes they were flying were obsolete and the enemy already had all the information these pilots would be able to give them. That's why it came as a shock to us to learn years later that Floyd had been Court Martialed for "collaborating with the enemy" when interrogated in his POW camp. There was always a stigma on him after that; so his career was probably down the tubes, and he got out before he otherwise might have. What an unnecessary loss to the Air Force; and what a way to treat someone who had given so much for his country!

~~~
~~~

When they finally released Ike from the hospital in Nagoya, he went back to K-46, eager to finish out his missions. The required number was fluctuating between 85 and 100 on almost a daily basis. He'd fly a few missions and the number would change. Finally, he got his 85 missions in while the requirement was still 85. He was Stood Down. But before he could be put On Report, the number went back up to 100. Oh, no! Well, nothing to be done but fly the other fifteen missions. But after he had flown three more missions, the number was dropped again to 85. Fortuitously, it stayed at 85 until he was put On Report! So he finished out his tour of duty in Korea, having flown 88 combat missions in the Mustang, 152 combat hours in the F-51-D, with an elapsed time of just a little over six months, including the month in the hospital in Nagoya.

~~~

Unable to put my hard-earned teaching certificate to use because of the uncertainties of Air Force life, I had gotten a job at the Kaiser Aluminum plant in Baton Rouge and worked the entire time Ike was gone. I had tried to follow Ike's wishes and wash the Olds every week and wax it once a month. It looked great and worked fine most of the time—it should have; it was brand new. But it had started having the familiar pinging sounds that I recognized as valve problems. I had taken it in several times to the Olds place to have them look at it. But the trouble with valve pinging is that it happens when the car is cold; when the engine warms up, the noise usually stops. So it would ping when I'd start it in the morning but stop by the time I got to the Olds place since the engine had warmed up. No amount of my telling them that I knew what I was talking about would faze them.

Sure enough, when finally Ike came home in August, I met him in New Orleans. He had shaved off the moustache and he looked great to me. As soon as we got in the car, he turned on the ignition and the pinging started up.

"This car needs a valve job," was his proclamation.
~~~

~~~

When we arrived in Baton Rouge, there was a joyful reunion with Mother and Daddy and Monk out on the front lawn. Monk had at first growled at the interloper: but then he recognized Ike's smell, I guess. As soon as he did, he went wild, jumping up and down, as high as Ike's shoulder. The rest of the day, Monk was all over Ike; and it took him hours to calm down.

The warranty on the Olds had expired just before Ike got home; but I had documented every time I had taken it into the garage with that pinging. So they didn't argue with him when he told them they were <u>going</u> to give him a free valve job. I guess I just hadn't said it in the right tone of voice. Fortunately, Ike's prediction about cars going out of production never came true.

~~~

People kept getting killed in Korea right on up to the Armistice Agreement signed July 27, 1953.

Chapter 7 – Back Home Again – Part 1

Happy to be back together again, we struck out for Ike's new PCS assignment: the 3625th Flying Training Wing (Advanced Interceptor) at Tyndall AFB, just outside Panama City, Florida. This was the first PCS he had ever had, since all of the others (besides combat) had been training assignments and were considered TDYs. They still had some Mustangs there as well as T-33s, the two-seated version of the Shooting Star.

To tell the truth, I'm unable to remember exactly what his job was there at Tyndall in the beginning; because, almost as soon as we got there and got settled into a sub-standard apartment, he was sent in October of 1952 on TDY to Moody AFB, Georgia, at Valdosta. He was actually to go through two schools simultaneously, Jet Transition and Instructor Pilot School. He had mixed emotions about transitioning into jets: he knew it was the newest, hottest type of flying; but he really loved the Mustang. He was happy that he had been able to have the experience of flying that wonderful bird but was ready to move on with the times.

~~~

We were in Valdosta until December, much of that time spent frantically looking for housing. There was none. Finally, in desperation we rented a room in a lady's house, the price including meals. It seemed like a good deal at the time, because she had a lovely home and seemed nice. But it didn't take us long to realize that she was a martinet and we were to be treated like children and have no privacy. She would walk into our room without knocking, even if Ike was sitting there in his shorts, and start reaming us out for having a chair too close to the wallpaper or something equally as ridiculous. But worse than that, Ike was starving to death. Since he had to report in at 7 a.m., he didn't get any breakfast at her house. Then he couldn't come home for lunch, so missed out on that meal. When he finally got home at night, he got a warmed-over casserole and had to take the maid home since she had missed her bus because
~~~

of him. Neither was he allowed to bathe in the morning because it disturbed Mrs. B's beauty rest. "Mrs. B." became Ike's nickname for me if I ever started putting too much emphasis on the physical aspects of the house. He preferred having a home, not a spotless house. I guess that's my excuse for never having honed my housekeeping skills very well.

So, very shortly, we were apartment hunting again; but there was still none to be had. We finally rented a huge room in the home of a very nice couple, who operated a nice restaurant downtown as well as the little café across the street, where we ate most of our meals. I even helped out in the restaurant at times when the landlady was having some health problems.

The perennial housing search soon started us thinking about long-term housing arrangements. In Ike's first three years in the Air Force, he had been assigned to eight different bases. Many couples were unable to stay together because of the unavailability of suitable housing; and, whether as a direct result of that or not, many of those marriages failed. Base housing was out of the question for two reasons: there wasn't much of it for junior officers in those days; plus, there is no housing provided for families on TDY assignments. So we began looking at house trailers, which were only recently becoming larger and more respectable. We spent most of Ike's free time on weekends looking at different models and narrowing the field down to what we wanted and could afford. By getting a trailer, we figured, we'd have housing wherever we went; and our money would not be going down the tubes for rent but into an investment.

~~~

Back at Tyndall in December, we settled into a nice little duplex apartment close to the beach, our neighbors in the other side being Gwen and Andy Henry. Andy was going through some school at Tyndall. Ike went to work on his new assignment as Instructor Pilot. As an IP, he tested the flying proficiency of the other pilots on base. There were very rigid standards that had to be met and a certain number of hours required in various types of flying: night, weather,
~~~

cross-country, instruments, and the like. Not only did Ike have to keep current in all of those himself, but he was in the air a lot testing all the other pilots on the base. Some of those check flights got almost as hazardous as his combat flying in Korea had been. But he was enjoying flying the T-33, or T-Bird. It's a good thing because he was to spend many hours in it over the remainder of his career. I got a Civil Service job in the School Secretary's Office on base, as well; so we were "permanently" settled in.

Not long after this, the Mustangs were phased out at Tyndall and were to be put in mothballs. The last day that they were flown, we and many others went out to the flagpole when they made their last fly-by. It was an emotional time for Ike—he stood there saluting with tears running down his face. He and that bird had been bosom buddies for two long, hard years.

Chapter 8 - Operation "Tiger"

Ike's transition into T-33s had taken place in the fall of 1952. No sooner was he back in the cockpit at Tyndall than he was sent on another TDY. This time I was not able to go because I was working; and it was a whirlwind tour, anyway. He was to take part in Operation "Tiger," a program designed to give AFROTC cadets on university campuses an idea of what it's like to be a hot AF jet-jock. At that time, it was not mandatory for ROTC graduates to go directly to pilot training; that was to come later. So lectures given by recent Korean War returnees were to provide the incentive they needed to sign up for pilot training. The Police Action in Korea was still going on, and replacement pilots were needed. Ike was told that he could pick the area of the US he wanted to tour with Operation "Tiger" and would probably be assured an assignment to ROTC duty on any campus he wanted after this TDY.

He chose the Southeastern United States, and for about three weeks toured many campuses telling war stories and giving pep talks about how great it was to fly a hot aircraft. There may have been others; but the campuses I remember where he lectured were The Citadel, Clemson, U of Alabama, FSU, LSU, Tulane, U of Texas, and his Alma Mater, SLI. Col. Napier, the Deputy CO of Air University, HQ AFROTC in Montgomery, wrote this letter to Ike's C. O:

...First Lt Isaac M. Hamilton, as a representative of your command, was excellent in his performance of this special duty. His manner, conduct and willingness to please left a favorable impression with not only the many cadets he contacted but also with the Air Force personnel at the various Air Force ROTC detachments he visited...Despite Lt Hamilton's strenuous schedule, and difficult work load in addressing so many students, his enthusiasm never waned. It is the opinion of the majority of our Professors of Air Science and Tactics that these presentations were successful in creating the desired interest for taking flying training by our cadets upon their entering active duty with the United States Air Force.

When he got back home—still all fired up—we discussed it; and he decided to apply for ROTC duty and was given three preferences. His first choice of all the campuses he had visited was Florida State in Tallahassee, as he had found that detachment to be the best organized and operated of all the ones he had toured. He didn't much care which other campuses he put down as second and third choice; but I had some very strong 'druthers. I had been frustrated at not being able to teach or get a Master's Degree. I influenced him to put down the University of Texas at Austin for his second preference, because they had a very strong Spanish Department, and I had dreamed of going there for my Master's work. This would be a PCS assignment, and I'd have plenty of time to get that degree. Then he put down Tulane, in New Orleans, for his third choice, as it was not far from either of our families.

I must confess that I was secretly hoping that he wouldn't get his first choice but his second. However, the Air Force, which sometimes seemed to take great pleasure in <u>not</u> giving you what you ask for in the way of an assignment, acted favorably on his desires; and he was assigned to Florida State. He was to report in in August of 1953 after attending the six-week Academic Instructor Course, part of the Air Command and Staff School at Maxwell AFB, Alabama, in June and July.

Our first PCS, less than a year long and interrupted by at least two TDYs, was now history.

Chapter 9 - The Long, Long Trailer

We had done a lot of research on house trailers for the past year and had come to the conclusion that now was the time to get one. This was a gamble as far as Ike's career was concerned, because he was an officer and had to have a certain air of respectability about him. A lot of folks still looked down on people who lived in trailers, thinking of trailer parks as "Tourist Camps," places for transients and "Po' White Trash." But we decided that the benefits would outweigh the disadvantages so went on with our plan. Our payments were going to be $173 per month plus about $15 for lot rental, quite a bit more than we had been paying for rent; but the loan would be paid off in four years. Then the trailer would be all ours, and we'd be paying only lot rental. We figured that we needed to live in the trailer for five years to break even, seven years to make the investment pay off.

Because it was made down South, in Grand Prairie, Texas, and we could go to the factory and have our floor plan customized to a certain extent, we had zeroed in on the Travelite brand. Air Stream made the biggest and nicest trailers, all of 50 feet long; but they were also the most expensive and outside of our budget, not to mention being too heavy for us to pull with our Olds 88. (It wasn't until several years later that the Air Force started moving people's trailers for them. We were pioneers in this new area.) Of the remaining brands, the longest anybody made was 42 feet. Of course, that was by 8 feet wide; nobody had even visualized the 14' and 16' by 60' double-wides that exist now. So to Grand Prairie we went, having already picked out a "Chinese Modern" interior that we loved because it was paneled with light-colored woods. There at the factory, we wanted to have a few changes made in the floor plan.

When we got there, we found that the Travelite people, without asking us, had just come out with some brand new models. That was okay with us, though, because they were really nice and modern looking and had light colored wood in all the interiors, not the dark-stained paneling that we had disliked in most of the ones we had seen when doing our research. The one we picked was three-toned on the outside: a dark green and a light green stripe separated by a silver stripe, really pretty and streamlined-looking. We had also bought on sale in Panama City a Sears' Kenmore bolt-down automatic washing machine to put in it. We would have it delivered when we got the trailer to Montgomery, Alabama, where Ike would be attending Academic Instructors Course for six weeks at Maxwell AFB.

We were back to the drawing board on the floor plan because this trailer was so different from the ones we had been looking at. We were going to get one with only one bedroom so that we could have the longest living room possible. (Doctors had told us that it was unlikely we would have any children of our own.) Next to the sink we had the builders leave space for our washer and also had a drain put in for it. This was practically over the dead bodies of the people at the factory, who said that a washer in a trailer would never work, the drain wouldn't work, and so forth. We were the first people ever to have an automatic washer in one of their trailers; so I guess we were pioneers in this area, as well. We told them to let us worry about that; and they went ahead with our plans. In Fort Worth, we bought a Simmons Hide-a-Bed for the living room to replace the rinky-dink, fold-down kind of couch that was standard in trailers at that time. The only other change we had made was the addition of a cabinet between the washer and the living room, the top half for storing our beautiful new Noritake china, and the rest to be drawer space. They would build the walls of the trailer around our couch because it was too big to go through the door. They agreed to meet us halfway between Grand Prairie and Montgomery, in Monroe, Louisiana, and not charge us any delivery fee. We had gone to Montgomery and picked out a nice trailer park in Prattville, a small town just west of Montgomery, and had had hydraulic brakes and a trailer hitch installed on the Olds. So we were hot to trot.

The driver met us in Monroe as planned. He helped us hook up and was about to take off when Ike, with a stricken look on his face, said,

"Wait a minute! Don't you have any pointers for me on pulling this thing?"

"No," the man nonchalantly responded. "Just take it wide around the corners." And he was off.

So, with fear and trembling because almost all of our worldly belongings were in that car and trailer, we took off that Sunday around noon for a new adventure in our life. We had neglected to ask him what the overhead clearance was, as well as a thousand other things that would have come in handy to know; but it was too late. We were on our own. I look back now and have to laugh. I can't help comparing our situation with that of Lucille Ball and Desi Arnaz in their hysterical movie, *The Long, Long Trailer*.

We got as far as the Mississippi River without incident. But not only was the bridge crossing the river at Vicksburg narrow; it climbed steadily upward because the riverbank on the Mississippi side was higher than that on the Louisiana side. There was also a big curve to the left just before reaching land. If memory serves me right, there was even a tollbooth there for which we'd have to stop. So it was impossible to get up any momentum to make it up the incline. Besides that, we were afraid we wouldn't clear the overhead part of the bridge. Ike was hanging out of his window and I was hanging out of mine, looking in all directions. It seemed we were taking up our entire lane and half of the other one. I was a nervous wreck!

Well, somehow we made it into Vicksburg safely; but the gas gauge had dropped alarmingly in just that short distance; so we had to stop to gas up. We had not realized how much gas the Olds would guzzle trying to pull that heavy trailer. We stopped at a service station ASAP. While the attendant was filling the tank, a policeman came up to Ike. He was nice and polite and said,

"Good afternoon, Sir. How's it going? Do you need any help?"

"No, we're fine, Officer. Thank you."

"Well," replied the policeman, "As soon as you can, please try to pull off the road. You are blocking two lanes of traffic at the intersection."

We looked back; and, sure enough; the trailer was still out in the road! How embarrassing!

Things were relatively uneventful after that, except that we had to stop for gas every time we turned around. We should have gotten gas in Selma, fifty miles away from Montgomery; but the Texaco station was around a corner on a narrow street, and we had only a Texaco credit card in those days; so we said, "We can make it." Famous last words!

We had decided to take the Old Montgomery Road from Selma and not go all the way into Montgomery by way of the newer, main highway, because Prattville was about five miles out on the northwest side of Montgomery. Bad mistake! The road was hilly and curvy, and it seemed the gas gauge was breaking the sound barrier going down. The route was not very heavily populated; and this was a Sunday afternoon, of all things. We started looking for a service station of any kind about halfway to Prattville but found none open. We were getting more desperate by the minute. We even stopped at one station that was closed but seemed to have living quarters behind it; and we tried desperately to rouse someone. Nobody answered. About that time, a family car stopped, and the driver asked us whether we needed any help. Boy, did we need help! We told them about our plight; so they agreed to drive along behind us in case we ran out of gas before we made it to a station.

Well, our Guardian Angel must have been looking over us. We really had no serious problem getting to our destination. The Olds waited until we spotted a service station at the top of the first hill in Prattville before running out of gas. It was well within walking distance; so we were soon back on the road, but not until we had thanked our Good Samaritans profusely. The only other problem was that we had to stop at three trailer parks (they all looked alike in the dark and coming from another direction) before finding the place we had reserved: Home Sweet Home for the next six weeks.

~~~

For the time we were at Maxwell, we placed membership at the West End congregation of the church, because it was right off the base and, therefore, the closest one to us. Van Ingraham was the preacher there; and he and Gloria had us over and became very close friends. In fact, every member in the congregation treated us like royalty. We never once ate a Sunday meal at home the entire time we were there.

~~~

Those six weeks flew by, with Ike graduating on 17 July from AIC. We settled into our new home and loved it. The only major problem arose when they delivered our household goods from Panama City, including the automatic washer we had purchased on sale. Guess what? It was about ¼" too wide to go in through the door! We had known the door was narrow; but so was the washing machine, since it was one of the older, bolt-down types with no outer shell as the newer models had. But the resourceful deliveryman got some pliers and bent down the protruding part of the brad on one side; and it slipped right in, fitting perfectly into the spot we had prepared for it with so much opposition from the Travelite people.

We had just thought that was an obstacle, though. When we put a load of clothes in it and cranked it up, and it got to the spin cycle, it rattled the blinds and nearly shook the walls down. I guess that was one of the things the Travelite salespeople had been trying to tell us. We were now in big trouble. What to do? With not much hope, we went shopping at Sears in Montgomery and, Lo, and Behold, found an apartment-sized washer—one of the newer ones with the square outer shell and so, hopefully, more stable—which just exactly met the specifications we needed to get it, not only through the door, but into the spot we had reserved for the other washer. The good folks at Sears gave us credit on the sale washer we'd bought in Panama City; and for only a pittance more, we were in business with a new washing machine. Since we had struggled through college with only a small tabletop agitator washer, then an old wringer-type one, and later had only a <u>semi</u>-automatic one, we felt as though we had finally joined the Twentieth Century. We were smelling like a rose again. Somebody Upstairs must like us.

Chapter 10 - AFROTC-FSU – Part 1

We arrived in the beautiful city of Tallahassee in August, 1953, raring to go. Although Ike had been given the <u>temporary</u> rank of 1st Lt on 27 May 1952 while still in Korea (not uncommon during wartime), he was also given the <u>permanent</u> rank of 1st Lt. on the same day he reported in for duty at FSU; but the "effective date" wasn't until May 6, 1954. Clear as mud? Yeah, me, too. Also on 4 September, he was awarded two Bronze Service Stars for the Korean Service Medal for service during his assignment there from 2 March to 31 August 1952.

Ike was now a card-carrying Academic Instructor, ready to stamp out ignorance in the first year cadets at AFROTC Detachment 145 at Florida State University. I was in my new job as High School English teacher at Havana High School in a rural, shade-tobacco-growing community sixteen miles from Tally. Since I had arrived jobless at the end of the summer, I felt lucky to get any position at all, even though it was to teach English and not Spanish, my first love, and it was in Gadsden County, the lowest-paying county for teachers in Florida. The salaries were still better than those in Louisiana, though; and I was happy to be working in my field after three years of knocking around since my graduation.

~~~

Would you believe Ike was to have one more TDY before school started?—an AFROTC Curriculum Workshop at Louisiana Tech in Ruston. I was antsy about not having my textbooks yet, but accompanied him anyway as far as Baton Rouge, where I stayed the three weeks with my folks. I was able to do some research at the Education Library at LSU, even though I still was clueless as to the textbooks I would be using. When we had driven through Havana on our way to Louisiana for the express purpose of picking up my textbooks, the janitor had been unavailable to open the bookroom; so I left Florida with none of the books I was to be teaching.
~~~

No problem. The school had <u>two weeks</u> of Pre-Planning before school actually started; so that would give me plenty of time to prepare, right? Wrong! <u>Every</u> morning for the entire two weeks was taken up with faculty meetings. About fifteen minutes of that entire time was useful to me; the rest of the time the faculty was hassling over the schedule. I knew nothing about schedules but was too timid on my first teaching assignment to beg off; so I suffered through it, thinking that at least I would have two weeks of afternoons to prepare for the beginning of school. Wrong again! Since I was the New Kid on the Block and everyone else there had been teaching the same thing from Day One of Creation and hadn't written a new lesson plan in recent history, they all felt obligated to come and visit me in my room! Polite thing that I am, I suffered through that, not feeling able to say what I should have said, "I'm sorry. I need to spend some time on my lesson plans. Would you excuse me?" So besides having the books ready to hand out and getting the room more-or-less ready, I got nothing worthwhile done during the Pre-Planning period. I worked like crazy at home, though, and had a sum total of <u>two days</u> of lesson plans ready when school actually started. Since my Methods class at SLI had been very generic—High School only, no specific subject—and since my Practice Teaching had been in Spanish, not in English, I had no idea how to teach English. I fell back on the same old way I had been taught in High School—alternating every six weeks between Grammar and Literature. Since I loved to read and felt a little rusty on my grammar rules, I decided to start off with Literature—a bad choice since I was a slow reader and could barely keep up with the assignments I had given the students.

Well, you get the picture. The students and I suffered through the first year, with my teaching on a provisional certificate since I lacked a Speech course and a Methods course in Teaching High School English. During the Spring semester, I did take a wonderful Methods course at night, taught by the author of the textbook himself, and learned some exciting new ways to teach English. A Speech course in Summer School finished off my requirements; and I began my second year of teaching feeling like I knew a little bit about what was I was supposed to be doing. At least I knew a lot of things <u>not</u> to do. And, in addition, I was able to talk the principal into letting me teach one Spanish class as well. So I was loving my new career.

~~~

Ike fit right into the ROTC unit there and hit the ground running. As Assistant Professor of Air Science, he taught all but one of the freshman Military Science sections, the other one being taught by Col. Paul Campbell, the Professor of Air Science (the "and Tactics" part of that title had been dropped since our SLI days). The Detachment personnel consisted of just a handful each of officers and enlisted men. Since there were so few officers, we were a close-knit group, even though Ike, as the newest 1st Lt., was always bottom man on the Totem pole. But we were treated royally, attending all the parties and having fun playing Charades with the bunch. Col. Campbell and his wife Vickie, as well as the others, were very hospitable. No one minded that we didn't drink, and they never got drunk; so all was well.

~~~

After living in a nice trailer park for a year, we found a spot to park our trailer about five miles out of town on a vacant, tree-shaded lot. The setting was beautiful and had hookups and a patio already waiting for us. We had people over a lot, with Ike buying a grill and cooking outdoors much of the time because of the extreme Florida heat. Although the trailer was air conditioned, we had to turn the unit down to freezing early in the morning in order to have it hold its own in the heat of the afternoon, even when not using the stove for cooking. Once we had Col. and Mrs. Campbell over for dinner; and everything went very well, if I do say so myself. They seemed impressed by our cozy trailer—that is, until they were leaving and Col. Campbell, a very tall man, whammed his head against the doorframe as he was stepping out onto the patio!

~~~
~~~

In the spring semester of that first year there, I caught the mumps from the kids at school and was as sick as the proverbial horse, missing two weeks of school and needing to have missed more. Since I, as the English teacher in the High School, had inherited the jobs of Senior sponsor, Beta Club sponsor, and Newspaper sponsor, I definitely had my hands full. Ike was in his busiest period, since Colonel Campbell had asked him to rewrite the entire freshman Military Science curriculum. He was burning the candle at both ends and unable to do anything but fix me a bowl of soup when he'd come home at night, before heading back to the office to work until the wee hours. I could hardly recognize him as the same guy who had gone to bed at nine p.m. every night at SLI. I lost fifteen pounds with that case of the mumps, but I don't recommend that weight-loss plan!

~~~

The summer of 1954 brought Summer School for me (I had to get that speech course out of the way for my Florida certification) and ROTC Summer Camp for Ike and his cadets at Tyndall. He was up to his old tricks of flying every possible minute. According to Major Roger R. Francis' Letter of Appreciation sent to Col Campbell,

Lt Hamilton was untiring, industrious and meticulous in performing his duties…Besides being the Operations and Training Officer he also handled the PIO guiding the Cadet Staff in the publishing of their Camp Book. He never missed a day flying with the Cadets in the T-33 type aircraft. I consider him to be one of the sharpest and most thorough pilots I have ever flown with…I consider him to be the most outstanding 1st Lieutenant I have ever had the pleasure of working with. He is well balanced, mentally coordinated, and quick in apprehension. I would consider it an honor to serve with Lt Hamilton anytime…I would suggest that every effort be made to encourage this officer to apply for a Regular Commission.
~~~

Chapter 11 - The Son of Promise

The second year of Ike's tour of duty at the FSU ROTC detachment was well under way. I was having a ball teaching Spanish and sponsoring the Spanish Club as well as all the other things I sponsored at Havana High. We had decided to try to work toward Master's degrees while on PCS at a good university; so we were taking a graduate level Tests and Measurements course together at night.

~~~

As if we didn't have enough going on in our lives, we had still been trying to have a child. We had already been married almost seven years and had been told it was unlikely we would have children of our own so we should adopt. At first Ike wouldn't even hear of adopting; but I had finally convinced him we should look into it. So we had gotten an application for adoption; but it was sobering: We would have had to sign papers saying we would live in the State of Florida for at least two years <u>after</u> we got the baby. Since he already had less than two years to go on his tour there, it looked unlikely that we'd be able to adopt in Florida.

Well, all that became moot the night I showed up late for our Education class after visiting the OB-GYN doctor and learning that—Wonder of Wonders—I was pregnant! It was hard to keep the excitement from showing during the class, since we sat up on the first row, right under the teacher's nose. So he let us share the news with the class; and everybody was happy for us. We finished that course but didn't get any farther on our plans for graduate school. Because of time limitations, we eventually lost the hours we had gotten at FSU toward Master's degrees. But we didn't care; we had other things on our minds now.

~~~

Havana, Florida, was still in the Dark Ages. When I told my principal in November that I was pregnant; he wasn't very happy. He was going to have to find a replacement for me for the second semester, one who could teach Spanish as well as English. He determined that I could not teach past the first semester. If it were now, I could stand my ground and teach right up to my delivery time if I chose to; but those were different times. He also declared that I was not to tell my students I was pregnant. How archaic can you get? These were farm kids, all of whom had little brothers and sisters and knew all about the Birds and the Bees. But I did my best to hold my tongue. Since I wore my clothes skin-tight in those days, I soon outgrew them. So Mother sent me some of her dresses to finish out the semester since she was somewhat bigger in the waist than I. A rumor had gone around about my being pregnant during my first year at Havana. Since it wasn't true, I had had no problem denying it. But this time when the rumor mill started grinding among the kids, I had to come up with something to tell them. My response when asked whether I was pregnant was,

"You know, it's funny how those rumors get started! The same one went around about me last year!"

Then I shut up and left them wondering. I was safe until after Christmas and the end of the first semester, which in those days was in late January. After I made the big announcement that I wouldn't be back the second semester and gave the reason, my Homeroom Seniors gave me a very nice shower before I left. The ROTC detachment ladies did, also, as well as the ladies at church.

~~~

So I was well stocked on baby clothes, although they had to be unisex because at that time it wasn't possible to know the gender of the baby before birth. When it got close to June 2, my due date, we moved the bed out of our bedroom, bought a baby bed and a baby chest of drawers; and with my old cedar chest, Baby Hamilton had a nice room waiting. We moved onto the Simmons Hide-a-Bed in the
~~~

living room, more thankful than ever that we had insisted on having a nice couch.

There was a young man we knew at church, named Don Lewis, who was working toward a PHD in Biochemistry. He had a friend doing a study on how to determine the gender of a baby before birth. Don asked me to participate in the study his friend was doing. At first, I was reluctant because, for some unknown reason, I didn't think I wanted to know the gender before birth.

"No, I don't think I want to know," I told him.

He said, "Well, what if we do the test and keep the results from you until after the baby's birth?"

I responded, "No, because you could say anything you wanted to after the birth, and how would I know whether it was true or not?

"Well, I tell you what," he replied. "We'll do the test; I'll put the results in a sealed envelope and give it to you; and you can open it after the baby is born."

I liked that idea; so that's what we did. For the test, I had to spit into a test tube the first thing in the morning once a week for six weeks; Ike would then rush it in to the lab where it would be kept under controlled conditions until all the samples could be run together later that day. When the test was over, Don gave me the sealed envelope, which I placed in the suitcase I was taking to the hospital.

Daddy was on a retainer from the Braun Company, out of Alhambra, California, the construction company he worked for, so had a few weeks off; and he and mother came to Florida for a month to await the arrival of their second grandchild. (My big brother Lane and his wife Pic had a precious 3-year-old girl.) Our landlady, Jo Osborne, lived next door and rented a room to my folks; so they settled in; and I didn't have to lift a finger after they got there. It was so hot that my ankles stayed swollen all the time, but Daddy always bent over and buckled my sandal straps for me. Mother did all the cooking and washing; and Daddy hung up all the clothes. He was afraid for me to do it since I might get the umbilical cord wrapped around the baby's neck. Talk about spoiled!

When Ike and I had been married seven years, four months and four days, I finally went to the hospital. It was early on the morning of June 4th, 1955, two days after the baby was supposedly due. My neighbor-landlady, Jo, was just coming off the night shift as a private nurse. She came into the labor room where I was and stayed with me all the way through the delivery, which took place at about noon. That was before the days of La Maze and husbands staying in the delivery room, and it's a good thing. There could be only one family member in the labor room with me at a time; so Mother, Daddy and Ike would take turns being with me. But when I would get the first little twinge of a labor pain, Ike or Daddy would bolt out of the door faster than the speed of sound! So Mother got most of the hand-holding duty. Jo was calming and solid as a rock. She kept me posted blow-by-blow on how things were progressing. That was good because I hardly knew anything. I had been given Demerol-Scopolamine, called Twilight Sleep, which was supposed to make me forget the pain. And it did its job well.

"Good. They're coming two minutes apart now," Jo would say.

"What do you mean? It's been at least 30 minutes since the last one," I would answer incredulously.

I also went sort of out of my mind. I kept worrying about some fish we had thawed out the day before to have for supper that night. If I told Mother once, I must have told her twenty times that those fish needed to be cooked right away or they would spoil. I was also overly concerned that Ike's uniforms wouldn't be put out for the cleaning man to pick up. He came a certain day of the week; and if that day were missed, Ike wouldn't have clean uniforms when he needed them. So I gave everyone a hard time about that, too, repeating my concerns multiple times, since the drug made me forget what I had just said.

~~~

After we had fixed up the bedroom in the Travelite for the baby, I put my open suitcase underneath the baby bed to have ready when I would go to the hospital. We had bred Monk when we got to Tallahassee and decided to keep the runt of the litter, a cute little female. We had been thinking of getting another male and calling him Chip, for Chip Off The Old Block. But someone told us that we should get a female because two males would have turf wars. So we had gotten a female and named her Chippie. Both dogs knew something was in the offing whenever a suitcase appeared; and they didn't want to be left behind. Whenever we left the bedroom door open for even a second, Chippie would dash in there, jump into the suitcase, and look up at us as if to say, "When are we going? Don't forget to take me!"

~~~

Also in the suitcase was the sealed envelope from Don Lewis with the results of the gender test. When I went into labor and it was obvious that it wasn't false labor, I figured that it no longer mattered about keeping the letter a secret; so Ike and I opened it. It was the most touching letter and read something like this:

"Dear David,

"Through a series of scientific tests, it was determined before your birth that you would be a boy. You can well marvel at the progress science has made in this field and I am glad that you have been a part of the discovery of new scientific procedures, …etc, etc, etc.

"If, however, Ann, the results did not turn out as we expected, you can still be glad that you are coming into the world at a time when science is making new discoveries every day, and it will probably not be long until gender can routinely be determined before birth …etc, etc.

"David or Ann, whichever you are, if you could have had a hand in choosing your parents, you could not have chosen two better ones than those God chose for you…etc, etc.

"Your Friend, Don Lewis"

When I delivered, they kept telling me it was a boy, and I kept saying, "Yes, I know. I read the letter." Just to make sure I understood, they spread his legs out and showed me that he was a boy—in all his glory!

~~~

Five days later we went home, and then the fun started. Since I was nursing Dave (something not being done by very many women in those days), I was the one who had to feed him. But bless Mother's heart! She slept each night on the couch cushions on the floor in Dave's room; and when he would cry in the night, she would get him up, change him, and bring him to me. I didn't even have to get out of bed! Such service!

I had never eaten breakfast on a regular basis after I was grown, but in the hospital I was ravenous all the time, especially since they'd bring the babies in to nurse at 5:00 a.m., and we wouldn't get breakfast until seven. My roomie and I were eating everything in sight—all the candy and fruit that people had brought us—anything that wasn't plastic! So from that day forward, I've always had to eat as soon as I wake up in the morning. My sweet Daddy would make bacon and eggs and toast in Jo's kitchen, so as not to heat up the trailer, and then would bring it over when I was up and ready to eat. He also hung on the clothesline every diaper that was washed. (Good disposable diapers had not yet come along; so cloth diapers and plastic pants were *de rigueur*.)

Ike was on his summer schedule (no ROTC classes in the summer); so he had to go to work only half of each day. Also, Mother had paid my occasional maid to come every day for a couple of weeks to help me out. So when Mother and Daddy had to leave
~~~

when Dave was about two weeks old, I really was in pretty good shape. Nevertheless, they had spoiled me so much that I thought the end of the world had come when they left. I assured them I'd be fine but then couldn't help tuning up as they drove off! Ike and I were on our own now with our precious, long-awaited little boy.

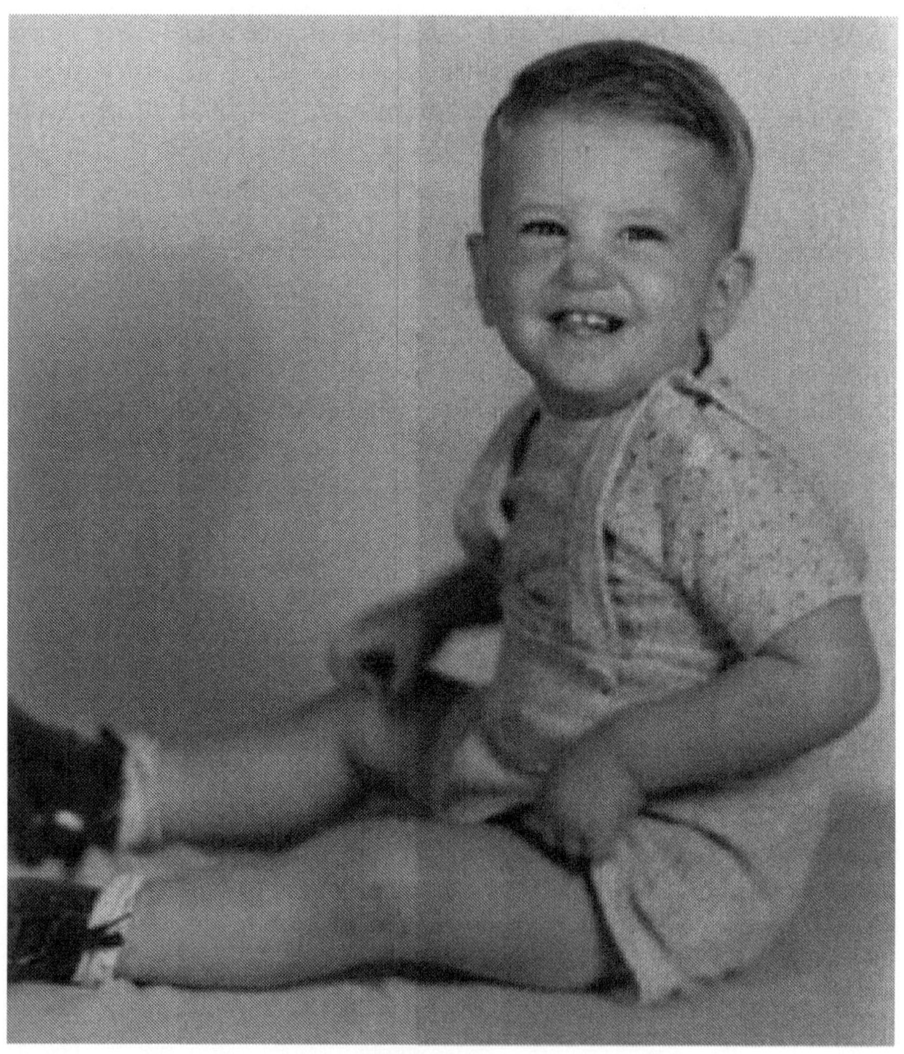

David Lane Hamilton, age 2

Chapter 12 - AFROTC – FSU – Part 2

Things soon fell into a routine; and life went on, albeit with our having to make many an adjustment to our lifestyle. Monk was now four years old and Chippie, nine months. Neither of them ever offered to hurt Dave in any way; but naturally, we kept a close eye on them. Monk, Ol' Mama's boy, thought I was spending an inordinate amount of time with the little interloper and got bent out of shape whenever I would sit on the couch and nurse Dave. Monk would perch on the back of the easy chair, with the front half of his body on Ike's shoulder, and glare at me out of the corner of his eye. Chippie appointed herself a committee of one to make sure that I was aware of every time Dave woke up and cried. She would run back and forth from me to the bedroom until I went to take care of her charge's needs.

~~~

For the last two years we were in Tallahassee, Ike played his violin with the Florida State Symphony, which was based at FSU. One year the artist in residence at the University was Ernö Donhyányi, the Hungarian composer. At one concert in which Ike played, Mr. Donhyány performed with the orchestra his *Variations on a Nursery Rhyme*, the *Twinkle, Twinkle, Little Star* theme. Another of the more memorable performances was the presentation of my favorite opera, *Carmen*. Since Ike sat on the outside in the orchestra, he was always easily spotted, looking handsome in his dress blues with white shirt and black tie.

~~~

The Letter of Appreciation from Major Francis at the 1954 ROTC Summer Camp at Tyndall, evidently put some kind of ball into motion; because in 1956, Ike finally received his Regular Commission. With the Reserve Commission received when graduating from the ROTC program, he didn't have the security a

Regular officer had. If there are cuts in personnel, the Reserve officers are the first to go. If you went into the Air Force on a Reserve Commission, you had to serve at least three years before the Regular one came through. He was still bottom man on the Totem pole at his work, but he was knocking himself out and doing a great job, getting superlative write-ups on his OERs. A new PAS took over the detachment when Col. Campbell left and was replaced. Colonel Withycombe and his wife Audrey were very down-to-earth, approachable people who always treated us with respect, as had the Campbells.

~~~

While living in Tallahassee, we were active members of the Gadsden Street church of Christ and made many more life-long friends there. The building wasn't very close to the campus; so we usually helped with our car in transporting the student members to the services. A few years later, a congregation was started just off the campus to make it more convenient for the university students to attend. Ike had not yet begun preaching when we lived there, but he did lead singing at times. In later years, when we would visit Tally, having friends in both congregations, we would attend services at whichever of the two Ike had been asked either to preach or to lead singing. He wasn't bashful about offering his services, either.

~~~

He missed full-time, front line flying but flew T-Birds every chance he could down at Tyndall AFB, our old base in Panama City. He and Paul Suttle, another pilot on the ROTC staff normally went down and flew together. They still had to get in a certain number of hours every month in order to stay proficient. Toward the end of our tour in Tallahassee, Ike was unable to go one time and Paul flew with someone else. The weather had socked in quickly while they were airborne, and many planes were having to circle the field in a holding pattern waiting for the weather to let up enough for them to land. With fuel running low, Paul and his partner tried to land but had a mid-air collision with another plane they hadn't been able to see; and they crashed. Both pilots in the second plane were fine. Paul's flying buddy got out with only a broken back; but Paul was killed. But for the grace of God, it could have been Ike in that plane.

There had been other deaths among our acquaintances, but this was the one that hit the closest to home for me. I suppose it was because we were such a small, close group there at the ROTC detachment. We had socialized a lot with Paul and Hilda; and they had two precious little children. We drove up to Spartanburg, South Carolina, for the funeral. I had seen it done in movies many times, but after the playing of taps and the twenty-one gun salute at the military burial, the flag from Paul's casket was folded and given to Hilda. I wasn't to understand completely until forty years later what a desolate feeling the widow has when handed that flag as a memorial to her husband.

~~~

Our three years at Florida State had flown by, and we were now awaiting orders for our next assignment. Ike had put in for a 3-1/2-month school for junior officers, Squadron Officers School, at the Air Command and Staff College at Maxwell AFB, Alabama. It seemed to make sense to us for the AF to send him there in between assignments; and sure enough, he got his orders to go. Then, out of the blue, those orders were rescinded, and he was told that he was needed quickly at his new assignment at Shaw AFB, South Carolina. On the basis of his first orders to go to Maxwell, we had driven up to Montgomery and paid down on a spot in a nice trailer park just off the base. But that made too much sense; so now we had to cancel that reservation and go directly to Sumter to report in to the base.

~~~

Since we had bought our trailer three years before, the government had started paying to move trailers for their personnel; so we no longer had to tow the Travelite ourselves. We had purchased a new 1954 Olds 88; so we were driving along behind the trailer all the way up there. Somewhere along the way, Tommy, the driver of the semi pulling the trailer, hit a stretch of washboard road a little too fast; and we saw the trailer make several big bounces. He stopped and we stopped and looked all over inside, outside, and underneath; but couldn't see that any damage had been done

When we arrived at the Shady Grove Trailer Park outside Sumter, where we had reserved a spot, it was dark by the time we got the trailer maneuvered into place and parked. We let Tommy go on since it was so late and Ike didn't want to level the trailer at night. But when he leveled it in the morning, it didn't take us long to see that major damage had been done to the frame. It was way up underneath and would have been impossible to see in the dark. There was a large buckle in the frame underneath the kitchen floor, right under the washing machine. We were sorry then that we had listened to someone's advice to wrap our china ourselves in towels and store it down in the washing machine to avoid the movers' possibly breaking it. Because of that big bump, our beautiful Noritake set of twelve place settings now had only seven. The washer also wore out prematurely because it was off balance the rest of its life.

We hassled for months with the trucking company Tommy worked for. They didn't want to pay anything to help out with damages because Ike had signed the release. But Tommy was an honest man with a conscience; and at the risk of losing his job, he went to bat for us with his boss, admitting that he had been driving too fast when he hit that bump. Eventually they gave in, and we got a mediocre settlement for the damage.

Chapter 13 - Shaw AFB, SC

Ike wasn't too happy with his new job as OIC of the 9th AF NCO Academy at Hq 363rd ABGp at Shaw. He <u>had</u> made temporary Captain in October of 1956, and that eased the pain somewhat. However, he felt that any officer, even a ground-pounder, could have been doing the job he was doing. And after being away from full-time flying for three years, he was chomping at the bit to get back into the action. But he tackled the assignment with determination to do a good job and did so. However, before long, with justification in hand, he approached his Commanding Officer with a request to be reassigned to a flying job. His boss understood and acted favorable on it.   After only four months at the NCO Academy, he was reassigned to the 17th Tactical Reconnaissance Squadron right there at Shaw.

~~~

South Carolina was practically a "mission" area when it came to the church. Most churches of Christ in South Carolina in the fifties were small and struggling, the one in Sumter being no exception. We pitched in and soon became Old Timers there. Since they were small, they were very close-knit; so we enjoyed a lot of good, close fellowship with the folks there. Phillip Morrison, the preacher, was at least partially supported by his "home" congregation of Old Hickory, Tennessee. He was (and is) a great preacher, great singer, and all-around good man, whom we enjoyed, along with his wife Mary Margaret. The "local" members were all solid as a rock. They appreciated any little thing we did to help out; so we got put to work right away. I had never taught a children's class; but they soon gave me a Second Grade Bible class, which I enjoyed—that is, when Dave decided to stay in his own class and let me teach mine. Once when he was being particularly obstreperous, I finished out my lesson with Dave sitting on my lap. Ike occasionally relieved Roscoe, the song leader. With the local ladies I learned to do hospital and other types of visiting. Different families took turns preparing communion and cleaning the small house that served as our meeting place.
~~~

~~~

Dave was fifteen months old when we went to Shaw in September of 1956. He was toddling around all over the place and "talking" a blue streak, although even I couldn't understand him most of the time. We had a big yard, which we fenced in so he and the dogs could have the run of it. We bought a thing called a Super-Duper Pooper Scooper, which helped us keep Dave and the yard clean. We had Dave trained to let the dogs in or out whenever they scratched on the door. He had a cute little playmate named Frankie across the way; so things were getting livelier around the place all the time. Dave, ever the Gregarious One, soon had broken through shy little Frankie's defenses, and the two became almost inseparable.

~~~

Ike had enjoyed playing with the Florida State Orchestra while we were in Tallahassee; so he looked around for an orchestra in South Carolina. There was none in Little Ole Sumter; so he began driving to Columbia, the capital, forty miles away, once a week for rehearsals with the state orchestra there. He must have done that a dozen times. Then when the time came for the performance—he was away on TDY and didn't get to perform with them! That put a damper on things; so he didn't play anymore while we were at Shaw.

~~~

We went to visit Ike's mother in Lake Charles and then my folks in the New Orleans area for the Christmas holidays. We were basking in the family scene at Mother and Daddy's the day after Christmas when Ike got a call from his CO saying that he was to report in on the third of January for the 57-A class of Squadron Officers School at Maxwell AFB, Alabama. We left Dave with Mother and Daddy and made a mad dash up to Sumter to throw a few things in the car to have for the 3-1/2 months we would be in Montgomery. It was just not feasible to try to move the trailer for such a short period of time;
~~~

so we had to rent an apartment in Montgomery while paying lot rent in SC. Grumbling at the Air Force for its poor planning in not having allowed Ike to go to SOS straight from FSU when we could have just pulled our trailer there en route to Shaw, we rushed to Montgomery. Quickly, we found an apartment and hurried back to pick up Dave where Mother and Daddy were meeting us in Mobile, about halfway between New Orleans and Montgomery.

Chapter 14 - Squadron Officers School – Part 1

Squadron Officers School is a part of the Air Command and Staff College based at Maxwell AFB, Alabama. This was now our third assignment in Alabama and second in Montgomery; so we were beginning to feel almost like Alabamans. The stated mission of the school was "to increase the abilities of selected Captains and Lieutenants to perform as squadron commanders and as staff members." It was very intensive for the guys, with lectures by the local faculty members as well as by distinguished guest speakers. The curriculum consisted of classes on Power and Policy, Communicative Skills, Leadership, Command and Staff, Doctrine and Employment, and Professional Development. There were also strategic military planning, problem-solving exercises, staff studies, lots of papers to be written and intensive sports competition. About half of the married men brought their families. So that the bored wives would leave their husbands alone and allow them to study, there were many activities planned for the wives: teas, coffees, picnics, tours, trips to movies, bowling, games, and the like.

The three sports played on "Mayhem Meadows" were soccer, volleyball and a game called flicker ball—a cross between football and basketball. The teams in the different sections of 20 students would compete against each other. The wives and children would usually dress in some sort of uniform and support their section's players at the games. This could get pretty intense at times, depending on the temperaments of the people involved. Fortunately, the wives in Ike's section were fairly levelheaded; so it didn't get out of hand, nor did we have to spend a lot of money on bizarre costumes for Dave and me, as we would have been expected to do in some of the other sections.

Since I was the English teacher and only typist in the family, guess who got to type all the papers and the staff study required of Ike? But Ike had a way with words, too; so I guess we made a pretty good team. He got A's on all of his papers, and his staff study won the prize for the best one in class 57-A. His section also won the highly competitive 24-hour "Tiger Trek," and the problem-solving exercise known as "Project X". His Section Leader, Col. Jay J. Taylor, wrote this about him on 12 April 1957:

Capt Hamilton fits well and deservingly into that niche of the outstanding squadron grade officer. His character and ethical standards are above reproach, his loyalty to the service and his fellow associates most admirable. He is truly dedicated in purpose and in deed. He invites challenging tasks and thrives on hard work and responsibility…While at SOS he strove to broaden himself in all areas. He welcomed the association with his peers and shared in their experiences, background and dreams of the future. He was an advisor and true friend to all who came in contact with him. He worked with painstaking thoroughness in all phases of the curriculum. His efforts in the communicative skills area were extraordinary. He made certain that his subjects for speeches and writing were of extreme importance to the USAF and highly interesting to his associates. His Air Power Report, the students' major writing effort, was outstanding and his Staff Study, which was equally as good, was selected as the finest in a group of 110 students. In addition to his exemplary individual efforts, he worked just as effectively as a member of the group. He was leader for the Unit Training exercise. The training program which was developed was selected as the best in the group. As Student Wing Commander for the Tactical Theater exercise he produced an outstanding Concept and Operations Plan. It was in the outdoor escape and evasion problem that he exhibited his metal (*sic*) as a leader and organizer. From the first moment in the section room to the final activities in the exercise, he led and directed the members in an impressive, effective manner. His sincerity and thoroughness brought grave realism into what could easily have been a mere school problem…

SOS "Project X," Maxwell AFB, AL, 1957
Ike Second from Right

~~~

Since we were living across town from the base, we placed membership at the Cloverdale church of Christ instead of at West End, right off the base, where we had attended while Ike was at AIC. We tried to get Dave started in Bible class; but he was still a little too young, I guess, and maybe too much of a Mama's boy, as well. He just wouldn't stay.

~~~

When graduation time rolled around, Ike's mother came from Lake Charles for the occasion; and we got to see Major General Lloyd P. Hopwood, Commander of Air Command and Staff College, award

Ike the DFC for "exceptional airmanship and courage" in Korea five years before. The occasion referred to was the rescue of a downed Marine F-4-U Corsair pilot on 25 June 1952. He also received an Oak Leaf Cluster for the DFC for "extraordinary achievement while participating in aerial flights against the enemy forces in North Korea" on 7 July 1952.

The letter that Col. Chitty, Commandant of SOS, wrote to Col. Nelson, CO of the 17th Sq. at Shaw, said, among other things, that

> ...Capt. Hamilton distinguished himself under intentionally competitive circumstances and was considered to be one of the 17 outstanding students in a class of 611 lieutenants and captains. I wish to congratulate him on his outstanding performance and exceptionally high degree of professional dedication.

Letters like that always look good in a fellow's record!

This very essential schooling behind him, we headed back to Shaw ready to tackle Ike's new exploit—transitioning into the RF-84 Thunderjet, his first swept-wing aircraft. His welcome promotion to the permanent rank of Captain came soon thereafter.

Chapter 15 - The Voodoo and Operation "Mobile Zebra"

Ike's transition into the photoreconnaissance workhorse, the RF-84 Thunderjet, went smoothly. This was the reconnaissance bird being flown by the Squadron he was assigned to at Shaw. Instead of guns mounted in the nose as on a fighter, there were cameras. In a combat situation, the recce pilots would fly in to "case the joint" and take pictures so that the fighter or bomber pilots could pinpoint their targets. Although Ike had come to an understanding with himself about the morality of war and believed his participation in it was justified in the defense of his county and smaller, more helpless ones, it still made him feel better to be pulling the "trigger" on a camera instead of on a gun. It didn't take him long to become proficient in the 84, although it wasn't his favorite aircraft. In fact, the pilots had nicknamed it the "Hog" because it had a tendency to wallow at low speeds. It wasn't to make a lot of difference to Ike anyway, because the squadron very soon transitioned into the latest and hottest bird, the RF-101 Voodoo, the recce version of the fighter.

Barney, the squadron Ops Officer, flew commercial up to St. Louis, where the McDonnell factory was located, and ferried back the very first Voodoo to land at Shaw, its new home. A funny story Barney liked to tell about was his boarding the commercial flight to St. Louis, wearing his flight suit and carrying his helmet and his parachute, and watching the looks on the passengers' faces when they saw him. He said he considered asking the pilot to show him his instrument card but thought better of it.

The entire squadron and their families, including Dave and me, were out on the flight line when Barney flew that first Voodoo into Shaw. We were flabbergasted. We had been told how huge it was but were still unprepared to see that tremendous bird being flown by one lone man. To add to the drama, Barney had attached a small American flag to the (midair refueling) probe and popped it up as soon as he taxied in to where we all were. It was quite an occasion

McDonnell RF -101 Voodoo

As soon as all the pilots got checked out in the bird and became proficient, they made several cross-country flights, even including some competition with other types of planes, out to Nellis AFB, Nevada, and George AFB, California. Ike had participated in some of those.

Then Operation Mobile Zebra was planned. In November, twelve birds and twelve pilots were to take part in a deployment exercise to the Far East—from Shaw through various interim bases, with the final destination being Tokyo. Only six planes and pilots actually went on that final leg, the additional ones going along as backup. Alternate pilots, an *en route* maintenance team, some KB-50 tanker planes, two flight surgeons, medics, communications people, and I-don't-know-who-all had to go along with them. It was one <u>big</u> logistical operation. Ike had been chosen as one of the pilots so would be gone TDY for quite some time, including over Thanksgiving.

Andy Henry and his wife Gwen, who had lived in the other side of our duplex in Panama City in 1953, were now stationed at Myrtle Beach AFB, South Carolina. Andy had some part in the communications for Mobile Zebra and was sent TDY to Shaw for the duration of the deployment exercise. He had to stay on base 24 hours a day, but Gwen came with him and brought their big, gentle

Weimeraner, Silver; and they stayed in the trailer with Dave and me and Monk and Chippie. That was quite a menagerie, but we all survived.

~~~

The team's first stop was George AFB; and the flight there was uneventful. The second stop was Hickam AFB, Hawaii. I don't remember whether they had to do mid-air refueling on that leg of the trip or not; but it, too, was uneventful. The next leg, from Hawaii to Tokyo, was the longest and required hook-up with a KB-50 tanker for mid-air refueling. They had all practiced refueling in mid-air out over the Atlantic; so it was no big deal, although somewhat tricky. The tanker, being a Multi, was naturally much slower than the Voodoo, a super-sonic jet aircraft. So in order for the refueling operation to take place, the tanker had to fly at maximum speed while the 101 had to fly up underneath and behind the tanker, slow down to practically a stall, pop the probe up, and connect with the refueling hose— somewhat like threading a needle while going hundreds of miles an hour.

On the flight out of Hickam, they were to refuel at about the halfway point, somewhere near Midway Island, where there was a US Naval Base. Everything was going hunky-dory for Ike until…Well, I'll let him tell it. I am including here verbatim his notes about his experiences on the flight out of Hawaii:

I took off from Honolulu International Airport at 2100Z <u>20 Nov 57</u>, the number 5 aircraft of a 6-aircraft flight to Anderson AFB. Approximately 10 minutes after take-off, the cockpit pressurization failed and the canopy iced up. The only visibility existing was the lower half of the windshield; so I took a position in the formation immediately behind and below the lead aircraft.

Approximately 15 minutes after T. O. the J-4 compass system failed, leaving the standby magnetic compass the only direction indicator. Failure of the J-4 compass system also made the radio magnetic indicator of the ARN 14D (omni navigational radio)
~~~

inoperative. Approximately 1 hour after T. O. the fuel quantity gage became inoperative. Approximately 2 + 30 after T.O. the ARC-34 (UHF radio) and the ARA-25 (UHF ADF) failed.

Tanker rendezvous for aerial refueling was at 2 + 51 after T. O. over Midway Islands at 15,000 feet. I descended in formation with the lead aircraft and sighted the tanker with which the lead aircraft was to refuel. The canopy was still iced up, so my visibility was still limited to the lower half of the windshield. As I slowed the aircraft down for refueling, I discovered that neither the refueling probe nor the wing flaps would extend. Both are necessary for refueling.

At this time I decided to turn back for Midway. Having no radio, I could not notify anyone of my intentions, nor could I signal from alongside another aircraft, as my canopy was iced up. As I turned back to Midway, I pulled ahead of the entire formation, hoping that someone would see me. Having no navigational equipment except the standby magnetic compass, I took up a reciprocal heading (051 deg) of the pre-briefed refueling heading. It was necessary to descend to 8000 feet for the canopy to de-ice. Immediately after reaching 8000 feet, the fuel low-level warning light illuminated, indicating approximately 2000 lbs. fuel remaining. This was approx. 3 + 00 after T. O. I estimated a maximum of 20 minutes before fuel starvation at this altitude. The APX-6 (IFF) was placed to the emergency position. The search for Midway was hampered by widespread patches of lower stratus clouds. I broadcast in the blind on Guard channel, just in case my UHF transmitter was operational.

After proceeding 10 minutes with the low-fuel warning light ON and Midway still not in sight, I began making preparations to eject.

Just then, however, I spotted Midway at 10 o'clock and took up a Northerly heading toward it. Being low on fuel, I landed out of a long base leg downwind on runway 24. Engine shut-down was 3 + 23 after T. O.

After landing I was informed that the spare tanker had seen me turn back toward Midway and had notified both the lead RF-101 and Midway tower. Midway had all available crash and rescue facilities standing by. The tower notified the lead 101 when I landed.

The reason I was south of Midway is that the tankers took up their outbound heading of 231 deg east of Midway instead of over Midway.

Investigation of the aircraft by pilot revealed that the cockpit pressurization line had broken in the left equipment bay and the following circuit breakers (37) in the same compartment were popped. (Then followed a list of the 37 circuit breakers that had failed—arh)

<u>21 Nov 57</u> (Thursday) Navy repaired broken pressurization line. Popped circuit breakers were re-engaged. Attempted engine starts unsuccessful. Battery discharged. Was charged during the night. Investigation revealed no AN/ARC-34 UHF radio or J-4 compass system maintenance facilities available this station.

<u>22 Nov 57</u> (Friday) Charged battery installed. Engine start successful. Engine run-up and taxi test revealed aircraft to be mechanically sound. Cockpit pressurization functioned properly. Following discrepancies of electrical nature: (1) Fuel Quantity gage inoperative; (2) ARC-34 transmits intermittently, and receives intermittently, on 243.0 only; (3) ARA-25 inoperative; (4) J-4 Compass system unreliable (making ARN-14D unreliable also).

Had Navy radio maintenance man familiar with ARC-27 (UHF radio) check over ARC-34, though he was unable to locate trouble.

<u>25 Nov 57</u> (Mon.) – During engine run up, cockpit pressurization line broke where temporarily repaired. Navy immediately began to improvise new fix.

<u>26 Nov 57 </u>(Tues) – Navy repaired pressurization line the 2nd time, and during engine run-up it broke again. Navy is going to try to improvise again.

It wasn't as dramatic on paper as it was when Ike told the story, embellishing on every little point, such as his decision to bail out.

What should he do? His fuel was running out a lot faster because of the lower altitude; so he knew he didn't have enough to turn back for Hickam, even if he could have navigated to there, which he couldn't because all of his navigational equipment was out, too. For the first time in his flying career, he began looking around for a place to bail out. A few other pilot friends of his had bailed out of aircraft before; but it was something you really thought long and hard about, for various reasons, not the least of which was the millions of dollars the plane cost.

Ike's choices were limited: Water and more water. He spotted a patch of water that was lighter colored than the rest and figured that it was probably shallower there. So he was considering bailing out there. Then he reconsidered, thinking that the lighter color possibly indicated coral reefs, and he could get all cut up on them. So he headed back out over the darker waters. Just when he thought that he'd better go ahead and bail out, a tiny patch of green peeped through the cloud covers at him—Midway Island! He headed straight for the runway there and made an emergency landing without even being able to radio ahead. He was unable even to circle the runway so just flew straight in—landing on the wrong end of the runway. Praying that his tail chute would work, he pulled it; and—Thanks be to God—it engaged! Otherwise he would probably have overshot the short runway, which hadn't been designed to accommodate an RF 101.

And the part about the crash vehicles on the runway at Midway— every emergency vehicle they owned—ambulances, fuel cars, fire trucks, the works, was out there. You can imagine their surprise when, out of nowhere, there zoomed in this humongous bird right over their heads, landing on the opposite end of the runway! They then tore down the runway to where Ike's plane had come to rest, inches away from the end of the runway and the water. He was in great shape, thanking the Lord for his escape from the jaws of death. He was prone to exaggerate (What pilot isn't?); so I don't know how much fuel was left in his tank. I imagine it was not much more than the thirty seconds' worth that he claimed.

~~~

The next nine days, compared to those few hours of excitement, proved to be b-o-ring. The Maintenance guys gave it the Ol' Navy Try on getting his bird back in the air; but they had never seen one like it before and were clueless as to how to fix it. The main entertainment on that base was sitting around watching the albatrosses, or Gooney Birds, mate and try to fly. Ike had his 8mm movie camera and took literally hundreds of feet of movies of the Gooney Birds. They were so funny and awkward; and when we'd watch those movies later, Ike would give the sound effects to go with the head bobbing they were doing. I did see a good looking nurse walk by with a pie in one of the shots; so I guess there was a little more to do than watch the albatrosses.

~~~

Then on November 28th, Thanksgiving Day, Ike really had something to be thankful for—his Squadron's *en route* Maintenance Team arrived at Midway to get his bird back in the air. They spent the day working on it and <u>thought</u> they had fixed everything. So the next day, he took off for Hawaii, happy to be back in the cockpit again. He soon learned, though, that his compass and some of the other navigational equipment still weren't working properly. So he was on his own again, flying by Dead Reckoning, better known as Flying by the Seat of Your Pants, back to Hawaii. Once again, by the Grace of God, he made it into the airfield without any major problems. He was stuck there the rest of the time until the guys came back through on their way back from the Far East.

~~~

As soon as he got back to Hawaii, Ike called me and started telling me all about what had happened to him. He seemed disappointed when he learned that I had been getting blow-by-blow accounts of his every move by way of Andy Henry. Andy was in constant touch with the communications people on Ike's team and had kept me posted on the progress—or lack thereof—of the squadron all the way, bringing me up-to-date frequently once Ike landed on Midway. His thunder stolen, all Ike had to do was see that his bird was air-worthy by the time he was to return—and have somebody take movies while he sat around in his new Hawaiian shirts sipping tall colorful-looking drinks with umbrellas in them!

~~~

We had gotten a brand new 1957 Ford Fairlane 500 in Columbia as soon as they came out in late 1956. (After all you couldn't let a car get more than three years old, now could you?). Then when Volkswagen first started making the Beetle, Ike wanted one immediately. The only second set of wheels we had ever had was his Vespa motor scooter; and we felt ready to get some other second set of wheels. But a Beetle???? I thought it was the ugliest car I had ever laid eyes on and didn't see how Ike could possibly be serious about wanting one. But want one he did; so nothing would do but we must have one. However, there was a six-months waiting period before we could get one. But he had gone ahead and put our name on the list. You guessed it—the six months' waiting period was up while he was gone on Operation Mobile Zebra. So I got to be the one to go to Columbia and pick it up.

I don't remember how I got there; I guess a friend dropped me off. But I signed the papers and struck out for Sumter. It was hard enough trying to get used to the four forward gears and having to lock the gear shift into just the right hole in order to put it in Reverse. There was another slight problem, too. That model of VW had to come to a <u>complete</u> <u>stop</u> before you could shift into First. What a drag! Even though I had been driving standard shifts and later, automatic ones since I was twelve—longer than Ike had been driving—I still had to get used to that arrangement of gears. So I chugged along and killed the engine, chugged along and killed the engine all through the town traffic until I finally got out on the open highway. The rest of the trip back was uneventful, but the car didn't have much gas in it. So I stopped at our favorite Esso station right across the highway from Shaw. The attendant knew it was a new car and serviced it for me (This was before the days of Self-Service only), then came to me with a stricken look on his face.

"Did you know that they let you get away from the dealer's without putting any water in the radiator?!"

Even though Ike had told me that the VW had an air-cooled engine, this guy had taken me by surprise. I was horrified, knowing that Ike would have my hide if I ruined the engine of his new toy before he even came back from his TDY. Then the attendant started laughing, and I remembered that, being air-cooled, the car didn't even <u>have</u> a radiator. He had gotten me but good! It took a long time before I could live that down.

Chapter 16 - Shaw AFB – Part 2

Back at Shaw, the guys settled into the routine of flying. Ike was having a ball flying his hot new aircraft. Dave was 18 months old, and Christmas was coming up. Nearly everything on base was to shut down for the holidays. Ike had some leave coming to him; so we took off for Port Arthur, Texas, where Daddy was on a new construction job. We had decided to leave Dave and the dogs with Mother and Daddy and make another trip down into Mexico after Christmas. We were driving the VW because it was new and much cheaper to drive than the Ford.

Off we went and had a great time sightseeing. But, although we had planned to spend three weeks there, we found that we were missing Dave more than we'd expected to. So we turned around and headed back to Port Arthur a week sooner than planned. Mother seemed really relieved when we showed up, because she said Dave was starting to get tired of her and be obstreperous. After several more days visiting with my folks, we went back to Shaw. Before Ike reported back in from his leave, we spent the time well and did two major things. He assembled the huge swing set we had bought Dave for Christmas—no mean feat. And we rented a locker in the frozen food plant and stocked it with a hindquarter of beef and lots of frozen vegetables, bacon, sausage and other goodies.

~~~

The day Ike reported back in, he received a big surprise: He was on orders to be assigned to Sembach AB, Germany! Wow! What a shock. Not only did we have a swing set we'd have to dissemble very shortly but we also had a locker full of frozen food to eat up in a hurry and a brand new Volkswagen to dispose of. But those weren't the least of my problems. I had a relapse of the "Scared Hometown Girl Syndrome," bigtime! I was scared silly over the thoughts of going oversees.
~~~

But when I started complaining to my friends among the squadron wives, I soon learned that they'd all have given their eyeteeth to be in my place. They said that duty in Europe in general and Germany in particular was the most desirable in the world. They started telling me about wonderful, cheap shopping opportunities over there, interesting things that I should collect, and so forth. So I began seeing the assignment in a different light and actually looking forward to it.

But many months were to elapse before we left. It was several weeks before we were to leave, and Ike was first to go through Survival Training at Stead AFB, Nevada. We got busy tying up all the loose ends we could. We ate steaks almost every day between then and when we left. Since it was only a few months old and Volkswagens were still so much in demand, we had no trouble selling our VW for exactly what we had paid for it. We were later to wish that we had also sold the Ford. If we had followed my uncle's advice we would have. He said never to take an American car overseas, because they make good cars there; and parts and repairs were hard to get for American cars. But the Ford was just a little over a year old and we loved it. He had said that the two possible exceptions to that rule were Fords and Chevrolets. So we wound up shipping the Ford.

~~~

To tell the truth, I was almost glad that we would no longer be living in the trailer. The walls had begun to shrink remarkably as Dave and the dogs had gotten older, especially on rainy days when they would chase each other from one end of the trailer to the other. It had been paid off for almost a year; but we had not lived in it the magic seven years that we had felt necessary in order to make a profit on it. So, since we had a wonderful landlord at the Shady Grove Trailer Park, Mr. Pitts, we decided to leave it there and pay him a little over the lot rent ($15/month) to keep it rented for us.

Having all those things settled and wrapped up, our passports, shots and such things taken care of, we left Shaw in April, 1958. Ike was to report to Stead AFB, Nevada, for three weeks of Advanced
~~~

Survival Training. Dave and the dogs and I went back to Port Arthur, to wait with Mother and Daddy.

Chapter 17 - Survival Training, Stead AFB, Nevada

While I was in Port Arthur, we lost Monk. We had never used a leash with him very much because he minded us so well and soon knew his boundaries wherever we went. But my folks had no fence around their yard, and I was finding it harder and harder to keep Monk in the yard. I had known for several days that there was a female in heat somewhere in the neighborhood because of the way he'd been sneaking off every time I turned my head for a minute. One day, it registered with me that I hadn't seen him in the house in about thirty minutes. I called him all around the house, inside and out. No Monk. I asked Dave whether he had let Monk out, and he answered,

"Yes, Ma'am. He scratched on the door and I let him out." He was proud of himself because that had been his job back in Sumter.

I drove all over the neighborhood, screaming for Monk at the top of my lungs. No Monk. I called the pound and every veterinarian in town and ran an ad in the local newspaper. The pound employees told me that if he were found in town dead or alive, they would know about it. But neither they nor the vets ever called me back. I got two calls on the newspaper ads. One was from a lady not far from our street who said that as we spoke, she was looking at a little dog that met that description and he was walking down the street in front of her house. I jumped in the car and dashed over there; but by the time I got there, he was nowhere to be seen, even though I canvassed the neighborhood. I got another call and went to check it out. It was a precious little black and tan Toy Manchester-Terrier mix that could have been Monk's twin. But it wasn't Monk. I was heartbroken and hated having to tell Ike that I had let our little dog we had doted on for seven years get away from us. I had to hope that someone had seen him and fallen in love with him—maybe the owners of the dog in heat—and would give him a good, loving home.

~~~

Ike, meanwhile, was struggling along at Survival School in Nevada. The training was pretty rigorous as expected and was climaxed by a three-day stint in the woods where the various teams were competing to see who could best survive. They were given pemmican, which he hated and gagged on, and one roll of Life Savers. He disciplined himself, allowing himself only two of the Life Savers a day. So with that and the berries he was able to find, he survived without having to kill anything. The hardest part of the whole thing for him was being put in a cramped black box with no air or light. It was supposed to simulate some of the torture he might receive if shot down and taken as a POW. He did not know how long he would be kept in it; and it was pretty scary, especially because he was prone to be claustrophobic; besides he could neither sit nor stand; so it killed his back. But once again, he disciplined himself and counted the time off by seconds until they finally released him. He had been in the box approximately twenty minutes, which had seemed much longer. He said that some of the men screamed and yelled and had to be let out before the time was up.

Ike's team won the competition and was treated to a night in a luxury hotel in Las Vegas, with all the thick steak they were able to eat. He could have enjoyed it more if his stomach had not shrunk so much during the three days in the woods.

~~~

There was about a month before he had to report to go overseas in May. Mother and Daddy were moving to the New Orleans area again; and Dave, Chippie and I would stay with them until we got our port call about two months after Ike got overseas. We took some leave and traveled around visiting our relatives and friends for about a month, since the tour in Germany was supposed to be three years long.

Finally, his departure was just a couple of days away. We took one last little trip, leaving Dave with Mother and Daddy. We crossed

Lake Ponchartrain, going as far as the sleepy little town of Covington on the north bank, where we looked at some property with a view toward retirement, went to see a Little Theater play and spent the night in a motel.

As soon as we got back, I learned that Mother had bribed Dave with the promise of a Tums and had managed to complete his potty training, which I had been working on for almost a year. She was sheepish about how it had happened; but I didn't care <u>how</u> she had done it as long as I wouldn't have to be dragging wet diapers along with me on our overseas trip! She had actually wound up giving him only a "lick" of a Tums and not the whole thing. I soon switched to Life Savers, and the little imp played that "lick" thing out for almost another six months!

Chapter 18 - Phalsbourg AB, France - Part 1

Ike had no sooner arrived at Sembach AB, Germany, than he was sent TDY to Phalsbourg-Bourscheid AB, France. The 32nd Tactical Reconnaissance Squadron was based there and was getting ready to transition from the RF-84 Thunderjet (or "Hog") into the Voodoo. The AF couldn't send him PCS to Phalsbourg because he had already had his one PCS transfer for that fiscal year; so he would be there on TDY until the 1st of July. It was all semantics— Phalsbourg was to be our "permanent" home for the foreseeable future. It was a very small base in the middle of nowhere (but in absolutely breathtaking scenery) in the Rhine Valley across the river from Germany. The closest large city was lovely old Strasbourg; and Paris was about five hours away.

~~~

As soon as our Ford was delivered soon after his arrival at Phalsbourg, Ike took a couple of the Squadron pilots with him and made a weekend trip to Paris. On their way back, he managed to have the one and only wreck he ever had in his life. The French law held that anyone coming from the right automatically had the right of way. It didn't matter whether the road from the right was a cow path and the main road was four lanes or more, the driver on the cow path had the right of way. The French drivers were very trusting about it (or fatalistic) and didn't even bother to look to their left when they pulled out into traffic. I suppose Ike had to have heard the little piece of information about that law before getting his French driver's license, but it evidently didn't register very well with him. The Frenchman pulled out in front of him without even looking; and, although Ike was able to slow down considerably (or there would probably have been fatalities), he wound up hitting the guy's car. Fortunately, no one was hurt. But the front of our Ford was bashed in; and the car had to be towed to Frankfurt, Germany, about four hours from Phalsbourg, to have the front end repaired. Since air conditioning was not needed often in our part of the world, and since we had foolishly sent oversees not only an American car but a razzle-dazzle model as well,
~~~

nobody knew how to repair it. It was to be tied up three months before we finally got it back. Many's the time we wished somebody had dropped that Fairlane 500 in the Atlantic on its way over to Europe! Good old USAA, our military insurance company, fought the good fight for about a year trying to absolve Ike of responsibility; but in the end he was charged with "failure to avoid an accident" and we had to pay through the nose.

~~~

The reason Ike was needed so badly at Phalsbourg was that he had more hours in the 101 than anybody else in Europe. They needed the pilots with the most hours in the bird to be the Instructor Pilots to transition the rest of the pilots into it. There were two senior Captains, Thompson and Strickland, who outranked Ike; but they didn't have as much Voodoo time as he had. So he had a big part in the transition program, with Thompson and Strickland, and Lieutenants Chuck Lustig and Scotty Schoolfield the other four IPs.
~~~

Chapter 19 – The Port Call

Finally, the big day came when Dave and I received our travel orders, and I was to report to the Engineering Depot in New Orleans to process. The first snag I hit when it was noted that my orders were for Sembach and Ike was now at Phalsbourg. I tried to tell them that he was to be reassigned PCS to Phalsbourg come July 1 and the new fiscal year, so please send us to France, not Germany. But no one listened to me. After all, what did I know? I was only the wife. So I went from desk to desk, going through all the bureaucratic steps that somebody had decreed had to be gone through.

Then came the household goods weight allowance problem. Since we had been living in our own trailer for five years, we had practically no furniture of our own to take with us. But we were going to need every stick of furniture we could get our hands on. For assignments to Germany, the weight allowance was only 2,000 pounds, whereas the allowance for France was 8,000. That was because base housing in Germany came furnished with "Deutsch Mark" furniture, while French housing was unfurnished. That meant that if I could take only 2,000 pounds and got sent to France, we would have to buy furniture after we got housing. So, although my plea to be allowed to take 8,000 pounds also fell on deaf ears, I was adamant (as only I can be when need be). Miraculously, some kind soul agreed that I should have 8,000 pounds and that the household goods should be sent to France, although they were still sending Dave and me to Germany.

All of this took a full day. While I was waiting in one of the interminable lines, I wrote a letter to Ike, letting him know about our arrival day and time at Rhein-Main AB, (Frankfurt) Germany. As soon as I got out, I mailed that letter, considering it foolish since I was also sending him a cable. Well, that letter proved to be providential, as, unbeknownst to me at the time, Ike had again been sent TDY (yes, a TDY from his TDY!) to Ramstein AB, Germany. Because of the wreck of the Ford and its being tied up in repairs in Frankfurt, Ike had begged a ride with a fellow TDYer and imposed upon him to swing by the post office on their way out of Phalsbourg so he could check his mail. Sure enough, there was my letter with our arrival information. Since the cable I sent him <u>never</u> <u>arrived</u>, I shudder to think what would have happened if he hadn't gotten that letter. Although not quite the Babe in the Woods I had been when we had first gone to San Antonio eight years earlier, I still don't know how I would have gone about tracking down Hubby in another country.

<center>~~~</center>

Dave had had his third birthday in June, and it was now a hot July. We said our goodbyes to Mother and Daddy, they put us on a plane to Philadelphia, and we were off. Arriving in Philly, we took the shuttle to McGuire AFB, New Jersey, as instructed. So far, so good. But the fun was just beginning.

The folks at McGuire had evidently never heard of air conditioning. It was as hot as the proverbial Blue Blazes there. Worse than that, there were long lines of women and children processing, with long waits in between their calling our names, and not enough seats to go around in the huge hangar-like terminal. We would process through one line, stand around waiting forever for the H's to be called in another line, and <u>finally</u> get a seat. Dave was getting heavier and heavier as the day wore on. So when a seat became available, I'd thankfully sit down, he would zonk out in my lap; and then they'd call my letter of the alphabet to go stand in another line. I saw the wife of a Major from Shaw there, with her little boy. They were also to go to Rhein-Main, although would be stationed at a base in Germany. They looked calm, cool and collected, as if they had just stepped off the cover of Vogue magazine; and Dave and I were getting grubbier by the minute.

After an interminable, blistering day, they <u>finally</u> called our flight. We were sitting on our carry-on luggage out on the runway when an announcement came over the loud speaker:

"Because of the current Berlin Crisis, <u>all</u> flights to Europe are canceled until further notice."

100

My heart sank! Not after all we had been through! The speaker went on…

"Blah, blah, blah"… and then: "This does not include Flight Number so-and-so to Rhein-Main, Germany, which is now boarding."

Whew! That was a close call; but we were going to get to go after all! But, wait a minute! Did I want to be on the one plane to go into the middle of a crisis of any sort? Shouldn't I be worried that they were letting this whole planeload of helpless dependents go on over and land in the middle of some International Incident? But the truth was, I didn't care! At that point, I just wanted to get on that plane and get over there to my husband! Enough of this separation business. I was ready for us to be a family again. I'd let my Nervous Nellie mother do the worrying for all of us.

So we boarded the big AF prop job transport, and off we went on a flight that, because of stopovers for refueling at Gander AB, Newfoundland, and a change of planes in Shannon, Ireland, was to take a full eighteen hours. This on top of the eighteen or so hours already elapsed since we'd left New Orleans in the wee hours that morning, was turning into quite a day. The flight turned out to be relatively painless. I'd been dreading problems with Dave, but I shouldn't have worried; because, as soon as those big noisy engines cranked up, he zonked out and slept almost the entire eighteen hours. I even had to start trying to wake him as soon as I'd hear the stewardesses rattling around in the galley, to make sure he would be awake enough to eat when they delivered our food. He had turned into a zombie, and I had trouble getting him to eat.

On that same flight with us was the Major's wife from Shaw and her Little Lord Fauntleroy. But I had taken a clean set of clothes for us in our carry-on; so, while everyone else was checking out the duty-free shopping at Shannon, Dave and I were cleaning up and changing clothes in the rest room. I couldn't help gloating when I saw that Major's wife and her little boy when we finally arrived at Rhein-

Main. They looked grubby like Dave and I had looked that morning, and <u>we</u> could have posed for *Travelogue*'s cover!

I had a few anxious moments wondering whether Ike had gotten my cable and would be there to meet me after all. But fortunately, Hubby was there at Rhein Main, along with the Major, to greet us. They had pulled rank or somehow ignored regulations and gotten around to a spot where they could see us going through the customs line. They were both bouncing up and down like a couple of Jacks-in-the-Box, they were so happy to see their families.

Family Reunion, Rhein-Main AB, Germany

Ike had borrowed the car from the fellow TDY guy, stranded now down at Ramstein. After an elegant meal at a swanky Frankfurt restaurant (where I had my first *Truite Meunière*), we spent a comfortable night before driving on to Ramstein for a couple of more days of TDY and eventually arriving at Home Sweet Home, Phalsbourg Air Base.

Chapter 20 - Phalsbourg AB, France - Part 2

"The Friendliest Base in France"—Phalsbourg AB, was at the Jumping-Off Place. It was five kilometers to Phalsbourg, a small town where there was one American housing area, and 8 Ks to Sarrebourg, where there was a somewhat larger one. But it was to be a long time before we could obtain housing. There wasn't enough to go around; so your name had to be on a waiting list seemingly forever before getting into either Phalsbourg or Sarrebourg. The interim housing, 2-bedroom Italian-made house trailers on the base, were also very much in demand and required a wait. So the thing to do was get something "on the Economy" until your name came up. But since we were vehicle-less, that wouldn't work for us. We were allowed to stay only one week in the Visiting Officers' Quarters and then had to leave.

Fortunately for us, Capt. Hudson, an officer in Ike's squadron, was TDY to England for several months. He and his wife lived in one of the trailers on base and had offered it for the use of anyone new to the Squadron who needed it while they were gone. So after one week in the VOQ we moved into the Hudsons' trailer, which was within walking distance of most places we needed to go. We had been planning to get a second car in France, anyway; so before long we ordered a new Renault Dauphine; but that, too, would require a wait. Still no word on the Ford.

~~~

Then Ike and the rest of the squadron took off for Nouasseur AB, Morocco, where the pilots were to transition into the Voodoo. The weather in the Rhine Valley was not conducive to flying, to make an understatement. There was some sort of precipitation almost 364 days of the year, exacerbated by the fog that emanated seemingly constantly from the Rhine River about fifty miles east of the base. So if they had attempted to carry out the transition program at Phalsbourg, it would probably have still been going on now. Arrangements had been made for the transition to take place at
~~~

Nouasseur, where the sun shone all the time. Dave and I were not only stuck there alone, we were without our own housing or transportation. I worried that the Hudsons would turn up wanting their trailer back; but that never happened. After about six weeks we got our own trailer and soon our Hold Baggage came in. Things were starting to look up for us.

I won't belabor the point on all the TDY's Ike had while we were at Phalsbourg. We figured up that the first year Dave and I were in France, Ike was away a total of seven months of the time. If I had $5 for every TDY he went on, I'd be rich now. We learned to cope, even while still afoot. I learned that the Protestant Chaplain was putting on a Vacation Bible School at the Elementary-Junior High School near where we lived; so I walked Dave over there every day for the two weeks it lasted. I didn't want him to forget about how to act in Bible Class; and it gave him a chance to be with other kids, as well. I asked the Chaplain, a good old Southern Baptist guy, whether there were any members of the church of Christ on base. Since it was a small base, he didn't know of many, only a "blond-headed nurse," an Airman who sang in the Chapel choir at the Protestant services every Sunday, and Col. Albert McChristy, the base Commander, who also attended at the Chapel. That was sobering!

On one of Ike's quick trips back to Phalsbourg one weekend, Dave developed a rash; so we all walked down to the Base Dispensary. (The base was too small to have its own hospital.) Who should be on duty there that Sunday afternoon but a blond-headed nurse? I hadn't even had time to tell Ike about my talk with the Chaplain; so it surprised him and her both when I asked her,

"You wouldn't happen to belong to the church of Christ, would you?"

"Why, yes, I do," was her surprised answer. "How did you know?"

I told her about my talk with the Chaplain and that we were members of the church. Her name was Colleen Thornberg, and we all became very close friends—even though she <u>did</u> diagnose Dave with the measles that day! From then on, she and Ike and I would meet together every Sunday we could, which wasn't very often because of Ike's many TDYs and her rotating Sunday duty with the other two nurses on base. When we did meet, we would sing a few songs, have prayer and the Lord's Supper; and Ike would take us through some passage in the Bible. You wouldn't really call it a sermon because he hadn't progressed to that stage in his spiritual growth yet. One Sunday when he was away, after we got a car, Colleen and Dave and I drove over to Nancy, France, and looked up the American church of Christ we had heard about there. We had been missing the good old fellowship of "like-minded brethren" that we had enjoyed in the States. That meeting with the handful of Christians there was like an oasis in the desert to Coleen and me. She and I later tried to get the Chaplain to let us go through his records to see if we could find other members of the church stationed there. But since he was only a Captain and the Catholic Chaplain, a Major who outranked him, was against it, we were not allowed to do that. After about a year, the Catholic Chaplain rotated Stateside and was replaced by a 1st Lieutenant. Our friend the nice Protestant Chaplain now was the ranking Chaplain; so he let us go through his records; and we found about thirty names of people who had put the church of Christ down as their preference! The only problem was that they were all men; and, since Ike was gone most of the time, Colleen and I didn't feel comfortable trying to look them up. Later on some other developments enabled us to do so; but that was downstream a bit.

~~~

Ike was able to make fairly frequent cross-country flights up to Phalsbourg so dropped in on Dave and me when he could. We never knew when he'd be coming or, for that matter, when he'd be leaving, because no one had telephones. There were no phones in the trailers on base; and Major Findlay, the 32nd Squadron CO, had the only one in the entire Sarrebourg housing area, where we finally got to move in about October. When it was time for Ike to go back to Nouasseur, the Air Police would come out and let him know.
~~~

Once he brought home with him from Morocco, stuffed into the nose-cone of his 101, a beautiful, plush 9' x 12' Moroccan rug, a large brass tray-table with folding lemon-wood legs, and a couple of "camel saddles" (small stools). We were finally beginning to get some furnishings of our own. Ironically, when our household goods arrived, their total weight had amounted to something <u>under</u> 2000 pounds. All that raving and ranting I had done in the New Orleans Depot seemed ridiculous now, except that at least what few belongings we had, had come to France instead of to Germany. Mother and Daddy had contributed a few small pieces of furniture; but the basics we had to check out from Base Housing. There was a supply of what was called *Deutsch Mark* furniture that had been brought down from Germany when folks had been transferred from there to Phalsbourg. There was a long waiting list for that, too; but we had the essentials. We now had the Ford back and had gotten the Dauphine, as well; so transportation was no longer a problem.

We had finally been able to move into Sarrebourg housing; Ike was, thankfully, at home; and our household goods were delivered—on Halloween Day. Typical of the weather at that time of the year, it was a cold, dreary, rainy day and night. But Dave, at 3-1/2, was not taking "No" for an answer on his first opportunity to go Trick-or-Treating. I was elected to drag around with him in the freezing rain from door to door in the housing area while Ike manned the door of our duplex apartment to give out the goodies to the other brave souls who ventured out. You can imagine about how much unpacking and arranging we got done that day and evening.

~~~

About the only thing positive you could say about Sarrebourg Housing was that it was more to be desired than Phalsbourg Housing. Both consisted of "ranch style" duplexes or four-plexes which some genius had thought would make us Americans feel at home in this foreign land. The style stuck out like a sore thumb among the beautiful old European buildings around us. Worse than that, though, was the fact that the housing was very poorly constructed and woefully under-insulated for that climate. The French had really done
~~~

a number on the American government when those houses had been contracted. The cheapest materials possible had been used; and the houses, only about four years old when we moved in, were already starting to fall apart and looked to be a hundred years old. Although Americans stationed in France at that time were given an extra stipend because everything was sky high in France, we still went in the hole every month because of the exorbitant electrical and fuel bills we had to pay. The heating units were poorly designed, the vents into each room coming out of the wall at ceiling level (and leaving black soot all around the vent and on the ceiling). They guzzled the fuel oil like the proverbial Drunken Sailor, while heating the top portion of the apartment to the stifling point and completely ignoring the bottom half of the rooms. If you sat for over a half hour, your legs would turn to blocks of ice; and if you stood up for very long you were in danger of fainting from the heat. Since Dave was always at the freezing level, we had to supplement the furnace heat with British-made Aladdin heaters, small portable units, also run on fuel oil or kerosene. They were very efficient, cheap and handy but also very dangerous; and they were later outlawed. We were warned against taking them into the bathroom with us and closing the door, because they could use up the oxygen in the room and that could be lethal. If you had kids, you had to watch them constantly to keep them from running into the top-heavy little heaters. When one Phalsbourg child was badly burned after knocking one over, the base finally got wise and fabricated some wire cage-like things to go around them, which made them a little safer. But that wire could also get very hot. The worst thing about the built-in heating system was that you never knew when it was going to run out of fuel. It took sometimes days to get the fuel truck to come and replenish the fuel. If the fuel ran out at night, on a holiday or weekend, you were out of luck until the office re-opened.

~~~

Security was a big thing on our base because of the constant threat of problems from the Russians and other Communists, especially since we weren't too far from Berlin, which continued to have one crisis after another. After all, our reason for being there, with all our
~~~

high-powered planes and ordinance, was to protect our Allies. So I sat through many lectures for dependents and tried not to resent the time it took. The lectures were about the possible danger we could be in (something Mother kept me aware of in every letter) and how we needed to be prepared at all times. We had to have a "survival" box (enough food, water, etc. for three days) prepared and ready to put in the car at a moment's notice. We had to carry a 5-gallon jerry can of gas in the trunk of the car all the time. This was unrealistic and actually dangerous because those cans always leaked, and, if too much pressure built up, could even explode. As it turned out, we dependents had only one actual alert during the entire ten months we lived in Sarrebourg Housing. As was to be expected, Ike was away on TDY at the time. At 5 a.m. one day, the APs went around knocking on doors (since we had no telephones) to warn us. We then had five minutes, I think it was, to jump out of bed, get our kids ready, get the "survival" box in the car, and line up with the others with engines running. We never went anywhere and eventually were able to go back to bed. Our escape route was supposed to have been the highway from Strasbourg to Paris, a major artery in France. We would have been easy to spot from the air and, therefore, sitting ducks; but I guess no one ever thought of that. I suppose it was all in a good cause, and I should be thankful that no real emergency ever occurred.

~~~

Unlike many of the Americans there, who had mostly been transferred down from Germany, the Land of the Big BX, and who hated everything French, we loved it in France. We were within three to five hours' driving distance from many of the major sights to be seen in France, Germany, the Benelux countries and Switzerland. We traveled every chance we got. There was also marvelous dining all around us. One week while we were stationed there in Alsace, both *Holiday* and *Look* magazines ran articles on some of the famous old restaurants in Strasbourg and other towns along the Rhine. Most of the other couples in the Squadron, though, never set foot off the base to eat, because they were afraid they would catch a bug. I guess they
~~~

thought they could get Montezuma's Revenge in the cradle of *gourmet cuisine*.

They also complained constantly because the people all around us spoke French and not English. On the other hand, I was thoroughly enjoying trying to dredge up my Elementary School French. I had been disappointed when we got our first overseas assignment and wound up in France instead of Spain, where I could have put my college Spanish to good use. I thought I had forgotten every word I had learned in the fourth, fifth and sixth grades in Louisiana when we had been taught French along with our other subjects. But as soon as I arrived in France, it all started coming back to me. In addition, since both French and Spanish had the same Latin roots, when I couldn't find a word in French, I would take the Spanish word and nasalize it and try to get by with it. Most of the time, it worked.

I learned a lot more French once I got into housing and hired a French maid three days a week. Maids were so cheap over there that you couldn't really afford not to have one. Mostly because they could afford them, the majority of the other wives in the Squadron had full-time maids. Josephine was the 70-year-old lady who worked for me three days a week and for Col. Wilson's wife the other three. I tried not to give her real heavy work to do; but she knew more than I did about how to keep the floors up and manage the washing in that culture. Dave gave her a run for her money; but he was also learning French fast. Once I attended a luncheon at the Officer's Wives Club at which some local French ladies were guests of honor. We were all having a struggle making conversation with them, since most of them didn't speak English. One of my friends said to me,

"Anita, you know French. Why aren't you talking with them?"

"Because they aren't talking about polishing the floor or cleaning the toilet, and those are the only things I know how to talk about," was my answer.

Unlike my experience in acquiring Spanish, which had been through the archaic Grammar-Translation Method, I was learning

French by the Direct Method. Instead of waiting until I knew the perfect conjugation of each verb before speaking, I just jumped on in and blurted something out. If I knew the infinitive, I used it for all persons. I figured that my listeners knew the right endings, so I'd let them finish out the verbs.

The result was that the French people really appreciated my attempts to use their language and were tickled to death to help me learn. As time went on, I'd pick up a correct verb ending here and another one there; and I gradually became fairly fluent in the language. Later on, in Colorado, when I took my first formal class of French, my instructor called my version "kitchen" French. I couldn't deny it. My pronunciation wasn't the greatest either. I never quite got the hang of the guttural French *r*; so I used the trilled Spanish *r* instead. The closest I ever came to being mistaken for a French woman was in the South of France when we were traveling through there on our way to Spain and someone asked me if I was Alsatian. The Alsatians where we lived never mistook me for one of them; but I was proud anyway of what I considered to be a compliment. At any rate, the way I acquired French had a lot to do with my teaching style once I became a teacher of High School and College Spanish and French after Ike's retirement. I always encouraged my students to "Say something, even if it's wrong," rather than be tongue-tied for fear of making a grammatical mistake as I had always been with Spanish before. My second year high school language students could carry on better conversations than I had been able to do after seven years of high school and college Spanish.

~~~

In November of 1958, the Squadron pilots and Voodoos, maintenance team and other support personnel came home to Phalsbourg from Nouasseur. A big to-do was made about it in the local media, in three languages at that. Plans were made for Ike to fly into the base, land, taxi over, get out of his plane and be photographed and interviewed by the reporters. However, the local Weatherman didn't cooperate; the field was totally socked in, as usual. So they got pictures of Ike taxiing from one end of the runway to the other and
~~~

<u>called</u> it a landing. Two girls in beautiful Alsatian costumes also greeted him.

Capt Ike M. Hamilton is welcomed to Phalsbourg Air Base, France, by Christine Schneider and Christine Lorentz in their traditional Alsatian costumes. Hamilton was among the first to fly an RF101 to the base.　　　　　　　　　　　　　　—S&S Photo by Grandy

Alsatian Girls Welcoming Ike to Phalsbourg, November, 1958

Phalsbourg had a <u>very</u> short runway, even for 84's, much less for the 101, a lot faster aircraft. There was a big high bank where the runway started. If a pilot landed short, he would crash into that bank. That had happened when, shortly before Ike arrived there, a Colonel flying an 84 had been killed that way. On the other hand, if the pilot didn't let down on the first two or three feet of the runway, he would overshoot and run out of runway at the other end, plowing into the cattle on the farm there. It took a lot of flying skill to fly in and out of that base. There were quite a few accidents because of those runway limitations. In his entire flying career, the only "incident" Ike ever had written up about him took place when he landed on the leading-edge lip of that runway, causing the plane to bounce up about 2-3 feet and then slam back down on the runway, springing the main gear. He was extremely fortunate that that was all it amounted to.

Somewhere around this time, we made a trip to Paris, hooking up with Bud and Bobbie Minter, friends we'd met at Moody AFB, Georgia in 1953. We did all of the *de rigeur* sights; but I drew the line at going up on the Arch of Triumph or the Eiffel Tower. I had come to the conclusion that I definitely had a bad case of acrophobia. Although I had never been comfortable going up to the top of the 34-story State Capitol building in Baton Rouge—the first place my parents always took visitors—I hadn't really diagnosed myself yet. But *en route* to San Antonio in 1950, I had had such a terrible experience on top of the San Jacinto Monument (it was <u>definitely</u> swaying!) in the Galveston area, that I had vowed never to go up on anything high again. But here I was in the City of Lights, with everyone pooh-poohing my fear and urging me to go up. The lady at the ticket window assured me that I could go sit inside the tearoom on *le premier étage* and everything would be all right. So, too dumb to realize that *étage* didn't mean "floor" but "stage," or even to look up and see that there was no second floor as in a building, I got in that elevator. I knew immediately that I was in trouble when it started climbing at about a 45-degree angle—ascending up the leg of that tower! But it was too late to back out now; I would just have to make the best of it.

As long as I was sitting inside the tearoom, looking down into my teacup, I was fine. But Ike and the Minters hadn't come there to look at tealeaves; they wanted to get out and view everything and take pictures. I stayed there alone in the tearoom until it got embarrassing telling the waiter I didn't want any more tea. Finally, I ventured out onto the platform. Big mistake! People were running all over the place, oblivious to all the danger I could see everywhere. I decided that I'd better go back down, and I started looking around for Ike to let him know not to worry about me. No Ike! I plastered myself up against the inside barrier and inched around looking for him. When I had made the complete circle and still couldn't find him, I said,

"Phooey to you, Ike Hamilton. You can worry about me if you want to. I'm getting out of here!"

But when I got to the elevator, it wasn't there. I had to wait. Given the state I was in, that wait made things worse and worse. Then I made the really <u>fatal</u> mistake of looking down to see whether the elevator was coming. Nothing but concrete! And seemingly thousands of feet below. I had forgotten that the elevator had to come up at an angle. That did it. I was now a veritable basket case, sobbing like a baby. I don't know what would have happened to me if Ike and the Minters and the elevator hadn't all arrived about that time. I survived the trip down on the elevator, vowing never to go up on anything like that again. And that's a vow I have kept. It made it hard as we would tour Europe, because almost anything that's worth seeing in Europe is high—the Zugspitz, the Jungfrau, the *campanile* at St. Mark's—everything. I'm sure I took a lot of the pleasure out of Ike's travels by being such a wimp; but I was <u>not</u> going to make a mistake like that again! Fortunately this fear didn't carry over to commercial flying.

~~~

Even though the base school went only through the 8th grade and I wasn't certified to teach Elementary School, I had looked into trying to get a teaching job at the school. But since it was operated by the Department of Defense, they hired only teachers who had been screened and hired by the DOD. It didn't make sense to me because I was already on the base; so they wouldn't have to bring someone overseas to teach there. But they pointed out that my status there was uncertain, depending upon the vagaries of Air Force assignments, and Ike could be transferred out at any time. I knew they were right about that; but I saw them have to ship at least one teacher out in mid-school year when she became pregnant without the benefit of wedlock. I figured I'd be a better bet than someone like her; but I wasn't in a position to argue. I also looked into working as a
~~~

secretary on base; but those positions, because of the U. S. Government's contract with France, all had to be filled by French nationals. So it looked as though I was out of luck when it came to finding a job around there.

However, I had made friends with Mary, the wife of one of the McDonnell Tech Reps attached to the Squadron; and she told me about another possibility. I learned that some positions in the Base Education Office had to be filled by U. S. citizens holding at least a B. S. from a U. S. college. Since I filled those two qualifications, and my degree was in Education to boot, I put my name in the system. Sure enough, in November of 1958, I was offered the job, and accepted it, of part-time Education Advisor, part-time Testing Specialist, and part-time University of Maryland Registrar—a three-in-one position that amounted to full-time work. But the weekend before I was to have gone to work on Monday, Dave came down with some virus or other and was pretty sick. I started getting cold feet about leaving my poor little boy at home with a French-speaking maid and going off to work. So the day I was supposed to have shown up for work, I called and bowed out. I recommended Mary for the job and she was hired for it. So much for my "career."

<center>~~~</center>

It was great to be in our own apartment in housing with our own belongings, few as they were, around us. We had opted not to bring our television set with us since U. S. sets were not compatible with French TV. We could have bought an adaptor but decided against that option. So we had to entertain ourselves and didn't have any trouble finding things to do. One night, Ike was practicing his violin when a loud knock came on the wall separating our living room from that of our next-door neighbors. We thought that maybe the neighbors were complaining of the noise. But soon, "Nellie" Nelson, one of the many Captains in Ike's Squadron came over with his own violin. He had been surprised to learn that Ike was a violinist. Nellie was a huge guy, at least a head taller than Ike, and anything but effeminate. I guess that's why the guys in the Squadron could get away with calling him Nellie. But he was a gentle man and genuinely

115

loved to play the violin. The only problem was that his violin was only a ¾ size one. His big old fingers would barely squeeze in on those strings. But Ike dragged out some of his old classical duets; and, whenever they would both be home from TDY at the same time, they enjoyed playing duets together. When the rest of the guys in the squadron found out about it, they teased them for a while. But it didn't get to either Ike or Nellie. At any rate, Nellie could have beaten every one of them up if he had wanted to. And both he and Ike could fly the socks off of most of the other pilots; so the guys quit bugging them about it after a short time.

~~~

After only a few months of living in Sarrebourg Housing and having to listen to the interminable backbiting and gossiping of the Squadron wives, I was climbing the walls. I guess I hadn't learned, as the Apostle Paul had, to "be content in whatsoever state I find myself." Before moving out there, one of the other new wives, still living in the trailers as I was, had asked me,

"When you get into Housing, which clique are you going to belong to?"

I was flabbergasted and answered, "Well, neither one!" But that had been very naïve of me. I didn't realize that by virtue of the fact that you weren't in one clique, you were automatically in the other. The two cliques she had been talking about were those who supported the Squadron Commander's wife, Mildred Findlay, and those who could find nothing good to say about her. The Findlays were very devout Mormons; so they didn't drink, smoke or Party Hearty as did nearly everyone else in the Squadron. By chance, the Findlays lived right across the street from us after we moved into Housing. They had five children and were constantly putting up pairs of the young Mormon missionaries who were traveling through Europe on their two-year required mission trips. Consequently, Mildred stayed busy all the time and did very little visiting around. Dave and her daughter Caroline were the same age; so they played together. I never set foot in her house except for a couple of times to use her phone in an
~~~

emergency, unless I was invited, which wasn't very often. Mildred, however, would frequently drop in on me for short visits; and we had a good time chatting about books we had read, languages, teaching, and the like. She had taught French; I had taught a little Spanish and was learning French. So we always got along really well. Neither of us drank coffee; but she would drink a Coke with me. That was it. But it branded me a Brown-Noser.

I had played cards all of my life until I got hooked up with Ike, a non-card player, but had never learned to play bridge until we were stationed at Shaw. There I had taken bridge lessons through the Wives' Club and was now a full-fledged, if extremely novice, bridge-player. With the husbands on TDY at Nouasseur and nothing else to do because of their full-time maids, the Squadron wives played bridge two or three times a week. Whether it was Beginner's Luck or some fluke, the first time I ever played with them, my partner and I won the top prize. So at first I was considered a pro, even though I knew very little about the game compared to some of the ranking wives in the squadron. And those gals played cutthroat bridge! Since they rotated everyone around from table to table, there was no way I could avoid playing with them. Once when I had one of the hardball bridge-players as a partner, I made a particularly dumb move. My partner blew her stack; and you would have thought I had given away State secrets or something equally as bad. After that, it was no longer fun for me, and I avoided playing bridge whenever I could.

In January or February of 1959, about the time I thought I couldn't possibly be any more miserable, Mary called me with the news that the baby they had been trying to adopt was finally available. She was on cloud nine, as they were leaving immediately to go to Karlsruhe, Germany, to get little Mark. But the Education Office needed someone to replace her right away; would I accept the job? I couldn't say "Yes!" fast enough.

I would need a maid/baby-sitter for Monday-Wednesday-Friday as I didn't feel I could ask Josephine to give up her other job with Mrs. Wilson. So I started beating the bushes to follow up on the other leads on maids that I had left over from November when I'd hired

Josephine. One of them was a girl named Nicole who was from another town, actually in Lorraine, but had given the address of her aunt in Bourscheid for the reference. Bourscheid was the tiny rural village on the other side of Phalsbourg's runway from the base. I drove over there, miraculously found the aunt's house (no easy feat); and who should open the door but Nicole. She was still job-hunting; so I hired her on the spot. Thus was to begin a wonderful long friendship with a remarkable young lady.

~~~

I wore three hats when I worked in the Phalsbourg Education Center. As Testing Specialist, I ordered the tests that I would later administer to the Airmen on base. They were anything from GED tests to ECI tests, in fact any kind of technical test offered through USAFI. I didn't score them but would send them to Frankfurt, and they'd send me back the scores and certificates.

As University of Maryland Registrar, I set up all of the college level classes. That was difficult as Phalsbourg was such a small base that it was hard to get enough students to make it worthwhile for the instructors to drive all the way down from Frankfurt to teach. It was also difficult for the personnel taking the classes to be assured that they wouldn't be sent TDY in the middle of the class and have to drop out. Many's the time I've twisted people's arms and called in all my favors just to have enough warm bodies for a class, and then had the instructor back out on me or one prospective student be sent on an unexpected TDY. Then it was Back to the Drawing Board on finding a course that would fit the needs of the majority of the people who were trying to earn degrees that way. The Air Force's goal in those days was for every enlisted person to have a High School Diploma or Equivalency Certificate and every officer, a Bachelor's Degree. Over the years it has changed to where enlisted men just about need a Bachelor's and officers, a Master's Degree. It wouldn't surprise me if now a doctorate were required for higher-ranking officers.

The Education Directors on larger bases were about GS-12s; but our base was different; so I was basically a flunky, with very low
~~~

salary. The position was not even considered a full-time one, although I worked forty hours a week. One of my jobs as Education Director was to counsel Airmen and sometimes Officers in the direction they should go in their careers and education choices and try to set them up with the courses or tests they needed. Many times I had their service schools evaluated and was able to help them get high school or college credit for them. I felt really good when I could call an Airman in and present him his High School Equivalency Certificate, or in some cases, even a Diploma from his high school back home.

In the spring of 1960, our last year at Phalsbourg, I even taught a night USAFI course in English to help get some of the Airmen ready to pass the English portion of the GED tests. Attendance was always spotty, between the many TDYs the guys had and the shift-work the medical people had to pull. But we actually finished out the six-week class.

Chapter 21 – World Travelers

One of the benefits of being in the Air Force was that Ike had thirty days' leave coming to him every year. We had seen a lot of the places around about us; and I was itching to get to Spain. Since my job was just an hourly one and had no perks—no sick leave, no vacation, no nothing—I could just take off whenever my boss felt it was a slack time. There were always a lot of rotations Stateside during the summers so not much activity went on in the Education Center. For a solid year Ike and I had been planning a trip to Spain. We had gotten all the brochures, maps and Michelin guides we could find. Whenever there was a quiet evening at home, we would drag those out and plan our trip. We had started writing ahead for reservations for strategic cities at least a year in advance. We wanted to stay as often as we could in the Spanish government's state-operated *paradores*, historical buildings kept as close to their original architecture as possible but with comfortable rooms and modern bath fixtures.

However, even with a lot of lead time, we were able to get reservations for only one *parador*, the one in Ciudad Rodrigo, Spain, right on the border with Portugal. It was a beautiful historical building of some kind, with statues, coats of armor, paintings and things that made us feel as though we were staying in a museum. I was disappointed about our not being able to book a room in the *Parador* San Francisco, an old monastery in the heart of Granada; but it was already booked up a year in advance. We did get a German travel agent to book us for a week at a hotel in a toy cove on the eastern tip of the island of Mallorca, because we didn't want to leave accommodations in such a remote place to chance.

The week before we had to leave, we attended a church Lectureship put on by American servicemen and missionaries in the Frankfurt area. It was wonderful to be with brothers and sisters again, hear good Bible lessons, and sing with all those voices harmonizing. It was like a little taste of heaven for us, especially since we had such a small group and on-again-off-again services at Phalsbourg. We met lots of people there and made some good friends. One couple, Earl and Eualice McMillan from Abilene (Texas) Christian College (now University) were there on a break from his studies toward his Doctorate in Religion from St. Andrews in Edinburgh, Scotland. They invited us to come visit them sometime.

Another friend we ran into there was Stan Young, a bachelor Airman who had been stationed at Shaw and was now stationed in Madrid, of all places. Since we were leaving early directly from Frankfurt to meet the schedule for our trip to Spain, he offered for us to stay in his apartment in Madrid and gave us the key!

So we were off for Spain. Since we had been traveling a lot in the northern part of France, we had planned to drive straight on through to San Sebastian with the minimum number of stops, spending only one night along the way. Our route took us through the city of Limoges, where the famous china is made. My folks had some antique Limoges china, which was a broken set; and I had been hoping against hope that I'd be able to find their missing pieces at the factory. But that was not to be: we learned the hard way that when folks said that everything shuts down for the month of August in France, they meant <u>everything</u>. We got there and the factory was closed for the entire month of August! What a letdown.

We soaked up all of the *de rigeur* sights in Madrid, including a bullfight. We also spent two days on side trips to the Escorial, to Alcalá de Henares, the home of Cervantes, and to Toledo, the home of El Greco. While in Toledo we toured the Bermejo Sword Factory, famous for making all of Spain's military swords and bullfighter's swords, as well as dainty *damascene* jewelry. On our way to Portugal, we visited the old city of Salamanca and the University of Salamanca, where Cervantes had attended. The world-famous *plateresco* doors of the University, built in the 16th Century, were breathtakingly beautiful.

Next stop: Ciudad Rodrigo, and then on to Portugal. My Spanish had been coming in handy in Spain, in spite of the fact that I spoke South American Spanish and they, Castilian. I had hoped, also, that my one semester of college Portuguese hadn't completely left me and that the three days we were to spend there would help me resurrect it. Failing that, I was planning to fall back on my Spanish, since the two languages are sister Romance languages. But that was not to be. While I was able to recognize some words and follow the road signs, I was unable to carry on a conversation in Portuguese. When I tried my Spanish, I quickly learned that Spanish-speakers are an anathema in Portugal. I had had no idea there was still so much bad blood between the Spanish and the Portuguese. But, surprisingly, they all knew French and welcomed conversations in that language. Since at that particular time I was more fluent in French than in Spanish, it worked out fine.

We desperately wanted to hear some *fados*, those plaintive songs similar to the *flamenco* melodies in Spain, but, to my ear at least, not as raucous. The only way we could do that, though, was to go to a dinner theater at about ten P. M. That meant we'd have to get a sitter for Dave. No problem. The hotel fixed us up with a French-speaking lady, who quickly won Dave over; and he couldn't wait for Ike and me to leave the room so they could get right down to playing. Never a shy child, Dave took to anybody and always got on the same frequency with them, regardless of whether they had a common language.

What a memorable night! We loved the *fados* we heard that night, bought several records before leaving the city, and became lifelong fans of the *fado* and Amelia Rodriguez, the foremost singer of them at that time.

The city of Lisbon was impressive, with its beautiful mosaics and tiled buildings. Even the part destroyed by an earthquake some centuries earlier had been restored and was connected to the other part by a huge elevator in the heart of town.

I don't know what the temperature was on August the 15th, the day we made the Lisbon-to-Seville leg of the trip; but the heat must have broken some records. And since we were unable to get gasoline with high enough octane to run the Ford engine properly, it had already started pinging badly and threatening to poop out on us entirely. We had already had the engine worked on in Madrid, knowing that we wouldn't find too many Ford places off in the boonies of Spain and Portugal. That's the time the air conditioning picked to stop completely. It had never been properly fixed in Frankfurt, but we hadn't needed it in the chilly part of France where we lived. Talk about hot! We couldn't wait to get to Seville; but, guess what? When we got there, there was no room in the inn—in any inn in the entire city. We learned a little bit about Catholicism that day. August the 15th is Assumption Day, the day that Catholics believe the Virgin Mary arrived in Heaven and was made Queen of Heaven. All of the faithful seemed to be in Seville that day, and there was no room for infidels like us.

We saw a few of the must-see sights; but we had no option but to head for the next city, the Ford pinging away. But God was good to us. Not far out of town, right off the highway, He had placed a <u>motel</u>, of all things, the only one we ever saw in our entire four-year stay in Europe. I guess the only reason it wasn't full was that a new highway had been put in, by-passing that stretch of the old highway, where we could just barely see the sign "Motel" sticking up at a distance. We thought it must be a mirage; but not only was it sitting there with a vacancy sign on it, <u>it had a swimming pool</u>! We couldn't get into that pool fast enough, as you can imagine. It was wonderful to be in that cool water after the day we had had.

Then, whom should we meet at the pool but an American couple, in the diplomatic service, who were assigned to the American Embassy there, and who, believe it or not, were members of the church of Christ. For two years, they had been there all alone, pining away for other American, and especially Christian, company. So we became immediate friends, visiting them the next day, Sunday, and having a worship service together with them. It was a great occasion for all of us.

The highlight of that trip, for me, and of all of our four years in Europe, was our visit to Granada and the Alhambra. Since Granada had been the very last stronghold of the Moors during their almost

800-year rule on the Iberian Peninsula, it had some of the most beautiful examples of the *arabesque* style of architecture, some of it going back to the thirteenth century. The Alhambra itself, while just looking like the big fortress it was from the outside, was full inside of the lacy plasterwork, fountains and mosaic courtyards that Moorish artists were famous for. Not only had I read all about the area in my Spanish history courses, but I had also taught Washington Irving in my English class in Havana, Florida, and was familiar with his intriguing *Tales of the Alhambra*, drawn from the folk tales, legends and myths he had learned about when he was U. S. Ambassador to Spain, first in Madrid and later in Granada. I bought an English copy of his *Tales* in a flea market in Granada, reading it while actually staying in Granada, and thereby making the visit even more memorable. The lunch we were able to have on the patio of the San Francisco Monastery *Parador*, was the icing on the cake for our visit to Granada.

We had picked up a hitchhiker on the outskirts of Granada as we came into town, and he had hooked us up with some good shopkeepers and given us ideas on the best restaurants and places to see. One day he took us to see Montealbán, the historic cave area of Granada where the gypsies lived. In one cave, equipped with electricity, a telephone and other comforts, they served us cold drinks and we were able to see two five-year-old children dance the *flamenco*. Those kids were precious and well on the way to perfecting that ancient dance. We later ate at a small café where we saw Gracia Montenegro dance the flamenco like we've never seen it done before or since. She had been dancing from childhood and had even spent three years, from age fifteen, dancing with the famous José Greco's dance troupe, touring internationally with him. We had seen him and his troupe dance at the Waldorf Astoria in New York in 1953 and figured out that it must have been during the time she was with his troupe. She now had her own troupe, and we were enthralled by her dancing. We had trouble, though, tearing our eyes away from the guitar players who accompanied her. One was her grandfather, the other two, apprentices of his. The grandfather never once took his eyes away from Gracia's feet while she danced; and the apprentices never once took their eyes away from the grandfather's hands as he played his guitar. The three of them sounded like one guitar. I don't have the words to describe the emotional high that experience gave us. It was with reluctance that we tore ourselves away from Granada to finish the rest of our trip.

Since he had spent a lot of his first year overseas in Morocco, Ike wanted Dave and me to see it, too; so we left the Ford in Algeciras and took a three-hour ferry ride across the Mediterranean to Tangiers, on the Moroccan coast. The best we could do in our 24-hour trip there was hire a taxi-driver/guide to show us around. The memorable parts of that visit, besides just the whole Moroccan atmosphere, were the visits to the Caves of Hercules and the *medina*, the open-market area, which brought to mind Charles Boyer's invitation to Hedy Lamarr, "Come wiz me to the Casbah."

Along the way from Granada up the East Coast of Spain to Barcelona, we stayed in the government-run *albergues*, or inns, as we had been able to get reservations in all but one of the ones we had asked for. These were small comfortable hotels, efficiently run, with the same floor plan everywhere. The thing I liked the most about them was that the food served in their wonderful restaurants was all regional. I learned to like suckling pig in one, *gazpacho*, in another, *paella* in another, and any number of the other delicious dishes typical of Spain.

Not only was Barcelona fascinating, with its *Rambla*, Gaudí architecture and replica of Columbus' *Niña, Pinta* and *Santa María*; but two side trips from there especially impressed us. One was to the Monserrat monastery, which inspired Wagner's opera *Parsifal*, and the other to *Pueblo Español*, the mock village built for the 1929 *Exposición Universal*, where every street represented a different region of Spain. There we were able to see artisans at work on glass blowing, lace making and other typical Spanish handicrafts. Since we had not been able to go everywhere we wanted on the tour of the peninsula, we were able to get some shopping done there from some of the areas we had missed.

By the time we got to Barcelona, we were pretty tired from all that traveling and rubbernecking. So when the time came to store our car for a week and fly over to Palma, Mallorca, we were ready. With the exception of the reservations we had booked in advance in Cabo San Vicente, we were on our own. We were soon on a bus headed for the other side of the island. It was a typical Spanish bus, chock full of all sorts of people and animals; but we survived the several-hour trip and took a taxi to the hotel. There, all we had to do was eat their wonderful food, sleep, and bask on the beach for a full week. It was hot, but a cool breeze blew in off of the ocean; so we didn't suffer. This was just the R & R we were needing before tackling the trip back home to Alsace.

Chapter 22 - Shifting Gears

A big change was about to take place in our lives, brought on, in part, by all of the TDY's Ike had had. He felt that he was missing out on a large part of Dave's childhood, being away so much of the time. Dave was learning to pray; and every night he was asking the Lord either to bring his Daddy home safely from his TDY or, if Ike happened to be at home right then, to give him a safe trip back to his TDY. He thought TDY was a place, like Baton Rouge or Lake Charles. As soon as Ike would walk in the door after being away, Dave would ask him when he was going back. This was tearing Ike up, as you can imagine. Then about that time, he was offered a job at the 66th TRWg, Headquartered in Laon, France, as the Wing IP, responsible for keeping all of the 101 pilots at the three bases in the wing current and safe. The pilot in him really wanted the job because it would be a feather in his cap: he was chosen out of all the other qualified pilots in the Wing. Every one of the senior captains in the Squadron would have given anything for that job; but Ike still had more hours in the Voodoo than any other pilot; so he was the one chosen.

But it would mean that we would have to move to Laon, the 66th Tac Recon Wing Headquarters, and Ike would divide his time evenly between the three bases, Laon, Phalsbourg and another one over in the Paris area. In other words, he would be away from Dave and me two-thirds of the time

We talked about it a lot and prayed about it, and he finally made his decision: He would turn the job down and ask to be relieved of front-line flying duties. This was a major turning point in our lives, as it meant that he would be getting out of the type of flying he loved most, in the hottest aircraft he had ever flown, and possibly even would be taken off of flying status entirely. But he was convinced that this action was necessary for the well being of the family. He had always had the courage of his convictions, and I had to admire him for taking this stand, although I was scared about the future.

The entire Squadron was shocked when they learned of his decision. Nobody could understand it; it just wasn't in their mind-set. What front-line pilot wouldn't have killed for such a job? Major Findlay was the only one who seemed to understand the reasons behind the step he was taking; and he was the one who stood up for Ike when The Powers That Be got into the action. They questioned him about the reasons behind his action, which they couldn't understand. Therefore, they concluded, it must be that old bug-a-boo Fear of Flying. He had encountered another form of this same concept with the doctors in the hospital in Nagoya, Japan; and here he was having to deal with it again. He tried to assure them that, not only was he <u>not</u> afraid to fly, but he wanted very much to remain on flying status. Not satisfied with these assurances on his part, they sent him up to the hospital at USAFE HQ in Wiesbaden, Germany, where they kept him under observation in the Psychiatric Wing for an entire month. They quizzed him up one side and down the other, but he continued to declare that he loved flying and just wanted to have a better family life. Dave and I were able to go up one weekend and he was given a pass for a few hours; so we got to be with him for a little while. Naturally, he was depressed but was determined not to cave in.

The thing that helped these men to make the decision they finally made was a letter from Major Findlay, Ike's Sq CO, telling about Ike's exemplary performance in every task he had been assigned to do under Major Findlay's command, and recommending that he be kept on flying status. Their decision was to allow Ike to remain on flying status; and he was reassigned as HQ SQ Commander on the base at Phalsbourg. He could do his proficiency flying; so he flew every chance he got, as he had always done.

~~~

About this time Ike applied to the Air Force Institute of Technology to get a Master's Degree, but he was turned down because of his poor showing in his first two years of college. His feckless days as a teenager at LSU were coming back now to haunt him.
~~~

~~~

Soon after Ike was assigned to HQ SQ, Col. McChristy gave him the additional duty of Housing Officer. Now he had two jobs, two offices and two staffs and was a very busy man. He had to go back and forth between the two offices; so very soon he started keeping a small pocket calendar with him at all times in order to keep up with his agendas at both places. Once he misplaced that calendar and the staffs in both offices had to drop everything and join the search for the little book, because Ike had become so dependent on it.

Among his duties as Housing Officer was that of allocating the available quarters as equitably as possible. Since there never was enough housing to go around, he made a few enemies doing this. He had soon discovered that the waiting list for the officers was very short compared to that for the enlisted men. Many enlisted men couldn't bring their families overseas because they couldn't afford to get housing On the Economy. This was working a hardship on many of the marriages of the young men in question. This was sad for Mr. Family Man to see; so he didn't do a thing but begin reallocating quarters to enlisted men as they became available. At first he tried to keep the officers on one end of the housing area and the enlisted men on the other, as had always been the policy. But soon, he even threw that policy out and assigned whichever unit became available to whichever person had had his name on the list the longest. That occasionally put an enlisted man in one side of a duplex and an officer in the other. There was some grumbling about this, but not much, as people could see that it was the right thing to do.

Another duty of the Housing Officer was to allocate the furniture and appliances. This was really a Bucket of Worms if ever there was one. This had been so inequitably handled that many higher-ranking officers had two refrigerators, two stoves and the very best furniture because they would latch on to whatever they wanted from friends' apartments when they would rotate Stateside, and nobody would do anything about it. The good stuff never made it back into the pool at the Housing Office; so the waiting list grew and grew. As soon as Ike learned of this bad situation, he had <u>all</u> of the furniture and appliances
~~~

inventoried, even what was in use in the quarters, and pulled out the excess pieces of furniture or appliances and put them back into the pool. You can imagine the Consternation in the Camp over that. But his boss, Col. McChristy, backed him up in all of it; so, in spite of his making a few enemies, Ike survived it. One particularly sticky case happened when a full Colonel was to rotate. Ike was supposed to sign off on everyone's clearance sheets before they could officially leave the base. He refused to sign this Colonel's sheet because he had given a couple of items to some of his friends, refusing to let Housing pick them up to return them to the pool. He raved and ranted and threatened to have Ike demoted and I-don't-know-what-all. But Col. McChristy stuck by Ike; and the Colonel finally allowed the items in question to be taken back by the Housing personnel. He came in sheepishly, and Ike signed off on his clearance.

So life went on, while I continued working in the Education Center and Ike held down two jobs, flying whenever he could.

Chapter 23 – The *Mademoiselle* from Toul-Rosières

We had been toying with the idea of venturing out on the Economy and had found the perfect house for our needs, in the city of Saverne, 25 kilometers away from the base, and only 40 Ks from Strasbourg. It was high on a hill overlooking the town and a cherry orchard. The front of the house faced that beautiful view, the master bedroom having a little balcony with French doors opening out onto it. The city was historic, with castle ruins on a hill on the outskirts, as well as good skiing in the nearby Vosges Mountains. Our house was still under construction, being built by a French couple that had spent ten years teaching in the French Congo and had saved their money to invest it in just this way. They would rent it out to *les Américains* for a while, thereby recouping some of their investment, then live in it themselves. Raymond and Yvonne Leyendecker were a lovely couple with three boys. The five of them, along with her parents, lived in a small apartment that wasn't as big as the main floor of the house we would be occupying. We had been planning to move before the trip to Spain; but the factory that made the indoor shutters (a very important part of a French house) was closed for the month of August, and the workers were also on vacation. So we had to wait until our return to move in.

The Leyendeckers' House in Saverne, France

We were able to take whatever furniture we needed from Base Housing. We had determined that, for the long haul, trailer living was no longer for us. When we rotated Stateside we would probably be eligible to live in base housing anyway. So when we had the opportunity to buy some beautiful Danish Modern furniture through the Officers' Club, we jumped at it. Danish Modern was all the go at that time in the States; and we were getting complete living room and dining room furnishings, including a lot of extras, for a song—only $1,600 dollars for all of it, about 1/3 of what it would have cost us in the States. It was made of teakwood by the DanskForm Company and came directly from Denmark. But it straggled in slowly; so we had no living room or dining room furniture for a while after moving into our lovely home in Saverne.

The house had only two bedrooms, but they were large. The French bathroom arrangement helped out. Just inside the front door, off a large *foyer*, was a small room with only a toilet and a teeny cold-water lavatory. The shower, lavatory and *bidet* were in a much larger room with entrances from both bedrooms. The floor space was completely doubled in the basement area, which consisted of an enclosed garage, a laundry room, and two other large rooms, unfinished, but as large as the two bedrooms upstairs. One room had a coal chute going into it and was where the French stored their potatoes in the winter. Needless to say we weren't raising potatoes; but we did use coal in the one little stove in the main *foyer* upstairs. To heat the rest of the rooms we'd just move our Aladdin heaters from room to room, thereby saving a bundle on heating costs.

~~~

Nicole Nopre, the 23-year-old young lady who had now been working for us for over six months, had become such a necessity in our lives that we couldn't visualize not having her with us. She was very fun-loving, getting pleasure out of the simple things of life, acting more like a 17-year-old than someone in her 20's. So we let Josephine go, and Nicole came to work for us full-time. Her home was in a little village in Lorraine, sixteen Ks from Sarrebourg (on the other side of the base from Saverne); so she commuted by train as long as we lived in Sarrebourg Housing. However, the train schedule between her village, Abreschviller, and Saverne, wasn't conducive to that; so she would have to live in with us. We got permission from the Leyendeckers to enclose a portion of one of the basement rooms to make a room for Nicole. So she began living with us, working full-time, and going home on the weekends.

~~~

Now that Ike wasn't having quite as many TDY's as when in TAC Recon, he was able to do follow-up on the men whose names Colleen and I had gotten from the Chaplain. He also had some help from Al Stephens, a medically discharged Navy vet, who had come with his family to the Paris area to be a missionary. He was in French language training but had some time to work with the American military personnel in France. Since we didn't have a "home congregation," we had been sending our monthly contribution to the Albuquerque church that sponsored Al, to help him get overseas. He was finally in France and happy to help us. Once his wife, Corene, and seven-year-old daughter, Colleen, came with him. Some of the guys had rotated home, and some were not really interested; they had put down "church of Christ" as their religious preference because maybe their grandmother had been a member and they couldn't think of anything else to put down. But we started holding services with the few who were interested. At first we were allowed to meet on base in the Courtroom; but the Protestant Chaplain was afraid he'd get into trouble with the government. We were supposed to have written authorization from our church "headquarters" in the States. That was interesting, since the churches of Christ <u>have</u> no earthly headquarters. We had been trying to get such a letter from the 12th and Decatur St. church in Washington, D. C., which was the recognized channel that the government used for these purposes. But so far it had not come through. Although our living room furniture had not yet arrived, we began meeting in our home on Sunday mornings, with everybody sitting on the Moroccan rug or a camel saddle. The big day was when we had eleven people present, including the babies!

~~~

Dave was becoming more and more fluent in French, especially once we moved on the Economy, because he played a lot with a little boy and girl who lived right behind us. He would also frequently go home with Nicole for weekends. No one in her village spoke a word of English, including Nicole; so Dave was on his own when there. But he never had a minute's problem with that. He was very outgoing, quite a brat, if the truth were known; but he stole the hearts of Nicole's entire family. Nicole's father, whom Dave learned to call *Papá*, ran a little train on a narrow-gauge railroad up into the mountains and brought back logs from the lumber camp up there. In his spare time he played the tuba in a German-sounding Oom-Pah-Pah band. Her brother Jean-Claude also played the cornet in the band. Nicole would often take Dave to band concerts or dances that they would have in the village square. Dave had a ball and learned to love her father's music. Whenever he heard that type of music, he used to call it *Papá*'s music. I was jealous because he was a lot more fluent in French than I and could gurgle those French *r*'s out like a native.
~~~

~~~

Dave was four years old, and still had no little brothers or sisters. We had now been married eleven and one-half years. So once again we started looking into adoption procedures. Mary and her husband, the Tech Rep, had been enjoying their Mark so much that soon after they got him, they had put in an application for a little girl. They had used a lawyer in Karlsruhe, Germany, not far across the Rhine from where we lived. Mark's parents had adopted him in Germany because it was not recommended that Americans adopt in France. The French law was such that the biological mother could change her mind at any time and take her baby back if she decided she wanted to. There had been some very sad cases of Americans who had adopted French babies and had that happen.

So Mary drove over with us to Karlsruhe and introduced us to their lawyer who had arranged Mark's adoption. He gave us a ton of papers to be completed and we got them all in right away—statements from the Base Hospital as to our health and our limited prospects for having our own kids; from the Base Chaplain as to our good character; from the Base Commander as to Ike's military performance; from the Base Finance Officer as to our financial stability; and from two people who had known us for at least ten years, as to our sterling character over the years. We had even had the Social Worker's visit, which was coordinated through the International Red Cross because we were American citizens, living in France, adopting a German baby. We had complied with everything we had to do. Now we just had to wait. We had decided we knew this time that we wanted a girl. So Mary and her husband would get the first little girl that came along, and we would get the second one.

While we were biding our time, our friends the McMillans, from Edinburgh, came and paid us a visit; and we gave them the royal tour of the area. Insisting that we go and visit them, they had gone back home; and I was bushed. I threw myself across the bed with fatigue. Boy, was I tired! I couldn't remember being that tired in a long time. Why was I so tired? Then I got to figuring back on my dates, which
~~~

I'd been too busy to keep up with while our visitors were there. Guess what? My period was late! Could I be pregnant? Probably not, since it was "unlikely that we would have kids of our own," or so we'd been told. But we had been told that once before and Dave had proven them wrong. I checked with the hospital and learned that, sure enough, I was pregnant! Ike was ecstatic. Now all we had to do was wait it out.

We had very few doctors in the Dispensary at the base: a couple of OB/GYN men, and two Flight Surgeons, and that was it. Ike had become buddies with Dr. Stack, one of the Flight Surgeons, because the flight surgeons were rated and had to keep up their flying time, too. He and Ike had gone on several Cross Countries together. So Ike asked him whether he ever took OB cases, and he said, "Yes, sometimes."

"Would you take Anita's case?" Ike asked him.

"Sure," Dr. Stack said. So that's how I came to be the only pregnant woman at Phalsbourg to have a bachelor Flight Surgeon for my OB doctor. I guess I was too ignorant to worry about how much he knew or didn't know about OB work.

~~~

I kept working in the Education Center until June of 1960, before the baby was due in late August. I behaved myself fairly well during the week so I wouldn't gain too much weight. My appointments were on Tuesdays at 2:00 p.m. I would skip lunch on Tuesdays, go for my appointment and the dreaded weight check, and then go and pig out on a sundae at the Snack Bar! I managed to keep within the weight limitations Dr. Stack had given me; so I guess I didn't get too far out of line.

~~~

Still flying the T-Bird at every opportunity, Ike was happy when, on 1 February 1960, he was able to trade in his plain wings for ones with a star above them, indicating that he had completed the 2,000 hours of flying time necessary to qualify as a Senior Pilot.

~~~

In June after I quit working, we made a big trip to Italy, by way of Oberammergau, Bavaria. We had planned a year before to attend the famous Passion Play that had been held there every ten years for centuries. The babysitters we engaged for Dave were two teenage girls and their grandmother. After seeing that awe-inspiring performance, we went to pick up Dave. Then we learned that the two girls had had walk-on parts in the play and had taken Dave to the theater with them. He watched the whole thing from the wings of the stage and was fascinated by it. He knew all about Jesus and the Apostles from his time spent in Bible classes; so now he thought that he was seeing the real thing!

I was seven months pregnant and, therefore, not the most comfortable in the world; but we continued on our way to Italy. Since some of the base personnel had been coming back from Italy with hepatitis, I asked Dr. Stack about the advisability of my going. He didn't have a problem with it, telling me only not to drink the water. It seems that the incubation period for Hepatitis was six weeks—very close to the time I was to deliver. Well, it was easier said than done to drink only bottled water. I quickly learned that in Italy it was next to impossible to get non-gaseous mineral water. Since I had trouble choking down the gaseous variety, I was suffering, having to drink Coke after Coke, which didn't really quench my thirst in that heat. To make matters worse, the air conditioning in the Ford had never worked again after the trip to Iberia the previous summer. So, although I was glad to get to see some of the world-famous sights, I can't say that the trip to Italy was my most enjoyable trip while in Europe.

Our first stop was at Lake Garda in Northern Italy, were the U. S. had a Recreation Area. We stayed two days in that delightful place, but eventually had to move on. We stopped in Verona, the setting for at least one of Shakespeare's plays, viewing an early Roman
~~~

amphitheater there. Venice was one of the most memorable places because of the canals, the gondola rides, and the famous artwork. Of course, Ike wanted to go up on top of the bell tower at St. Mark's; but true to my vow, I stayed on *terra firma*. I did allow him to take Dave, because I didn't want to take the pleasure out of things for him as well as for Ike. But, knowing how oblivious Ike was to anything when he was taking his 8 mm movies, I did worry that Dave would get too frisky and climb up to look over, Ike would not see him, and Dave would fall off. But they made it down all in two pieces; and, as usual, my worrying had been in vain.

It was <u>very</u> hot, and I was dying of thirst. Dave and Ike would sit there in front of me guzzling tap water with ice and making my mouth water. Then it dawned on me that there was not just a danger of <u>my</u> getting hepatitis. The time of the birth of my baby would not be a good time for either or both of <u>them</u> to come down with hepatitis, either. So I decreed that they should not drink any more tap water. Maybe it was selfish; but I really did have the best interests of the whole family at heart.

Rome was wonderful but would have been better if the streets hadn't been all torn up. The Olympics were to be held there later that year; and we couldn't go two blocks without running into detours. I am positive that, given the number of streets under repair and the extent of the problems at that time (June), there is <u>no way</u> that those streets were finished in time for the Olympics. I never talked to anyone who attended, though; so I have no way of knowing how it turned out. We still managed to get around and see the main things there were to see. When we went to St. Peter's, we were turned away because I had on a sleeveless maternity top that exposed more of my upper arms than was allowed. We had no alternative but to leave. But the guard took pity on us, produced a lady's headscarf from somewhere, and gave it to me to cover up my nudity. It barely reached around me and wound up covering only about an inch of my upper arms; but it satisfied the guard; and we were able to go in and see all the wonders of that beautiful place.

~~~
~~~

About this time, things were starting to change between Uncle Sam and the French Government. The U. S. was going to start gradually phasing down its bases and pull out of France. We would all have to be transferred someplace else eventually. We had already decided that we loved Europe so much that, although we missed our families, we wanted to extend our European tour another year. This was usually done at the end of the second year of a three-year tour; and Ike had already requested an extension, which had been approved. We didn't know where we would go. He had been given three choices; so he put down his choices in order of preference: (1) Ramstein AB, Germany (only about two hours from where we were presently living); (2) some other base near Paris, the name of which has escaped me; and (3) Aviano AB, Italy. We had invited Nicole to move with us; and she had given it a lot of thought. She finally decided that if we got Ramstein or the French base, she would go with us; but she wouldn't go with us to Aviano. I guess you've figured out by now which base I was hoping we <u>wouldn't</u> get!

Ike had no sooner been approved for his extension than he received a letter from Gen. Withycombe, his old CO (then a Colonel) at the ROTC unit at Florida State. He was now the Commandant of the fairly new Air Force Academy outside Colorado Springs. He was asking whether Ike wanted to work with him as an Air Officer Commanding over one of the 24 cadet squadrons at the Academy. An AOC was responsible for their military training and every other aspect of the cadets' lives except their work on their academic degrees. It was a plum of an assignment, even for a graduate of one of the other military academies, and much more so for a lowly ROTC graduate. Ike reluctantly had to write him back and tell him about his extension, while thanking him for having the confidence in him to offer him such a prestigious position and the honor of serving under Gen. Withycombe again.

~~~

Dave was approaching his fifth birthday and was still sucking his thumb. Fortunately, he never pulled forward on his teeth while he did
~~~

it; so no real harm was done. I preferred thumb sucking to a pacifier; since pacifiers are hard to keep up with. Once at 2:00 in the morning, Rosie Schoolfield had come knocking on my door, frantically asking whether I had a pacifier she could borrow. Her little girl had lost hers, Rosie couldn't find it, and the kid wouldn't stop screaming at the top of her lungs. I didn't have one, and neither did anyone else; so Rosie, in desperation, cut the finger out of a rubber glove, stuffed it with cotton and tied it tightly with string. Her little girl finally went back to sleep. The next day Rosie found the pacifier in a corner on the floor way up under the crib.

But I had been trying for some time to break Dave of his thumb sucking. I had done all the right things and probably all the wrong things, but to no avail. He knew that I was going to have a baby; so I started using that as leverage, telling him that thumb sucking was for babies. He was no longer a baby, I pointed out; and, anyway, one baby in a family is enough. He gradually started trying to quit, falling back on it only when he was very tired. He got to where he would go behind a piece of furniture and hide when he felt the need to suck his thumb. Soon he stopped even that; and about the only time I caught him sucking his thumb was when he was going to sleep. He gradually slacked off; and by the time the baby came, the habit was 99% gone.

~~~

We were not allowed to have our babies at the Dispensary at Phalsbourg because they were not equipped to handle any emergency that might come up. So up until just a couple of months before I was to deliver, Phalsbourg's pregnant ladies had to be air-evacuated to another base on the other side of France, Châteauroux. Since the OB doctors at Phalsbourg were notorious for missing the due date by a country mile, some of those poor girls would be gone from home for up to six weeks. The husbands would have to take leave and hold down the fort at home if there were other kids. But fortunately for me, that was changed; and now, expectant mothers were going to Toul-Rosières AB, only a couple of hours away, near Nancy, France. Monday was Phalsbourg's day at the Toul hospital; and we ladies would go over there a week to ten days before the due date to be
~~~

checked out by Dr. Weiss, the main OB guy there. If doctor Weiss thought you would deliver before the following Monday, he'd keep you there; if not, he'd send you back home. What resulted was that some girls wound up staying up to two or three weeks before actually delivering; others were sent home and had to return the next Monday—unless they went into labor before Monday.

That's what had happened to my next-door neighbor, Caroline Fink, in Sarrebourg Housing. They would absolutely not deliver her baby at Phalsbourg when she was inconsiderate enough to go into labor between Mondays. So they sent her to Toul in an ambulance, a nurse and a Medical Corpsman winding up delivering the baby in the ambulance on the way over. It was a wild ride and the instruments were thrown on the floor of the ambulance at one point; but a healthy little baby boy was delivered safely. When they got to Toul, the hospital wasn't going to admit them because they would "contaminate" the babies in the nursery and the other mothers. That's when Lt. Fink, the Base Information Officer, normally a mild-mannered man, blew his stack. He let them know in no uncertain terms that his wife and baby were going to be accepted there or he would see that things got really bad. He threatened to sue the whole Air Force, get his senator in the act, and I'm not sure what else. They finally admitted Caroline and the baby, curtaining off the end of a dead-end hallway and giving them their own "private" room, which, I was to learn, was better than what the others had.

My baby was theoretically due on August 31st; so I was sent to Toul on Monday, the 22nd, nine days before the due date. Remembering the Fink fiasco, we had decided not to take any chances but to drive over the night before and stay in the VOQ. My appointment was for 9 o'clock; and I didn't want to start the day behind in my sleep. So I reported in and was finally called in to see Dr. Weiss, on whom I had never before laid eyes. He was purported to be a great doctor; but then you never knew. He and his nurse walked in the door laughing and joking. He then examined me and said,

"Do you want to have this baby today or tomorrow?"   Not knowing whether he was kidding or not, I asked him,

"You mean I have a say-so in it?"

He replied, "Sure. Do you want it today or tomorrow? It's just right there. I'm surprised you didn't have it last night."

Knowing that Ike had to return to work at Phalsbourg that day, I answered,

"Today, of course. My husband has to go back to Phalsbourg." But I really didn't know how it could be today if he was giving me a choice. But he then said,

"How long were you in labor with your first child?"

I answered, "Nine hours." To which he replied,

"Well, you'll have this baby in about four. I'll induce labor." With that, he proceeded to break my water, start an IV and send me on down for the delivery.

The "nesting instinct," I suppose, was making me pretty nervous about the whole affair, especially since our transfer was pending, and I had no idea where I would be going home to. Ike could get his orders any minute and be gone by the time I got out of the hospital. As if that weren't enough to worry about, months before we had offered for the Vernon Boyds, a family coming to be missionaries in Strasbourg, to stay with us in Saverne until they got transportation, found suitable living quarters, etc. They were supposed to have arrived that very weekend, but we had heard nothing from them recently so were wondering what was going on with them. So my frame of mind going into the delivery was anything but calm. I had more than spoiled fish and dirty uniforms to worry about this time.

Ike, of course, stayed until after the delivery, which turned out to be almost on the dot of four hours after Dr. Weiss induced labor.

Except for the short labor, it was no picnic for me, especially since they broke off a needle when doing the episiotomy. But I was pretty well out of it; so Ike probably suffered more than I did. When a nurse came running past him out of the delivery room, calling out, "Where is it? Do you have it? We need it right now!" it scared him to death. The nurse came back in a few minutes rolling along a portable x-ray machine. Ike, frantic, asked her,

"What's the matter? Is my wife all right?" The nurse just laughed at him and said,

"Oh, it's nothing. Dr. Weiss just broke off a needle in her, and he's going to have to x-ray to find out where it is." As if that was going to calm Ike.

But our little girl, Rebecca Ann, was not harmed in any way and was the epitome of good health. Ike, very much relieved, went on back to Phalsbourg and would be coming back to get us on Wednesday. They took Ann to the nursery, where she was to stay for about twelve hours, and me to my room. That is, they took me to <u>our</u> room, as there were eleven other mothers and babies in that ward. I'm talking primitive! There was a partition for every two beds, but the partitions didn't go all the way up to the ceiling; so the decibel level got pretty high.

When they finally brought Ann in to me, I thought they had surely brought me the wrong baby—she had flaming red hair! It turned out to be not as red as it first seemed to me, but a beautiful Strawberry Blonde shade. It surprised me, though, I guess because the sun was shining through the window on her head, which seemed to light up. Besides, she <u>was</u> nine days early and a little redder all over than I remembered Dave having been. When I thought about it, I guess it wasn't so strange to have a redhead, as there were several that I knew of in Ike's family. And although Ike's hair was blond, when he grew a beard, it was red. In later years, when people would ask Ann where she got her red hair, she would answer, "From my Daddy's red beard."

At any rate, it was love at first sight, and I kept her. Even when I would rather someone had taken her away, I kept her. I had no choice; because this was a "rooming-in" arrangement, meaning that, once they brought your baby in to you, it was never to be taken back to the nursery again because it would "contaminate" the other babies. It also meant that no one there was ever again to lay a finger on her but me.

I hope I never have to live through another night like that second night. Between nursing the baby, changing her, having to yank her up and suction out her nostrils on the frequent occasions when she would choke on phlegm, and listening to all twelve babies cry, I literally did not shut an eye that night. My elbows were raw from lifting myself up and my diaphragm felt like a Mack truck had run over it all night. Then there was my episiotomy and the results of the search for the broken-off needle; but I won't go into that. We had been told to "drink a lot of liquids;" but then they didn't bring us enough liquids. Once when all 23 of the other humans in that ward were <u>finally</u> asleep, I could have finally gotten a little rest; but I was dying of thirst and had no water. I refused to ring the old-fashioned hand bell for the nurse, because I surely didn't want to awaken everybody, especially Ann. So I got up and went to the only nurse I could find to ask for some water. She chewed me out royally because she was at the entrance to the nursery; and I had unwittingly "contaminated" all of the babies in there!

Although no visitors were allowed in the OB ward, not even the fathers (remember the "contamination" problem), Mary and her husband happened to be TDY at the base at Toul; so she somehow conned her way in to see me. She was a sight for sore eyes. I also received some lovely red roses, a trans-Atlantic wire from my sweet parents. Mother had offered to come over and help me out with Ann's birth; but since I had Nicole, I really didn't need her. I thanked her profusely and told her to come on if she wanted to and that I would dearly love to have her, but I could get along o.k. without her. So she didn't come. I think her feelings were hurt.

Never was I so glad to see anyone in my life as I was Ike when he came to get me on the third day. I was so fed up with that place by then that, if he hadn't been able to come that day, I'd have gotten up and walked out and gone home some other way. But he came, bringing Dave and Nicole, all three of them beaming from ear to ear. From that day forward, Nicole always referred to Ann as "her" baby. She and I had had a fight over how to spell her name. Nicole wanted it spelled "Anne," the French way. But I wanted a little American girl; so I prevailed. In later years, Ann started putting on airs by spelling it "Anne." Dave's first words when he saw me carrying her were, "Does she have a pony-tail?" She could almost have had one because she had a full head of <u>very</u> thick hair—and still does.

Before we could leave the area, we had to go by the *Mairie* in the tiny village of Rosières-en-Haye, right outside the base, to register Ann's birth. She was to have joint French and U. S. citizenship until age eighteen, when she would have to choose between the two. The secretary being on vacation (remember this was August, the month when nothing gets done in France), the *Maire* didn't want to fool with us. But Nicole convinced him that we couldn't come back later, and he went ahead and entered the information about Ann's birth in the Registry, leaving a space for the secretary to sign it upon her return. We made a spin through the village (it didn't take long), taking movies of the manure piles in front of each house (they were status symbols: the bigger the manure pile, the better off the family was) and of me holding Ann beside the sign with the name of the village. In later years, Ann was not to appreciate those manure piles for some reason!

At least I was going home to the same place I had left in Saverne. Ike had meantime gotten his orders—to go to Ramstein AB, Germany, his first choice of new assignments. And we didn't have to leave for five more weeks; so I would have a little recuperation time. We didn't hear what had happened to the Boyds until months later: they had been unable to obtain missionary visas; so never came to France after all.

Dave, 5; Ann, 3 Weeks

~~~

No sooner had Ike delivered us all home to our house in Saverne, than he had to go TDY for a week to Ramstein, where he attended the week-long Air Ground Operations School in which he was to be teaching once we arrived there.

Because of the original arrangement between the U. S., Germany and France, the *Deutsch Mark* furniture that we had checked out from the Phalsbourg Housing Office now had to be returned to Germany where we were going. All the furniture from the base that we took to Ramstein with us had to be turned into the pool, and we had to wait our turn for the pieces we wanted like everybody else. That meant that we were unable to keep the nice bookcase headboard for our double bed. I guess they had a Housing Officer as hard-nosed as Ike on that base!
~~~

Chapter 24 - The Land of the Big BX

Ramstein AB, Germany, was a huge NATO base with everything needed to support and maintain all essential personnel, aircraft, and facilities. There were not only American personnel but also French, Canadian and German. Ike was assigned as Assistant Commandant of the USAFE Air Ground Operations School. The student body of the school consisted of key men, mostly officers, from all the American military bases in Europe, as well as from other NATO countries. They gave lectures on the mutual support between the air and the ground forces and had a lot of static displays to illustrate it all. They took the "show on the road" from time to time; so Ike continued to have frequent short TDY's. He also flew every spare minute he had in order to keep current in the T-33.

~~~

We had a two-bedroom, one-bath apartment in a four-story, 24-unit apartment building with no elevator. Fortunately, we were on the second floor so didn't have to wag groceries, boxes, babies, and the like up more than 1-1/2 flights. There were four of these big buildings taking up an entire block. They were back-to-back with a huge quadrangle/playground out in the central area. Each building had maid's quarters in the basement. They were small but adequate bedrooms with two large central baths for the entire floor. Most of the time, Nicole was the only maid occupying quarters there, but occasionally one or two other maids would stay there for a while.

~~~

On January 3rd, 1961, I went to work half time as Testing Specialist in the Education Center at Ramstein. There was a big staff there, with a full-time American Education Director and a full-time German University of Maryland Registrar. There were also several secretaries and a couple of Airmen. My job was just to order the tests the guys needed, monitor them, and then send them back to Frankfurt for scoring.   I was still involved in helping obtain the GED Equivalency Certificates and High School Diplomas, which I viewed as the most rewarding part of my job.   I was having my cake and eating it too: I was home with Ann in the mornings to feed her, bathe her, play with her, and so forth.   Then about the time she went down for her nap, I would go to work for four hours.   Sometimes she was not even up from her nap when I got home at 5.   So I didn't feel too guilty about being a "working mother."   Nicole, fun-loving kid that she was, would sometimes be down in the living room floor rolling around with the kids when I'd return from work.   There was a huge meadow not far from our apartment building where she would take Ann in the stroller and Dave could work off a little energy.

We had started Dave in Kindergarten at Phalsbourg AB, but he had just been attending there for two weeks when we were transferred.   We were then disappointed to learn that there was no American Kindergarten at Ramstein.   So he was out of luck.   But it was okay since he was still taking long naps in the afternoons at age five.

However, in November I learned that there was a French school on the base.   All of the NATO personnel had to have schools for their kids.   The Canadians had their own school; the Germans sent their kids to schools in the nearby towns; the Americans had their school; and the French had a school for kids through age twelve.   After that, they packed them off to boarding schools across the border in nearby France.   But I learned of the *école maternelle* through an American lady whose little boy went to it.   There was a husband and wife team who taught the French kids, she teaching them from ages <u>four</u> through seven, and he, ages eight to twelve.   When I went to see this lady and asked whether I could enroll Dave in the *école maternelle*, she said it was fine as long as he was fluent in French.   He was certainly that; so Dave was officially now in school.

That lady was no slacker; she kept those little kids for <u>six</u> hours, three in the morning and three in the afternoon.   They were taught to write cursive from the very beginning, not manuscript.   Of course, the formation of some of the letters wasn't the same as ours; but Dave did well in writing, as well as in math and other subjects. The teacher would send home notes when she wanted us to buy him some school supplies from the French *librérie* there. Once she sent a note asking us to send with him some pen staffs, pen points and a large plastic sheet to cover the desk. I was dumbfounded and had grave misgivings, expecting him to come home from school covered with ink from head to foot. But the kid never came home with one spot on him. I don't know how she did it. But anyway, Dave was not getting behind the kids in the States who were going to Kindergarten; in fact, I think he must have been ahead of them. One of his classmates, a little French boy names Yves, lived in the building right behind us in housing; so he and Dave became inseparable friends. Dave then went on to the First Grade at the American school the next year.

Dave at *Ecole Maternelle*, Ramstein AB, Germany

Ramstein was just one of scores of U. S. Army or Air Force bases in about a fifty-mile radius around the largest city in the area,

Kaiserslautern, in the Pfalz region. The shopping was great in all of the BX's and PX's, hence the Americans' nickname for the country. We had already sampled the wares while in France, since our BX there was tiny, and shopping on the Economy was out of the question because of the unfavorable *Franc*-Dollar exchange ratio. But things were different in Germany. We got four *Deutsch Mark*s to the dollar in those days; so shopping on the Economy was also economical. We had had to send most of our furniture into storage since we were coming to the 2,000 pound-weight-limit-for-household-goods area. No sooner had the last pieces of our Danish Modern furniture arrived in France than we had to send it into storage for the remaining two years of Ike's tour. The only piece we brought with us to Ramstein was Ike's Hi-Fi cabinet. I think he would have left the kids and me behind before going anywhere without that cabinet. Through the Hi-Fi club at Phalsbourg he had gotten into Hi-Fi equipment big-time, and listening to music was his only leisure-time activity. We had gotten used to watching no TV in France and never missed it. Therefore, even though the German television with compatible with American TV sets, we decided not to pursue getting a set.

One thing we did purchase on the Economy was huge quantities of Rosenthal china, Wheat pattern, because our Noritake set had been incomplete ever since the breakage on that move from Tallahassee to South Carolina. To allow for the inevitable breakage, we got sixteen dinner plates, cups and saucers, as well as lots of serving pieces. We now had two kids who would be getting married someday; so this was an investment in the future.

~~~

In Kaiserslauter, affectionately known as K-Town by the irreverent Americans, there was the meeting place for the largest congregation of the churches of Christ outside of the U. S. That was because of the area's having the largest concentration of American military bases anywhere in the world at that time. We had to commute about 25 miles one way to go to services; but it was mostly Autobahn; and, anyway, it was well worth it. After the two "dry" years at Phalsbourg, we were ready to get back into fellowship with
~~~

our brothers and sisters. Hans Nowak, a German citizen who had been converted right after WWII and studied in a Christian College in the U. S. and married an American girl, had been sent there as a missionary to the Germans, but preached for the Americans, too, out of the goodness of his heart. There were just a handful of Germans meeting but about 150 Americans. Soon after our arrival there, we moved into a lovely new building in the center of town. The auditorium was still unfinished; so every Saturday we had to go to the building, clean it up and reposition the rows of hard old wooden seats (donated by some base's movie theater during renovations) so that we could have worship on Sunday. The Germans and Americans would all pitch in; so I started picking up a little German that way and getting to know some of my German brothers and sisters.

Hans Nowak was a dynamo. He had to be in order to meet the killing schedule that he kept, at least on Sundays, when he preached five times in three different places. He preached on Sunday mornings and evenings for the English congregation that met in K-Town, and at five p.m. for the K-Town German congregation. At two he drove to Sembach AB and preached for the American congregation there and *en route* home for a congregation at another American base. He and his wife, Peggy, had four boys, the second one, Clifton, being the same age as Dave. They lived in a two-bedroom apartment in the church building. Peggy, very fluent in German, taught the German ladies' and children's classes. So it was that, when Hans went to the States to get his American citizenship, he asked <u>me</u> to teach the Ladies' Bible Class he had been teaching. I tried to recommend that Peggy teach it; but she refused, saying that we ladies needed the experience and opportunity ourselves. I guess I was the logical one then, since I had a full-time maid and also had been an Education Major. So I became the teacher of that class.

What I didn't have was very much Bible knowledge. Ike and I had been basically warming the pews before coming to France, where we had made no great strides in our spiritual growth. So I had to really buckle down and study, sometimes five hours or more for the 45-minute class; but Boy! Did I learn more about the Bible?! It was a wonderful experience. Those ladies were really dedicated; we had class "in spite of rain, snow, sleet or hail." Sometimes I'd make the rounds of the little villages around Ramstein picking up the ladies who had no transportation. We would often get stuck in a snow bank. The ladies would get out and push; and off we'd go to Bible class. Once we even had class on Thanksgiving Day; because it was on a Thursday, the day we always had class.

Ike, too, was learning to teach and preach. Hans had a Men's Training Class that met on Wednesday nights. Sometimes those men would treat us to an evening of several ten-minute sermons. That's how Ike got started preaching, although he had already had quite a bit of public speaking training and experience. Hans also nudged us from the nest in sending us out to Sembach once to show some evangelistic filmstrips in somebody's home. All this training was to stand us in good stead later on.

Because of another Berlin crisis (those happened on and off the entire four years we were in Europe), the National Guard had been called up. There were a lot of men from Tennessee and Arkansas now serving in Germany—without their families, since it was supposed to be only temporary. Those two states being full of congregations of the church of Christ, a lot of those men were members. They rode to church with us because they had no transportation of their own. By now, Ike had found reasons to go ahead and get the two cars we were planning to take back Stateside with us; so we had both a Mercedes and a Volkswagen. We would take both cars for worship services, cramming as many people into each as we could fit in. Once I counted thirteen bodies in the VW. Ann's place was always the "cubbyhole" in the back, over the engine; but Dave would join her there on occasions like this. We had one other newborn baby, held by her mother; but all the rest were adults!

For Thanksgiving, we had four of those guys over to our apartment. I decided to do something different and cook a duck instead of a turkey. I got a huge one that looked as though it would feed an army. However, never having cooked a duck previously, I had no idea that they shrank so much in cooking. That duck looked like a small fryer when it came out of the oven! I got rave notices on it; and with the other food Nicole had fixed, we had enough; but I had despaired of even being able to feed everyone with that puny little duck.

~~~

Nicole could now go home to Abreschviller only about once a month because of the poor train connections. I would put Ann in the Base Nursery for the afternoon when Nicole was gone. Occasionally, she would take Dave home with her for the visit with *Maman, Papá*, and Nicole's brothers, sisters, nieces and nephews. She would dress him up to look as much like a little French boy as possible (hard to do since he had a burr haircut). Dave, being his verbose self (I wonder where he got that?), would talk a mile a minute, in French, of course, regaling his fellow travelers with all sorts of stories. When they would get off the train, Nicole would casually say,

"By the way, this is a little American boy." She enjoyed seeing the incredulous looks on their faces.

~~~

Memorial Day Weekend, 1961, Ike had the long weekend off; so we decided to leave the kids with Nicole and make a trip to see Berlin. We drove up there, via the "Berlin Corridor," a highway that ran through East Germany and had multiple check-points we had to pass through before getting to the Western part of Berlin. Those guards would look at us as if we were criminals, really giving us the creeps. Even the people living in West Berlin were practically prisoners; since the only way to get out of the city was by air or that corridor. We hired a taxi driver to take us on a two-hour tour of East Berlin. That was really enlightening. He drove us down the main street, Unter den Linden, where the Communists had refurbished and modernized everything with their universal façades. But that's all they were—façades. The taxi driver drove us around in the back of those buildings and showed us what a shambles they still were. The famous *Reichstag* Building was a pile of rubble and Brandenburg Gate was really sad to see. By contrast, West Berlin had already made great strides in repairing the damage done during WWII. Only the shell of the *Marienkirche* had been left as a memorial to all the bombings. We went home considerably sobered and thankful for the freedoms we had. Less than three months later, the Communists were to put up that infamous Wall around East Berlin.

Chapter 25 - The Boondoggle

Some of the foreign countries that sent students to the classes offered by the Air Ground Operation School had similar schools of their own; and an interchange of ideas was fostered. England was one of those countries; and from time to time, AGOS would send one of the staff members to their School of Land-Air Warfare in a faculty exchange program. In 1961 Ike was chosen for that assignment. Unlike Ramstein's school, which was only a week long, England's school was two weeks long. We decided to make a family vacation of it and tack two weeks' leave on to the end of it. We hoped to travel around England and even over to the Scandinavian countries, which Ike had seen briefly but I hadn't.

I could not have gone if we hadn't taken Nicole, because I had been having terrible pain in my joints, especially my shoulders, and had been diagnosed with Rheumatoid Arthritis (a diagnosis which was later to be proven wrong). I could barely lift Ann, who at ten months, was not walking and was like a big sack of potatoes. If I got her up on my shoulder, I couldn't get her back down because my left shoulder would lock up. So Nicole was a must.

But which car to take? The ferry from Calais to Dover charged by the weight of the car, and the return ferry we were planning to take from Southampton to Le Havre charged by the length of the car. Either way, the VW was the only way to go. So we had to cram five people's bodies, all of our luggage, plenty of baby food and lots of disposable diapers for Ann in that car. I had written Eualice McMillan asking about the availability of baby food and disposable diapers (which were just coming on the market and were still not as reliable as good old cloth ones—but the only way to go on such a long trip). She told me that they were available but hard to find. I just wish she had told me that the baby food was not found in grocery stores but in the Apothecary's and that diapers were known as "nappies" in that part of the world. Just to be on the safe side, we filled two cardboard Coke cases with baby food and built up Ann's cubbyhole with them, covering it with her carriage pad, which made a fine bed for her. (Car seats and seat belts, and the laws pertaining thereto, had yet to be invented, thank Goodness.) When the engine would start up right underneath her, she would konk out. Trouble was, when the engine would stop, she would wake up!

We had bought luggage racks for the top and back of the VW and still had trouble getting all our luggage on there. Ike was getting grouchier by the minute trying to load it all in. When I brought out Ann's Fold-a-Rolla stroller, he balked. No way was there going to be room for that stroller. But I insisted, pointing out that Ann was getting very heavy; and Nicole and I wouldn't be able to carry her all of the time. He would have to do his share of the carrying. Since his back was not in very good shape, he gave in. I don't know how many times on that trip he thanked me for making him see the light about that Fold-a-Rolla!

Our first night on the road, we stopped at some US Air Base in Normandy and stayed in the VOQ. We were running way behind schedule, and it was 11 p.m. by the time we got there. Everyone was tired. But Nicole and I had very efficiently packed—one suitcase for every person. When Ike learned he'd have to lug in all five suitcases every night we were on the road, he hit the ceiling. So Nicole and I had to repack all five suitcases, putting in only enough clothes for one night, but for everybody, in <u>one</u> suitcase for those One Night Stands.

Lack of rest notwithstanding, we enjoyed the ferry ride over the English Channel—*La Manche* (The Sleeve), as the French call it— and those famous White Cliffs of Dover were a breathtaking sight. Our first weekend there was spent in London, which lived up to its name in every way. While there that weekend, as well as the next when we came back, we saw as many sights as we could and also were able to get tickets for *The* World *of Susie Wong* and *My Fair Lady*. Imagine seeing that wonderful musical with a <u>real</u> English cast!

~~~
~~~

In Amesbury, the closest town to Old Sarum, where the RAF School of Land-Air Warfare was located, we got rooms in The George Inn, a <u>ninth</u> century coaching inn. We felt as though we were living in a museum again. The bathroom facilities, across the hall, were fairly modern and adequate. We got two rooms, one for Ike and me, and one for Nicole and the kids. The only "fly in the ointment" was the cold. This was the month of June; but we nearly froze to death the entire month we were on those islands. We got an electric heater from the management, but it ate those schillings or pence or whatever they were as if they were candy.

~~~

I'm calling this chapter The Boondoggle because that's exactly what it turned out to be. Boondoggle is Air Force slang for an assignment that requires little or no work, is just a sightseeing trip or some other fun-type outing. No wonder the Brits had to have two weeks for their school. They didn't start until 9 a.m., broke for coffee at 10:30, broke for lunch, broke again for tea, and dismissed the class at 4 p.m. It was good for Ike to see how the Brits ran their school, but he didn't learn anything vital from it. He enjoyed it, however; and, after all, Uncle Sam was paying for it.

The Commandant's wife had the student wives over for tea one day; so I went. I was a little nervous at first, as I usually was with higher ranking wives. But I needn't have been. That lady was a delightful, charming, witty person. Who says the British don't have a sense of humor? She had me cracking up with laughter over her hilarious remarks. I thought she was marvelous. Since I was doing more laughing than anyone else, I began to wonder whether I was making a spectacle of myself; but she seemed to appreciate me, and I couldn't help it anyway.

~~~

Most of the days, Ike took the car, while Nicole, the kids and I just walked around in the local area, waiting for his return at 4:00 p.m. to pick us up to go sight-seeing. Occasionally, I kept the car and took him to school so I could do some shopping or something else. Since it didn't get dark until about 10 p.m., we had hours and hours to go around looking at all the lovely old manor houses in the vicinity. Stonehenge was only 2 kilometers away from Amesbury. Salisbury, where Christopher Wren had built that beautiful Cathedral with 365 windows, was only a few K's on the other side of Old Sarum. Old Sarum was an interesting place in itself, its history being mysterious. There had been a settlement there, up on a hill, now in ruins. In the 13th century its population had suddenly abandoned it, for reasons that had never been discovered. In a flea market in Salisbury, I bought a used copy of Thomas Hardy's *Tess of the D'Urbervilles* and read that sad story right there in the shadow of Stonehenge, where the heroine finally died. How romantic!

Left-side-of-the-road driving with a car having a steering wheel on the left side is no fun. Especially if you are in the passenger seat and the driver is trying to get you to let him have permission to pass the car in front. The roads were winding and hilly around in that area; so I could seldom find a suitable place for Ike to pass. He couldn't see a thing; but he'd get tired of waiting and pull on out and start passing even though I hadn't given him the go-ahead signal. We had some narrow escapes, and his normally hair-raising driving habits were compounding my anxiety.

~~~

Completing his "duties" at the Old Sarum school, Ike was free for the next two weeks. We headed North, toward Edinburgh and a visit with Earl and Eualice McMillan. On the way, we stopped off for two nights in Stratford on Avon. The English teacher in me was in hog heaven. We visited Anne Hathaway's cottage and other haunts of The Bard. We were able to get tickets both nights to plays at the Royal Shakespeare Theatre, right on the banks of the Avon River. Christopher Plummer was the rising young star on the acting horizon at that time, and was already gaining an international following, having been featured on the cover of both *Look* and *Life* magazines the very week we were there. He acted in both the plays we saw those two nights. The first night he was *Richard III*, and the second,
~~~

was in *All's Well That End's Well.* He did such a good job of acting in both of those plays that it was hard to tell that he was the same person. What a wonderful treat!

~~~

Heading on up North, we arrived at Edinburgh, where we stayed several days with the McMillans. They threw themselves into showing us the sights, not only in Edinburgh, but up in the Highlands. We left Nicole and Anne at their house in the city and spent one night in a Bed and Breakfast on the out-and-back trip to the Highlands. Earl, having been a history major in another life, was full of fascinating information about every castle ruin, abbey and cemetery we saw along the way. If you ever need a good guide for the Highlands, call him up. He was fantastic.

~~~

Since we had been unable to get tickets for the ship crossing over to Scandinavia, we headed in the other direction, passing through Glasgow on our way to catch a ferry to Belfast, North Ireland. We were able to visit Robert Burns' birth house before the Ireland trip and his death house afterwards. I particularly wanted to go to Belfast because my brother, Lane Rivers, had been stationed there for a while when training for his participation in the Normandy invasion and subsequent duty with the Engineer Corps attached to Gen. Patton's army. We were once again afoot in Belfast, having left our car in Scotland, so rode double-decker buses most everywhere. We did a one-day tour up to Giant's Causeway, way up on the northern tip of North Ireland.

Returning to pick up our car, we headed for Southampton, passing through the Lake District. My favorite period of English Literature had been the Romantic Period; so the haunts of those Romantic Poets were most inspiring to me.

~~~
~~~

Our only other stop *en route* home was Paris. Even though by now we had already made several trips there, country girl Nicole had never been to Paris. We spent two nights there and told her it was her visit, so we would do whatever she wanted to do. Predictably, she wanted to see some of the same things that everybody sees there: the Eiffel Tower, the *Champs Elysée*, Versailles, the Louvre, etc. We didn't mind seeing those again since one never gets to see everything in the allotted time. But when she wanted to see the *Galleries Lafayette*, we thought we would be bored. She ordered most of her clothes from a *GL* catalog; and they were just cheap, ordinary clothes that didn't impress me. But when we walked in that store we were in awe. The entire layout took up a whole square city block. Inside the main part of the store there was a beautiful circular staircase leading to the next level, with a breathtaking stained-glass dome above it all. That store had <u>everything</u> in it, costing anywhere from a few *francs* to millions. We could have stayed there forever, and Nicole had to drag us away. So we were glad we had our little country girl along with us on that visit to Paris or we would never have experienced the *Galleries Lafayette*.

Chapter 26 - Operation *"Kinderlift"*

Our visit to Berlin had made us sensitive to the plight of the people stuck living there in West Berlin. So when the Base Chaplain at Ramstein put out a call for families to participate in Operation *Kinderlift*, we signed up for it right away, in spite of the fact that we had only two bedrooms, one of which Dave and Ann shared. This was a pilot program to provide a way for German children living in West Berlin to get out into other parts of Germany and learn a little bit about "how the other half lived." Many of them had never in their lives been anywhere except West Berlin. Hans and Peggy had been urging anyone at church who could to take some of the kids; so nine of the kids were to go into homes of members of the church. By coincidence, the kids were to arrive the very day that we started Vacation Bible School at church. Most of the wives picking up the kids at the chapel were to have taught classes in VBS; but we thought we'd have plenty of time to get our children and make it on time to teach our classes.

As it turned out, the bus bringing the children was very late, and we had to wait a couple of extra hours. When it finally arrived, they matched the kids up with the people who had signed up, and I picked up Rainer, the eight-year-old boy who had been assigned to us. Hans and Peggy had signed up for two boys. But the people at the other end had sent along two more kids than had been bargained for—two strapping teenage boys who looked as though they would eat you out of house and home. It was heartbreaking to see them standing there with the Chaplain pleading for someone to take them. Peggy couldn't stand it; so she raised her hand and said she would take them. This was a family that already had four boys, remember. But relieved, we all took our kids and headed out for the church building and the first day of VBS.

Rainer looked awful. I learned later that he had been carsick the entire overnight trip down from Berlin; and they had had to stop several times for him to vomit. What he needed was rest. But what did I do but take him to VBS? In about five minutes, I exhausted my

German vocabulary, telling him how many people were in my family and their names. He told me about his family and that was that. How were we going to last through five weeks of this?

When we got to the building, Rainer thought he was arriving at his new home. Fortunately, Peggy took all of the German kids into one classroom and just played games with them. So Rainer was having a good time and was all right for a while. Then, when it came time to go home, he learned he had to go home with <u>me</u>. But he didn't want to go with me; he liked Peggy better. I didn't blame him; but a deal was a deal. So we headed out.

But we were not to go home yet. I had to take a lady home who lived on another base, and she had to do her Commissary (grocery) shopping before I dropped her off. So Rainer and I sat out in the car while she shopped. He was looking pretty green around the gills and was crying. I tried to comfort him but didn't know how. I understood only two words of everything he said: *Schlect*, which means bad, and *Mutter* (Mother). He felt bad and wanted his Mother. I didn't blame him. I was wanting my Mother by then, too.

Not to worry. We arrived home where we were greeted by Nicole, who, thankfully, spoke German. I introduced them, looked at my watch, which said 12:55 p.m., and headed off to work for 1:00, barely making it on time. At least Rainer was in good hands with Nicole. When I got home from work, Nicole and the kids were out on the meadow and Rainer was acting as though he felt like a human being again, but was saying,

"I'm going home. I don't like it here. I'll stay tonight and then I'm going home tomorrow."

But by the next day, he was having such a good time that there was never any more talk of his going home. By the end of the five weeks we almost literally had to drag him on to the bus to send him home. He and six-year-old Dave hit it off beautifully, coming up with some kind of international "play" language. Ann had her first birthday while Rainer was there. He loved her to pieces and called her his *Schatze* (Darling).

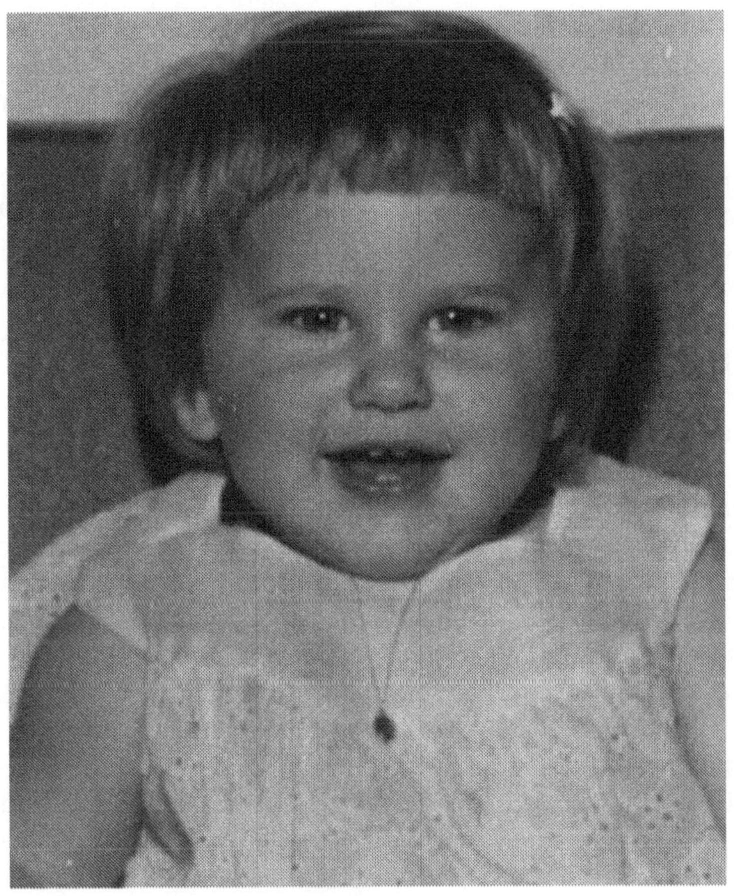

Ann on Her First Birthday

We did have a couple of problems that resulted from Rainer's being there. He and Dave had to share a single bed. One of the first nights Rainer was there, Dave came into our bedroom in the middle of the night sobbing,

"Mommy, I wet my pants! But there's something wrong. It's in the back!" It took me only a minute to figure out that Rainer had wet the bed, getting Dave wet in the process. He was a bed-wetter; so we had to make adjustments for that.

That's not the only time Rainer got Dave into trouble. Certain things that Dave was never allowed to do, Rainer not only did, but persuaded Dave to do, too. We would fuss at Dave, even spank him, but let Rainer off Scot free, which, of course, wasn't fair. Ike was of the persuasion that, if he had to spank a kid, the kid should know that he'd been spanked; so he always pulled Dave's pants down when he spanked him. Through Nicole, we had been warning Rainer that he was going to get a spanking if he kept on doing the things he was not supposed to do. But I guess we put it off so long that he thought we weren't really serious. Finally, the day came when it could no longer be postponed—Rainer had to have a spanking. I can still see it now: the four of us—Ike, me, Nicole and Rainer—standing there in the doorway between the living room and the kitchen. Ike went into a long English explanation as to the reasons he was having to spank Rainer. Rainer was taking in every word; but, of course, he couldn't understand any of it—except the fact that Ike was angry. His eyes were bigger than saucers. They shifted to me when my time came to translate it all into French for Nicole, since she was the only German-speaking one of our family. When Nicole began explaining it to him in German, he finally got the picture—he was really going to get it. It's comical now but it wasn't then. Ike then proceeded to give him a much lighter spanking than he would have given Dave under the circumstances; but you would have thought that Ike had killed him. He sobbed broken-heartedly for a long time. But after that he was a little angel and never gave us any more trouble.

When Rainer finally went back home, it was heart-wrenching for all of us, as he had really become a member of the Hamilton family. I kept in touch with his parents for some time to come; but it was difficult because of my lack of German skills; and we finally lost touch with them.

Peggy Nowak had had a crystal ball when she took those two big boys into their home for Operation *Kinderlift*. She and Hans studied the Bible with them; both of them were baptized; and Peter even later became a gospel preacher.

Chapter 27 - Back Home Again, Part 2

Ike's crystal ball had been working overtime about cars again. The U. S. was on a "Buy American" kick, and American cars were starting to be sold through the BXs. We had been hearing for some time that the U. S. Government was going to change its policy and stop shipping home foreign cars for the military people. We had had a bellyful of American cars, what with all the valve problems with our GM cars and the horrendous troubles with the Ford. Ike didn't need much of an excuse to scrap our plan of waiting to buy new cars until the last minute before our rotation Stateside. He couldn't wait to unload the Ford. Nor had the Dauphine been as good a car as we had been led to believe it would be. It was going to be German cars for us for the foreseeable future.

Long before Ike got his orders, he was scouting out the best bargains. Somehow he found a place in Switzerland where VW's were even cheaper than in Germany, where they were made. He had his heart set on a black Mercedes with red leatherette interior and wouldn't budge on that color, in spite of the fact that I hated black, since every taxi driver in Germany had a black Diesel Mercedes. He was trying to appease me by letting me pick the color of the VW. I chose powder blue, my favorite color for a car to this day. So he and Dave took off on a trip to Switzerland to trade the Dauphine for our second Beetle. When they came back in a day or two, he was driving the most hideous, pea-green Volkswagen I had ever seen! He claimed that it was the only one in stock that had American specifications (miles versus kilometers on the odometer, among other things). So much for my powder blue car.

The Mercedes he bought in Oslo, Norway, of all places, because he was able to get the one he wanted there for only $2,900. No, that is not a typo: Twenty-nine hundred dollars—unbelievable with today's prices. They were not even that cheap in Germany, where they were made. I suppose it had something to do with the exchange rate. Ike had flown up to Oslo in a T-33 on a cross-country with a buddy, picked up the Mercedes, and driven it back home.

When he reached the border between Norway and Sweden in the middle of the night, the guard routed him around to the left lane. But it didn't register that he was supposed to <u>stay</u> in the left lane. So he got back in the right lane and was heading on down the road. Although he was supposed to have "broken in" the car (by keeping the speed below fifty for the first few hundred miles), knowing Ike Hamilton, I imagine he was floor-boarding it. Soon he saw a huge truck coming at him, in the right lane.

"Boy, he sure is staying in my lane for a long time," Ike was thinking. When it finally dawned on him that maybe <u>he</u> was in the wrong lane, he had only seconds to spare before being hit head-on by that big semi! Miraculously, he made it back to Ramstein in one piece, with our beautiful new Mercedes. We practically had to give the Ford away—a lesson learned the hard way.

~~~

We had long since made the decision to sell the Travelite trailer when we went home. We had also been bitten by the camping bug, as we had seen how much the Europeans enjoyed camping out. But being the softies that we were, we wanted a travel trailer that was completely self-contained and had as many comforts as we could afford. We subscribed to RV magazines, wrote off for brochures, and did an in-depth study for about a year, just as we had done on the trip to Spain. We had finally narrowed it down to one specific trailer and brand, which was in our price range, was light enough to be pulled by the Mercedes (not as heavy a car as we had imagined at first), and had as many amenities as possible. It was a 16-1/2' x 8' Fan trailer with a bed in an overhang. Through correspondence with Mr. Pitt, the manager of the Shady Grove Trailer Park back in Sumter, SC, who had been renting out our Travelite for us, we made a deal to trade the Travelite in on the Fan trailer we wanted. It would be ordered from the manufacturer by the Trailer Sales guy right next door to Mr. Pitt. We would pick up the Mercedes, go directly to Sumter, make the switch, and head for home. Things were falling in to place for us. We got excited just talking about it.
~~~

~~~

When Nicole had begun working for us, she was engaged; but that engagement had been broken off by the time we moved to Saverne, and she started living in with us. We asked her then whether she would like to return to the States with us. By then Ann had stolen her heart and she loved Dave, also; so she was amenable to the idea. But she said something, which seemed strange at the time, but later proved to be prophetic:

"I'll either go home with you or get married, one or the other. But if I get married, I'll wait until just a few days before you go home. I won't leave you without help."

Sure enough, when we got to Ramstein, she started dating one of the French Airmen stationed there. They got pretty serious; and I thought that was going to be it. But that love affair blew over, too; and my hopes went up again. Then on one of her trips home to Abreschviller, she met Yves Wiart, visiting a friend who lived there, and that was that. They started courting long distance, except for her monthly trips home, and were soon engaged.

~~~

Ike finally got his orders—the Stateside version of AGOS, at Keesler AFB, near Biloxi, Mississippi. He would be doing basically the same thing he was doing at Ramstein, only probably without the international overtones. We were excited and so were our parents, since Keesler was only an hour or so from the Louisiana state line. I was going to be happy to be that close to my folks again after having been gone for four years, and they would get to be with their grandchildren often.

About the time we had gotten used to that idea, here came another set of orders for Ike, rescinding the ones to go to Keesler. This time he was to go to the Air Force Academy, Colorado. General Withycombe hadn't forgotten about Ike! We had assumed that, since

Ike wasn't able to take him up on his kind offer for the previous year, he was now out of the running for a job as Air Officer Commanding at the Academy. But it didn't take us long to get excited about the wonderful possibilities of such an assignment. When I learned that Base Housing there had built-in dishwashers, I was completely sold on the idea and told Ike, "This assignment is costing you a dishwasher!" I knew that once I got one, I'd never want to go back to washing dishes by hand again.

~~~

Both cars had to be taken to Bremerhaven, Germany, the port for shipping them to the States. The government was still paying to ship one car, even a foreign-made one; so we let them ship the Mercedes, which was heavier and therefore more expensive to ship than the VW. We were to pick it up in Philadelphia, after landing at McGuire AFB, NJ. We kept the VW a little longer before shipping it to Houston, where we would pick it up *en route* to Colorado from Louisiana, since my brother lived in Houston.

~~~

True to her word, Nicole set her wedding date for three days before we were to leave. She had gone on home a couple of days before in order to get ready. We borrowed a car from friends and drove down for the day. The whole town, especially the Nopre household, was excited about the wedding and about our coming. *Maman* and Nicole's sisters had been cooking for days and had veritable feasts prepared for all the guests. *Maman* usually cooked on only the wood stove because it was cheaper, but she had put her seldom-used gas stove into use, as well, for this occasion. Every table had been brought into the small living-dining area and been supplemented by boards over sawhorses, so that both rooms were filled with one wall-to-wall table. Every chair they owned or could borrow had been brought in.

The civil wedding ceremony at the *Mairie* took place at ten a. m. Only Nicole and Yves and a very few people went for that one. Then the religious ceremony took place at eleven a. m. at the Reformed Church that Nicole belonged to. Her folks were not too happy about her marrying a Catholic; but since he was willing to be married in her church, they weren't putting up too much of a fuss. (We had been invited to attend her brother Roger's Confirmation there some time before. Between that and now the wedding, we could not tell any difference between the Reformed Church and the Catholic, although to them there was a lot.)

When the time came for us all to travel on foot down the block or so down to the church building, as was their custom, we all made quite a procession. Nicole, who was petite and attractive, if not really what you'd call a beautiful girl, looked marvelous and radiant that day; and Yves was handsome in his suit. The Hamiltons marched behind the Nopre clan, Ann almost stealing the show as the adorable 20-month-old toddler she was, all decked out in a pretty blue outfit that Mother had made for the occasion. Ike got marvelous 8 mm movies of the entire thing.

Yves and Nicole Nopre Wiart

The rest of the day and into the wee hours of the night were spent eating and socializing. About seven or eight courses were served throughout the day; but they took their time between them. There were dozens of bottles of wine and *Orangina* on the table; so no one went thirsty. Nicole would look sad and cry whenever she thought about our leaving, but then couldn't help being happy. It was a bittersweet occasion for all of us, especially for the Hamiltons and Nicole. We finally left about 7 p. m. to drive back to Ramstein, not a dry eye left among the bunch.

~~~

We took leave of Nicole, Europe, Ramstein AB, and our brethren at the church in K'Town with mixed emotions. We had thoroughly enjoyed the two years in France and the two in Germany. We had learned to love a lot of good people there. At the same time, we were happy to be returning to "The Land of the Round Doorknob," and our families there.

Our departure was delayed one day because our flight out of Rhein-Main had been canceled for some reason. Learning that the great Spanish guitarist, Carlos Montoya was performing in Frankfurt that night, we moved heaven and earth to get there to see him. The kids could go into the Base Nursery, but only until 10 p.m. Without wheels of our own, we had to ride two buses and later a taxi to get to the concert hall. Then we had to do the same thing in reverse to get back to pick up the kids before the Nursery closed. The performance had Standing Room Only. We didn't care, so bought two tickets anyway, even though we got to see only about 45 minutes of the whole show.

It was well worth all the trouble. That man was amazing. It was hard to believe there was only one person with only one guitar on the stage. Montoya played all over that instrument, simulating horses' hooves in the Sevilla *Feria* parade by beating the rhythm out on the wooden guitar case. In another piece, if you closed your eyes, you could imagine yourself going through all the phases of a bullfight.
~~~

We were so spellbound that we almost didn't make our connections back to Rhein-Main. That unforgettable concert was the icing on the cake for our entire tour in Europe.

~~~

Our seven-hour flight home the next day was relatively painless and a far cry from the 18-hour flight Dave and I had had in that Prop Job four years before. We slept only a few hours in a room in the VOQ at McGuire. Since we had gained seven hours on the return trip, it was still broad-open daylight. The heat was ferocious; and Ann, thinking for a reason that it was daylight, preferred playing to sleeping.

Taking a shuttle bus to the port in Philadelphia to pick up our Mercedes, we were soon on the road. We began to experience reverse culture shock when we saw all the billboards and other eyesores along the highways. None of that sort of thing existed on the roadways in Europe, which we had come to take for granted. Our first full night on U. S. soil was spent in our cute little Fan travel trailer that was waiting for us when we got to Sumter. Mr. Pitts did allow us to go take a peek inside our old Travelite house trailer, which was parked out in a field, wasn't leveled and looked depressing to us by flashlight in the dark. It had served us well, and now we were abandoning it.

It didn't take us long, driving and pulling the Fan with our ball hitch, to realize that we were going to have to stabilize it a lot better. Whenever Ike would get over about 25 MPH, the trailer would start fishtailing; and the whole rig would threaten to spin out of control. Since he insisted on driving at least forty, the kids and I were in a constant state of hysteria. We badly needed an equalizing hitch; and even Ike admitted it before long. But we didn't find a place to have one installed until Montgomery, Alabama. So we lost a lot of time having to drive so slowly, and then another four hours or so while the new hitch was installed. We had already had to call all our relatives about the canceled return flight, and now we had to call them again about this delay.
~~~

We finally did make it, though, to our first stop—Starkville, Mississippi, home of Ike's sister Lydia Blanche Terrell, and her family. I was carrying Ann when we got out of the car; and when the Terrell's two Boston Terriers ran out toward us barking, Ann squealed, "Tou-Tou, Tou-tou!," French baby-talk for Doggie. Lydia Blanche's husband Earl was so taken by that, he always called Ann Tou-Tou from that day forward. She was bi-lingual in her baby talk, so was cute and made a hit with everyone. They thoroughly approved of Dave, also, not being able to believe what a young man he was turning into. After all he had been only three when we left for Europe in 1958, and now was seven and growing quite tall. Only his snaggle-toothed look gave him away as a little boy. He had lost one upper front tooth to the dashboard of Mother and Daddy's car in New Orleans just before we left to go overseas. Then a year later, the other front baby tooth had needed pulling when it started to abscess. His permanent teeth were taking their own sweet time about coming in; so it would turn out to be two more years before we could send Nicole the picture she had requested of him with all of his front teeth.

Our next stop was Shreveport, where Daddy was working as Superintendent on the construction project for Interstate 20. Mother and Daddy were more than taken with their fourth—and last—grandchild. Ann was at an adorable age, smart as a whip and getting into everything. After we had been in their apartment about twenty minutes, Mother heaved a big sigh of relief. We then learned for the first time that she had been worried to death about Ann every since I had come down with a <u>bad</u> case of Asian flu when only about three months pregnant. I had exacerbated her anxiety when I would write home things like, "Well, the lazy thing hasn't even turned over yet" or "Dave walked at 11-1/2 months and here she is over a year and *still* not walking." (She had finally walked at thirteen months.) Mother had concluded that my case of the flu had caused Ann to be retarded. Now Mother (and all) knew her for the precocious child she was.

Not only were we glad to see Mother and Daddy after a four-year absence, but Chippie was a sight for sore eyes, too. We hadn't been able to take her with us to Europe because of an animal quarantine that was on at the time we traveled over there. So Daddy had built a doghouse for her at Mom Hamilton's home in Lake Charles; and we had left her there. It didn't work out for her to be an outdoor dog; so Mom had to let her revert to being a housedog. She had loved Chippie; but Mom was getting old and not too steady on her feet; and little old Chippie was constantly tripping her up. I don't know exactly how they worked it out between them; but not very long after our departure from the States, Mother and Daddy had become Chippie's guardian.

Mother doted on Chippie; and Daddy did, too, in his quiet way. But Chippie, always a "Man's Lady," had latched on to Daddy and would never let him out of her sight when he was at home. She recognized the sound of his truck; and long before Mother knew Daddy had arrived home, Chippie would be at the door waiting for him, jumping up and down as if on springs as only those little long-legged Toy Manchesters can do. He couldn't sit down and relax to read the paper or watch TV that Chippie wasn't right there glued to him. I think Mother was jealous. Chippie would allow Mother to spoil her and make over her when Daddy wasn't there; but let him come on the scene, and Mother wasn't even alive for her. She was almost that way with Ike and me, too.

Although we had left the country with very strict orders not to give Chippie table scraps or anything but dry Purina Dog Chow, she had somehow gotten to where she "wouldn't eat" unless Mother poured gravy over her food. If there was no leftover gravy, Mother would <u>make</u> some for her. Chippie had, naturally, gotten gobby fat. Ike put a stop to that the minute we left Shreveport with her. He said,

"When she gets hungry, she'll eat."

And he was right. It took her only about three days to discover that we weren't going to pour any gravy over her food and that she'd better eat the dry stuff or she wasn't going to get anything. Before long, she was back to her precious little slim, trim self again. She was now almost eight years old.

~~~
~~~

Our next stop was Lake Charles and a visit with Ike's mother. She had been getting quite senile and unable to live alone since about halfway into our European tour. We could tell by her handwriting in the letters she wrote us whether she was in one of her more lucid periods or not. Floyd Williams, Ike's sister who lived in Lake Charles, had secured the services of a Mrs. Pentecost, who lived with Mom and took care of her. It was sad for us to see the person who had always looked like she had stepped out of a bandbox when she went out, even to the corner grocery store, having become so careless in her personal grooming. She would be wearing a purple belt with a red-flowered dress, and her hair was unkempt.

We enjoyed our visit with Floyd, James and twelve-year-old Martha. Since the Williamses were the only members of either of our families who belonged to the church of Christ, and they had been instrumental in our conversion to the church, we were always especially close to them.

In Houston, where my brother, Lane Rivers, lived with his wife, Pic, and their two children, Rikky, ten, and Bill, almost seven, we had great times in their home. My Daddy's youngest brother, Dr. Frank Musser Rivers, also lived there, so we were able to get reacquainted with him and his family.

~~~

We had planned it so that the VW would arrive in Houston while we were there, so that we could drive it on up from there to Colorado Springs. But when we went to the port to pick it up, it wasn't there. For some reason it hadn't been put on the ship it belonged on. We got antsier the whole time we were there; but it never came in. Our only recourse was to give Lane a Power of Attorney so that he could take care of it for us. Long after we had gotten settled in at the Air Force Academy, it came straggling in; and Lane hired someone to drive it up to Colorado for us. I think it cost us about $80.
~~~

With family visits over, and report-in time fast approaching, we headed out on the long trip up from Texas to Colorado. We came to appreciate again that these United States of America are BIG! We had been used to crossing international borders as frequently as we crossed state lines here in the States. We were overwhelmed with the beauty of Colorado from the very first. Colorado Springs is a beautiful old city at the foot of the Rampart Range of the Rocky Mountains, with spectacular views all around. The Academy, out on that same Rampart Range twelve miles North, in the direction of Denver, sprawled on hundreds of acres of land before us as we arrived. It was awe-inspiring!

Chapter 28 - USAF Academy, Colorado – Part 1

When Ike reported in for his new assignment at the Air Force Academy, he learned that we wouldn't be able to get into our quarters in the Douglas Valley Housing area for another couple of days. So we found a trailer park in the Springs and stayed there for the interim. Ike would get up and dress in uniform, go to work, come home and flop across the bed. It took his body two or three days to get adjusted to the altitude there. I've forgotten the exact altitude of the Academy, but it was considerably higher than the "Mile-High" city, Denver, about fifty miles up the road from us.

Finally in our quarters—a nice three-bedroom, two-bath house, with a dishwasher in the kitchen (!) and washer and dryer in the large basement—we settled into a routine. Ike was made Assistant Air Officer Commanding of the 12th Cadet Squadron, one of the 24 they had at that time. I learned recently from the Internet that they now have 36 squadrons. But these were early days for the Academy. Summers were very busy times for the Doolies, or fourth-classmen. They had very rigorous training, similar to Boot Camp, for six weeks. It could make a young man or break him. Some dropped out during or right after that summer training, never even enrolling in the classes for which they had come there. There was stiff competition among the squadrons in every respect, including sports and military exercises as well as academics. The kids and I would go out and root for Ike's cadets whenever there was a game of some sort. Only the 1st classmen were allowed to have cars; and even the 3rd and 2nd classmen had a lot of restrictions—such as only so many trips off campus during a semester. The Doolies had a lot more restrictions than did the upperclassmen, and were not allowed to go off base at all during that first six weeks training period, nor to be invited out into anyone's home. Even when the cadets <u>were</u> able to dine out on base, it had to be in an officer's, not an enlisted man's, home.

At the end of the first six weeks, all the officers on base were advised that on a certain night, the Doolies could be invited into their homes for dining. We were encouraged to invite as many of them as possible. If we didn't specify names, the number of cadets we had requested would be assigned to us randomly. There was a memorable line in that letter that said, "Remember: Cadets eat huge quantities!" Ike always joked about that, saying that they hadn't specified of <u>what</u> the cadets ate huge quantities. It was true; they did eat a lot. I had never cooked for more than about six or eight people; but we would have 25 to 30 cadets over at a time out there; so I was soon to learn how to cook in larger quantities. I was intimidated at first by the fact that ever since it had opened, the cadet dining hall at the Academy had won the Hennessy Award for the Best Dining Facility in the entire Air Force. It maintained that title the whole three years we were there. At first, I would knock myself out trying to have a completely home-cooked meal, making cakes and pies from scratch— no convenience foods or anything like that. I was really missing Nicole's help, and especially her gourmet French cooking! Once I bought an institutional-size can of pie cherries and made six lattice-topped pies, no mean feat for a girl who had never been able to make a decent piecrust in her life. I was so tired when the guys got there that I couldn't really enjoy the visit.

For that first "Dining Out" evening in the summer of 1962, we had put down the names of about twenty 4th-class cadets who had listed "church of Christ" for their religious preference when signing in on base. They were scattered throughout the 24 squadrons and most of them didn't even know each other. They were wondering why we hadn't invited guys all in the same squadron as everyone else had done. We had also invited Lynn Shelton and his wife. Lynn was the preacher for one of the five congregations of the church in the area, and had gotten permission from the Air Force to hold services on base for the cadets who were members of the church. But the only time slot he could get was at 6:00 in the morning. Sometimes, he would drive the twelve miles out from the Springs in snow a foot deep, struggle up the hill to the campus area, only to find that none of the cadets had bothered to get out of bed that early. But he was dedicated and kept on doing it. Ike began working with him in that ministry and they grew quite close.

That first night in our home, when everyone had been introduced around and seated, Ike broke the news to them that we were members of the church as were all of them. They were elated; and, the ice broken, they started getting to know each other and us, and our kids, who went over big with the guys.

After dinner, we were sitting around in the living room chatting; and one cadet said,

"Brother Shelton, I would like to talk to you sometime about baptism. I have been meaning to be baptized, but I've just never gotten around to doing it."

Lynn said, "Well, I'd be glad to talk to you about it any time."

About that time, another cadet spoke up and said,

"I've never been baptized either, and would like to be." So we had a good old Bible discussion right there, with Lynn determining that they knew what they were doing and, therefore, should be baptized ASAP.

Ike then did something that would have gotten everybody, especially himself, in a lot of trouble if it had ever been discovered: He said,

"There's no time like the present. Let's go."

So we didn't do a thing but pile all those cadets into our three cars, go into town to the Central church building where Lynn preached, and watch while Lynn baptized those two young men. What a joyous occasion! Our Guardian Angel must have been looking after us again; because no one ever found out that those cadets, who were not supposed to go off base for many more months, had left base.

Over time, a close bond grew up between us and all of them. As Doolies, they were all required to go to a Sunday Protestant Chapel service, either the early service, with breakfast afterwards, or the later one, with breakfast before. Ike got permission to take some to church services with us in town; but because of the schedule, only those who had early chapel could go, skipping breakfast. We would take both cars, bring along lots of Pigs-in-the-Blanket and tall Tupperware glasses of milk (with lids); so they could eat breakfast in the car. Since Dave and Ann sometimes had to sit in their laps because of crowding, it was inevitable that one day somebody's elbow would jostle somebody's glass of milk and douse somebody's uniform. To my recollection, it happened only once, though.

Since we had known nothing about the congregations of the church in Colorado Springs before going out there, we asked around about them among some of our friends. Somebody knew a lady in the West Pike's Peak congregation, a Sister Derryberry; so we called her up as soon as we hit town. She was a nice lady and had us over for a meal; so before school had even started, we placed membership at that congregation. The minister there was Major Kenneth Ratcliff, a lawyer with the Staff Judge Advocate's office at the Academy. Ken was the only other Academy officer besides Ike who was a member of the church. He and his wife Eugenia shared with us the opportunities to have the cadet members of the church over for meals and fellowship. We enjoyed them and the members at West Pike's Peak, even though, if we had known about the ministry that Brother Shelton had at the Academy, we would probably have placed membership at the Central church, where he was the preacher. It would have made for closer coordination in a lot of the activities we did with the cadet members.

~~~

Construction on the modernistic Chapel, not "completed" until 1963, had begun in 1958. Even through it was open for use while we were there, the architects were constantly having to figure out ways to control the many leaks from that striking A-line glass roof. At any rate, the AF Academy is the biggest tourist attraction in all of Colorado; and the Chapel is the biggest attraction at the Academy.
~~~

~~~

Ike continued to fly every chance he got, the designated air base being Lowery AFB, in Denver, fifty miles to the North. Sometimes he was able to fly into and out of Stapleton Field, in Colorado Springs. I notice now on the Academy's website that they have their own airstrip and train the cadets in the flying portion of their schooling right on the spot. Perhaps that would have been Ike's home "base" if it had been there then. At any rate, he was always Gung Ho about flying and was racking up a lot of hours in the two-seated T-33, since he wasn't in front-line flying. He still had to get a variety of types of flying time: weather, night, cross-country, instrument, to name at least part of them. He could go anywhere he wanted in the US on his cross-countries as long as the other pilot was compatible. He and the pilot he usually flew with fell into the routine of going where Ike wanted to go one time and where the other pilot wanted to go the next time. Once they flew down to a base near the Mexican border, rented a car, crossed the border, and did their Christmas shopping. Another time, they flew into England AFB, Louisiana, at Alexandria; Ike's sister and brother-in-law Floyd and James Williams met him there and took him down to Lake Charles for an overnight visit and then back to England Sunday afternoon for the flight home. He was home before they got back to Lake Charles!

~~~

One Sunday afternoon in October of 1962, after we had reported there in August, Ike had just gotten back from a cross-country and was undressing before taking a shower. I was in the bathroom and noticed that one of the dozens of moles that covered his torso looked inflamed all around it, as if he had been scratching it. I asked him what the problem was. He replied,

"Oh, that darned thing has been giving me fits all weekend."

I was shocked and insisted that he get himself into sick call the very next morning. It must have been bothering him a lot; because, although he usually tuned me out when I made such a suggestion, he did go the very next morning. A doctor looked at the mole and ordered a Medical Corpsman to cut it out for a biopsy. Thursday morning, the hospital called Ike and told him that the mole had proven to be malignant, Melanoma, at that, and he would have to have immediate surgery. It is well known that Melanoma is usually the fastest-growing kind of cancer there is—once it gets into the blood stream, you are history. But, according to the surgeon who operated on him the following Monday, that Corpsman had saved Ike's life. If he had cut into the mole itself, the virulent cancer would have gotten into the blood, and Ike's months would have been numbered. But the young man had very carefully cut around the mole, leaving a margin about 1/8 of an inch around it. The surgeon said that that margin was completely clear; but he wanted to see a larger area around it to make sure that it was also clear.

Surprisingly, we didn't get terribly worked up about the scheduled surgery. There wasn't a thing we could do about it, anyway, except to leave it in God's hands. We prayed about it, of course; and then we left it for God to take care of. We later said that the Almighty must have had more things in mind for Ike to do. The surgeon had taken out a section 2" deep, 2" wide and 5" long on his chest near his left armpit; and it had proven to be completely free of any cancer cells. Ike remained in the hospital about ten days and then was released. But he was taken off of flying status for the next eleven months. That worried me; because I figured that, if they felt it was too risky for Ike to fly, something could still go wrong with him. But for the next five years, he kept meeting the Tumor Board at regular yearly intervals, and was always given a clean bill of health. Over the years, any time a doctor on a new base or anywhere else would look back over his records and discover the part about that Melanoma, he would look up at Ike incredulously and say,

"Do you know what a lucky man you are?"

We didn't think that luck had anything to do with it. We gave all of the credit to God.

~~~
~~~

But the whole thing had made such an indelible impression on Ike that a change started coming over him right away. There seemed to be more of a spiritual urgency about him. I guess he felt that he was living on borrowed time and had to give more back to the Lord than he had been doing before. He started reading his Bible more, teaching a Bible class, taking part in evangelistic home Bible studies, and thinking in terms of getting out of the military and dedicating the rest of his life to service to God. At that point, he had been in the Air Force twelve years, with only eight more to go for twenty, when the retirement benefits would be available to him. But he was considering chucking it all and going into full-time preaching.

Lynn Shelton, the preacher from the Central church in downtown Colorado Springs, can take the credit for Ike's not resigning his commission at that point. Lynn said,

"Ike, please don't do that. Think about what it would mean. Right now, as an officer in the Air Force, you are in a position to have a lot of influence on these younger men. You can get into a lot of doors that I can never get into as a minister, because I am being paid to teach the Gospel."

That made sense to Ike, so he decided to heed Lynn's wise advise; and for the next eight years, he considered himself "a missionary at government expense." As an active-duty officer and later a retiree, he and his dependents had a comfortable living without losing the benefits he had worked so hard for. He began to do more and more preaching, filling in from time to time for the preachers in all five of the congregations in the area: West Pike's Peak, Central, Eastside, Prospect Avenue, and a suburb of the Springs, Security. Those five congregations had a very close relationship with each other and would rotate the hosting of singings on Sunday afternoons in every month with a fifth Sunday. The Prospect Street Church was a black congregation that purposely met separately from the others in order to be able to serve their neighborhood better. Ike had already done fill-in preaching there several times when their preacher left. They were without one for about three months so asked Ike to fill in for them until they found another one. So the whole family temporarily moved our membership over there to help them out. We figured out later that Ike averaged preaching somewhere in those five congregations once a month for the entire three years we were there.

~~~

My so-diagnosed Rheumatoid Arthritis had continued to get worse for the last couple of years we were at Ramstein, and later at the Academy. I had been given Cortisone, with its attendant side effects (facial hair and "Moon Face" among them); doses of up to twelve aspirin daily, which eventually brought on a peptic ulcer; Chloraquin, which had done a little good but bleached out my hair; and any other medication they could think of. Most of them had bad side effects, and few eased my pain to any noticeable degree. Ulcers were treated a lot differently back in the early 60's; so a major cramp was put into my life-style when I was diagnosed with one.

When we went home to Louisiana for Christmas that first year after we returned to the States, Ike had pretty well recovered from his surgery and I was somewhat better from my ulcer problems, but not completely well. *En route* to Louisiana, traveling through Texas, I got deathly sick with uncontrollable vomiting and had to go into the Emergency Room of a small clinic in Childress, Texas. The doctor gave me a whopping shot to break the cycle of vomiting and told Ike to get me into bed ASAP or he wouldn't be able to. Ike rented an unscheduled motel room where I immediately crashed for the night.

Still wobbly, I wasn't the best company throughout the holiday with family in Baton Rouge and Lake Charles. Mom Hamilton and Mrs. Pentecost ("Penny") were not getting along well. Ike and I decided to offer to take Mom out to visit us for a few months to let them have a vacation from each other. When we told Penny what we were going to do, she said,

"Oh, that's good, because I was going to have to give you my notice anyway."
~~~

Ike's three siblings had gone through three or four other sitter/companions before getting one that would stay even as long as Penny had. So the decision was made for Mom to come and live with us, becoming Ike's dependent so as to have the benefit of medical care through the Air Force. Medicare was not to go into effect for at least another five years; so now was the time. Ike and I had talked about it before and knew that, of her four children, he was the one in the best position to have her as a dependent. We had to pay for at least 51% of her upkeep, and the other three children would pick up the other 49%.

We had fully intended for her to live with us. When we broke the news to her that this was to be, not just a visit, but a permanent move for her, she was elated. Ike was her "baby" and had always been her pet; so she was loving this. Dave gave up his private room for Mom, and we moved him in with Ann. But I had woefully underestimated two things: how much physical care she actually needed; and what weak physical shape I was in. I was unprepared for having to dress her almost completely, groom her, bathe her and help her find her way around the house, where she was completely disoriented. I had hired a full-time maid (we could afford one since the other three kids were helping to pay for Mom's expenses) and could go about my business during the day. She was even used to going to bed very early; so I would put her to bed the same time I put the kids down every night, about 7:00 or 7:30. Then I thought Ike and I would be able to sit down in the living room, relax and have a little time together alone. But the next thing I'd know, here she would come into the living room, looking for the bathroom. I'd take her, and then put her down again; but I was never able to relax fully, for fear she would get up again. One night she woke us up in the middle of the night <u>in our bedroom closet</u> looking for the bathroom. That did it! From then on, I was unable to sleep.

The floor plan of our house had a central hallway with <u>five</u> doors leading out of it: the three bedroom doors, one bathroom door, and the door into the basement. I couldn't sleep for fear she would open the basement door and pitch down those stairs; so I had to get help sleeping. I suppose I went into a depression, although I didn't realize it at the time. (It was years later before people were to be diagnosed routinely with clinical depression.) I had always been solid as a rock, nerve-wise, while Mother was the Nervous Nellie in the family. I would do fine during the day, but at sundown every day, I would start crying. This went on for about two weeks, during which time I practically turned into a basket case.

Realizing that I needed help, we called—who else?—Mother. Ike talked to her, but I was listening on the extension. When he asked her to come out for a little while and visit and help out, she didn't catch on immediately and said,

"Well, Ike, I'd like to, but Dad has been having a little arrhythmia with his heart, and I'd be afraid to leave him alone." Hearing that, I started bawling into the phone,

"Oh, no, Mother! Don't you dare leave Daddy alone! We'll be all right!" As soon as she heard me sob that into the phone, she was on the next plane to Denver.

For the first three weeks of January of 1963, the temperature at the Academy was 25 degrees <u>below</u> zero, the coldest it ever got while we were there. The day Mother was supposed to come into Denver in the evening, I had been out in the Volkswagen. The defroster on the driver's side had chosen that day to go out on us. But, since there was a <u>blizzard</u> (I'm not kidding!), Ike took the VW instead of the Mercedes to Denver because the Mercedes was bad about slipping and sliding on ice and snow. So all the way there and back, Ike was driving in the snow and ice, leaning over and looking out the passenger's side of the windshield. You can imagine the state of Mother's anxiety. When she walked in the door, I threw myself at her, sobbing, and felt that The Reserves Had Arrived.

We thought things would be all right then; but I continued to be depressed and start crying every evening at sundown. Finally things came to a head; I was in sad shape; so Ike and I decided that I needed to go to the hospital. But I refused to go unless my favorite doctor, Dr. Reich, was on duty as the Medical Officer of the Day. Ike called the hospital, but learned that he wasn't on duty. More wailing on my part and consternation on Ike's part. Finally, in desperation, he called Dr. Reich <u>at his home</u> (something that is definitely <u>not</u> done in the Air Force), explaining the state of affairs to him; and Dr. Reich agreed to meet us up at the hospital. But before we could get into our car to go up the steep hill to the hospital, he called back from his home in Pine Valley—<u>way</u> across on the other side of the huge base—to tell us that his engine was frozen up, and he couldn't start his car. So Ike got in the VW, drove the long way around to Pine Valley (there were too many hills along the shorter route), picked up Dr. Reich, and drove the long way back to Douglas Valley to get me. Along the way, Ike got stuck in the snow and ice about three times, and Dr. Reich had to get out and push. When they finally showed up, I threw myself into Dr. Reich's arms, feeling that my worries were over because my Savior had arrived!

Dr. Reich kept me in the hospital about a week. I guess I was pretty sick, physically, as well as mentally; because I remember throwing up several times and fainting once when I got up to go to the bathroom. Finally, I got to go home.

Mother had been holding down the fort at home; so I could go to bed and relax about everything and get better. But, unbeknownst to me, while I had been in the hospital, she had convinced Ike that he needed to get Mom into a nursing home. Mother had been appalled when she learned that I'd been helping Mom get in and out of the tub for a bath every night. Mom, although just around five feet tall, was very heavy and a dead weight in trying to manage her in the bath. It's a thousand wonders I hadn't dropped her and broken every bone in her body. So Mother had immediately gone to sponge baths as soon as I was out of the picture. She and Ike had secretly gone around and looked at nursing homes, had found one that would take her, and arranged to take Mom to it the day I came home from the hospital.

So, no sooner was I home than they brought Mom, all dressed in her best clothes, into my bedroom and broke the news to her and to me that she was going to be taken to a nursing home. She, naturally, didn't want to go; and we both started squalling. But take her they did; and after a certain adjustment period, she settled down and didn't seem to mind it too much. It took me at least six months, though, to get over feeling guilty for having promised her that she would be part of our home and then dumped her in a nursing home.

~~~

In the fall of 1962, Ike and I had enrolled in a French course taught on campus through Pueblo State College. We had different teachers, mine being Col. Miele, a native Frenchman who was the head of the Academy's Foreign Language Department. Ike was doing well when he had to have his surgery in October. He consequently missed several classes; but I tutored him even in the hospital; so he completed the quarter with a B. He had also started taking a night course out of Denver toward a Master's; but with all the goings on in our family, he had to withdraw from it.

I was enjoying my course with Col. Meile; and since I wanted to add French to my teaching certificate eventually, I continued in the quarter that had started in January. I had missed the week that I was in the hospital, but I went back to class soon after returning home, though unstable on my feet.

We normally parked the Mercedes under the carport and the Volkswagen out in the "cluster" in the center of the five houses in our *cul de sac*. That night when I got home from my French class at 10:00, the wind was blowing pretty hard; and I should have parked the Mercedes under the carport. But, Ike, for some reason, had the VW parked there; and as I was still weak and in no mood to change the cars, I went on in and went to bed. Wrong move. That night we had one of the worst Chinook winds come through there that anyone in the area could remember. Since the Academy was on the east side of the Rampart Range, in the foothills of the Rockies, the wind would whip down that mountainside, and whoosh through the housing area. Our house was right in the path of the Chinook, being at the top of a hill, with an open stretch of street and no other houses blocking us from the wind.
~~~

All night long that wind kept *whumping* into the back of our house. I feared for our German wine glass collection on the teakwood divider in front of the living room window, because the windows were buckling in with every gust of wind. I hardly shut an eye all night long. When Ike got up in the morning, he took his cup of coffee out into the front yard and looked around to survey the damage. He noticed someone's metal chimney in the front yard of the house across the cluster from us. He then started taking stock of chimneys in the cluster and found that they were all in place. Then he realized that is was <u>our</u> chimney that had wound up over there! Worse than that was the condition of the Mercedes: almost every one of the pebbles from the flat-topped roof of our house had landed on that car. It was pockmarked on the front, back and one side of the car and every window surface on those three sides was shattered. It cost USAA $900 to restore the Mercedes (remember this was 1963); and our rates went sky high.

We learned later in the day, when I discovered water leaking into the basement from above, that the suction from the wind had gone down through the vent in one of our bathrooms and <u>stripped the plumbing </u>entirely. When they took stock of all the damage on the base, it turned out that our house had received the most damage on the entire base.

~~~

Ike remained off of flying status for eleven months after his surgery. Since his flight pay of $225 a month was also cut off, that put a serious crimp in our budget. We had foolishly committed about that amount of money to pay for the travel trailer we had brought from South Carolina when we returned from Europe. So, as I got to feeling better, I decided that I should go back to teaching and help supplement Ike's income. I was hired for the 1963-64 school year to teach eleventh and twelfth-grade English at Air Academy High School.

~~~

The Black Forest School District was the best one in the Colorado Springs area. A lot of people were moving into the Black Forest subdivision across the highway from the Academy in order to get their children into the schools there. There were three elementary schools: Black Forest (across the highway, near the housing development), Douglas Valley (near where we lived on the Academy) and Pine Valley (on the other side of the base, where Dr. Reich lived). There was only one Junior High-High School, and that was in Pine Valley. So the kids in the High School where I taught were a mixture of military dependents and local civilians' kids. All of the schools were top-notch ones, and I felt privileged to be able to teach there for our last two years in Colorado.

~~~

Dave did well in Douglas Valley Elementary the three years we were there. We were glad to learn that he would be studying Spanish there, although I hated for him to give up his French. I tried to keep conversing with him in French after we came home from Europe; but he refused. I guess he figured, "Why should I talk French with my mother?" Anyway, although he went on to do lots of good things with several other languages, he later regretted not continuing with his French.

~~~

I had trouble keeping good help at home to take care of Ann and clean house for me. Since we were twelve miles out from Colorado Springs, the maids would have to have their own car. Many's the time she would just not show up; and at the last minute I would have to yank Ann out of bed, dress her, plow through her long thick hair with a brush, stick a box of dry cereal in her hand, and drag her over to the Base Nursery, which, fortunately, was right next door to my school. I felt guilty, too, (as only I could do) when she would come home singing a nursery song that I hadn't taught her.

~~~
~~~

But other than that, I was enjoying teaching again. I had one Senior English class and three Junior English. I was able to put into practice the good things I had learned in the Methods of Teaching English course I had taken nine years earlier at Florida State, using thematic organization instead of chronological, and incorporating all four English skills—reading, writing, speaking and listening—into each unit instead of separately.

~~~

Ike had worked as an Assistant Air Officer Commanding the first year we were there; but at the beginning of the 1963-64 school year, he received his own Squadron, the 7th. That squadron ranked 24th out of 24 in almost everything—academics, sports, military skills, whatever—and they were proud of it! They were known as "Seagram's Seventh" because liquor bottles were constantly being found in their quarters. You name the rule, Seagram's Seventh broke it! Ike and his Assistant AOC, Capt. George DeCell, definitely had their work cut out for them!

Well, those guys didn't know Ike Hamilton. They thought he would go around looking for faults everywhere, as their previous AOC's had done. But he wasn't about to play their little games with them. He went into the job with the attitude that they were the best guys at the whole Academy until proven otherwise. He did not look for trouble. But, Boy! When they were caught in an infraction, he threw the book at them! One of the things the cadets always liked to do was to break into the quarters of the Officer of the Day at night (24-hour duty in the Quad), steal his pants and run them up the flagpole. Ike slept in his uniform; so they didn't get to have even that pleasure with him. He had other such tricks, too; so they finally stopped trying to catch him up. Once one of the cadets said to him, "Capt. Hamilton, you take all of the fun out of it!"

Gradually, Ike and George started building up the self-esteem of the 7th Squadron. They put a lot of emphasis on getting them to perform better, not only in their academic studies, but also in their military courses, physical fitness, sports, or whatever. Since Ike had
~~~

always been a track man and loved running, he was fitting right into the Air Force's current push in the sixties for all of their officers to be in tip-top shape and pass certain fitness goals each year. Ike jogged every day and kept in shape. When, once a year, the squadrons competed in a run (I'm not sure what distance, maybe two miles) from the Quad out to a place called Chimney Rock, Ike set the standard for his cadets by being the first one to arrive there each time, even though he was now well into his thirties.

The mascot for the 7th was the Cougar. Somehow, Ike learned of some Marine organization in Colorado Springs that had a bobcat they were willing to lend the 7th for the period of the summer competitions. So that bobcat became "Charlie the Cougar" and moved into a cage in our front yard the summer of 1963. I didn't like it at all, thought it was dangerous, and didn't want a thing to do with it. But, I was only the wife; so what say-so did I have in the matter? I thought sure the authorities on base—who were so strict you had to get special permission to put up even an FM antenna—would veto it; but they were mysteriously quiet. The cadets would come over and feed Charlie and clean up after him; so thankfully, I had no part in that sort of thing. But I worried that the neighborhood kids (or ours) would stick their hands in through the barbed wire and get hurt. Eventually, somebody put a second fence around the outside of the one he was in; and I slept a little more easily then.

I don't know whether it was the influence of Charlie, or what; but the 7th won their games for the first time that summer. Even though Charlie decided to take a nap at the propitious moment when he was supposed to look ferocious, he still gave the Squadron *esprit de corps*. Nevertheless, I was relieved when Charlie went back to the Marines.

As part of their extensive summer training, each new class of Doolies had to take part in a three-day Survival Training. They were told how to get food in a wilderness, dropped off in the woods, and picked up again three days later. When they returned to the Academy in the early morning of the third day, they were fed steaks at the dining hall. Through some monumental SNAFU in the planning our second year, the first evening the Doolies could go for dinner into the homes of officers on base coincided with their return from survival training. We had done our usual thing and asked for all of the young men who had put down the church of Christ as their preference. The Sheltons and Ike were doing shuttle runs to the Quad to bring about thirty cadets to our house. When one carload showed up, I greeted them at the door; and one of the cadets, whom I had never even met, said,

"Mrs. Hamilton, I'm feeling sick. Do you have a room where I could go lie down for a while?"

"Yes, of course," I answered, and showed him to our bedroom.

The next carload showed up, I greeted them at the door; and the same thing happened:

"Mrs. Hamilton, I'm feeling sick. Could I please go lie down somewhere?"

So I showed him to Dave's room. When the third person showed up sick, I showed him to Ann's room, wondering what I would do if any more came in sick. Fortunately, there were only three sickos that night. But all of the cadets were "off their feed;" and I had lots of food left over that night. The planners of that Dining Out night never made that mistake again.

~~~

Chippie was getting older along with Dave and Ann, being nine months older than Dave. At nine years, she was still a feisty little thing and loved to rule the roost. We had always boarded her and Monk out whenever we would go on trips. Since they were so small, they would stay together in one cage; so we could board two for the price of one. Although Monk never did, Chippie had developed a pretty bad "kennel cough" which usually was exacerbated whenever we would leave her at the vet's. We were also starting to have her teeth pulled one by one because of bad occlusion and gum problems.
~~~

There was a huge St. Bernard dog that lived next door to us. Fortunately, the yards were fairly big; so they didn't encounter each other very often, Chippie being an indoor dog. They pretty well had an understanding between them, I guess.   But once when those neighbors had company, and a strange German Shepherd was visiting the St. Bernard, six-pound Chippie decided to go over and charge both of those huge dogs. One of them nipped her in the rear and sent her scurrying back home. He actually broke the skin near her anus; but she would not let us touch the wound, or her either, for that matter. She curled up on her towel in our bathroom and stayed there. I guess she was in shock, because she wouldn't even let us take her outside even to go to the bathroom. After three whole days of that, she got up, ate and drank, went to the bathroom outside—and immediately ran over to take on those two big dogs again! I guess you can't keep a good Manchester down.

Chapter 29 – The ZI Field Trip

During one of their summers at the Academy, the cadets of a squadron go, together with their AOC, on a tour of military installations around the "Zone of Interior"—the continental 48 states, or ZI. Ike spent the summer of 1964 on that field trip with his cadets. The kids and I decided to go spend that time with relatives down South; so we headed out in the VW for a l-o-n-g summer's trip. Since Ike would end his duties at Ft. Benning, Georgia, we were to meet him there when he had completed the tour.

~~~

We spent our first night on the road with Ike's cousin, Dorothy Dee Winfield and her family in West Texas, and our second with our old friends Earl and Eualice McMillan (of Scotland days) in Abilene, Texas. It was good to catch up on everybody's news, see how much their kids had grown, and in general make up for living the vagabond life of an Air Force family. From there we went to Houston, where my brother, Lane Rivers, lived with his wife, Pic and their two children: Rikky, 3 years older than Dave, who was now nine, and Bill, six months younger than Dave. Ann was turning four in August and was at a real cute stage. Lane and Pic owned a beachfront house down on Galveston Beach; so we spent a few days down there, trying to learn to water ski. From there we went for an overnight visit with Ike's brother Randall and his wife Mimi in Port Arthur. The oldest of their three boys, Randy, was married, lived in Baton Rouge, and had two boys of his own, between Dave and Ann in age. Houston, Randall's second, was already out of the home, as well as I remember, and only Floyd, their youngest, was still at home. On to Lake Charles and a visit with Floyd and James Williams and their daughter, Martha, now fourteen, and other Hamilton-Hewitt relatives in the area.

~~~

Next stop: Baton Rouge, where we were to spend the bulk of the time while Ike was to be gone. Since we were settling in somewhere for a little while, I tried to get Dave set up with swimming lessons. We had signed him up for them at the Academy the summer before; but he never got to take them. He had had a serious fall on his bike, sliding halfway down the hill on one side of his leg, badly abrading it. It had not healed enough for his lessons; when he showed up the first day of swimming class with his leg oozing, they turned him away.

Now a year later, we were trying again on the swimming lessons. But we learned that, because of the race problems in Baton Rouge, the public swimming pools had all been closed down. We finally found a private pool through a friend of Mother and Daddy, and I enrolled Dave in lessons there. But that effort proved to be vain, as well.

One day when Dave was out playing in the front yard with a toy bow and rubber-tipped arrow, he came running into the house exclaiming,

"Mama, I got bitten by a squirrel! Or maybe I scratched myself on the bark." I looked at his little finger, saw that it was bleeding a little but not badly cut, washed it off, soothed Dave's fears, and went on about my business. In a few minutes, Dave was back in the house, crying,

"Mama! Mama! It was a squirrel! And it's lying dead on the ground next to the tree!"

I ran outside; and, sure enough, there lay a dead squirrel at the base of the big oak tree where Dave had been playing with his bow and arrow. He said that he had put his left hand on the tree trunk to balance himself when he leaned over to pick up the bow. That's why he wasn't sure whether the squirrel, which had been on the tree trunk, had bitten him or he had scraped his finger on the bark. When I quizzed him about whether he had been shooting at the squirrel, he denied it; but I couldn't tell whether that was the truth or just his fear of possible punishment showing. At any rate, I didn't see how he could have actually killed a squirrel with that feeble little rubber-tipped arrow. So the only other thing I could imagine was that the squirrel was rabid.

Mother and I then swung into action—she to take Dave to a doctor and I to take the squirrel to the Health Department. Backwoodsy Baton Rouge didn't have the capability of testing the squirrel for rabies; so the Health Department would have to send the head to New Orleans for testing, with a three-day wait for the results. I then dashed over to the doctor's office, where the nurse had cleaned Dave's finger with antiseptic and discovered four little puncture wounds consistent with a squirrel's bite. The doctor didn't get excited about it at all and wanted to wait until getting the report on the squirrel. Since I wasn't even sure we had the right squirrel, I was ready to go ahead with the rabies shots. But the doctor wasn't ready to take such drastic steps; so we were in limbo.

The world's two biggest worriers were really at it now. Wanting some help with my decision-making, I tracked Ike down in California, where he was currently with his cadets on the ZI Field trip. But I didn't get much help from him. His response was,

"Honey, you are there and I'm not. I trust your judgment. Do what you think best." Great! The ball was back in my court.

Mother's best friend, Ruby Anderson, always had coffee with Mother on her way to her work in a pediatrician's office. When she came by the next morning and heard the story, she told her boss, Dr. Albritton, about it, and asked him his opinion as to what we should do. He immediately replied,

"If that were my child, I'd start him on the rabies shots immediately."

That's all it took for me to have Dave over to Dr. Albritton's office the same day. Dave was only nine years old and naturally afraid; but he already knew Ruby "A," and she had a way of joking around with him so that he hardly felt even the first four of the daily shots go into his intestinal wall. He never complained, even when she had to start back around and give him shots in the four places that were still sore from the first shots. When the word came back from the Health Department that the squirrel we had found had tested negative for rabies, Dr. Albritton thought we would probably be safe going with just the fourteen shots of the basic series instead of the twenty-one shots necessary with a positive test.

At any rate, Dave never developed rabies, for which I'll forever be thankful. When asked whether Dave could complete his swimming lessons, Dr. Albritton said that he could, but if he started feeling bad in the water to discontinue them. Dave went to a couple of more lessons, got nauseated one day while swimming, and had to drop out. So much for his second try at learning to swim.

~~~

According to schedule, at the end of the six-week trip, we met Ike at Ft. Benning. We decided that we were about as close to Florida as we would get for a long time so made a trip down that way to visit Tallahassee friends and even to Coral Gables, in the Miami area, to visit a cousin of mine, Lillian Byrd, and her family.

Tired by now of traveling, we still had a <u>long</u> way to go before returning to the Air Force Academy. In Lake Charles, we decided to take Ike's niece, Martha Williams, back with us for a visit to Colorado, with Floyd and James driving out later to visit Mom, see the sights, and pick up Martha. So she crammed into the back seat of the VW with Dave and Ann. They got along fine but got pretty bored before the trip was over. Once we got to Colorado, but still had quite a way to go to the Academy, Dave made this oft-quoted statement,

"I'll be glad when I see a sign that says Air Force Academy – one inch!"

We finally did see that sign and were glad to get home after such a long, tiring, but rewarding, trip. We enjoyed having Martha as a third child—she was five years older than Dave—and when Floyd and James got there we did the Colorado sightseeing thing in a big way.
~~~

Ike's other sister, Lydia Blanche Terrell, her husband Earl and their two kids came out and turned it practically into a full-fledged Hamilton family reunion. Since none of them had seen Mom since Christmas of 1962, it was a happy occasion when they were reunited with her.

Chapter 30 – USAF ACADEMY – PART 2

August, 1964 – the start of our third and last year to be stationed at the Air Force Academy. Ike received a welcomed promotion to major on the 19th, just as he was beginning his second full year as AOC of the 7th cadet Squadron. I was beginning my second year as English teacher at Air Academy High School.

The Seventh was coming along. They were beginning to pull out of their self-imposed slump and actually started winning different competitions. By the end of Ike's last year there, his second working with them, they had come up from an overall ranking of 24th out of the 24 squadrons to third. They were no longer calling themselves "Seagram's Seventh," and were now really proud to be the 7th Squadron. Ike felt good about it all; and, of course, it didn't hurt his OERs any, either.

~~~

When Dave turned nine, he <u>finally</u> got in the second of his two upper front teeth. Having looked at him snaggle-toothed since the age of three, we hardly recognized our own son. We were now finally able to send Nicole the picture she had requested of him with all of his teeth.

Since Dave was getting so big now, we thought that he should have a *bona fide* violin teacher. In a sporadic way, Ike had been teaching him the rudiments of the violin; but we hired Sgt. Greenhouse, a member of the wonderful USAF Academy Band, to teach Dave violin. They got along well, and that was the beginning of the development of Dave's talent, which was to give us all a lot of pleasure in the years to come.

~~~

Things had been going on in the world around us. My first year teaching, 1963-64, was the year that President Kennedy was shot. I was in one of my English classes when the announcement came over the intercom system that he had been shot. At first, we held out hope that the President might live; but soon those hopes were dashed. It was quite a shock to me and to my students, as it was to everybody else.

The Bay of Pigs incident in Cuba had happened in 1962; and there was a time when we worried that it might lead to another war, in addition to the one that was going on in Viet Nam. Ike was vulnerable now for a combat assignment, as it had been ten years since he had served in Korea.

~~~

For almost the first time in his career, Ike was in a position, at least to a certain degree, to direct his career. In spite of the fact that he had not made it to Air Command and Staff College at Maxwell, he knew that the Air Force schools there were vital to an officer's career and had decided that he very much wanted to go there and teach in the Squadron Officer's School. Since he was not an ACSC graduate, he felt that his chances were not as good as those of someone who was; but his stellar performances in every area of his career up to this point stood him in good stead. So he turned in his "Dream Sheet" for that assignment, at the same time knowing full well that he could get assigned to combat in Viet Nam. We had a family portrait made to go along with the "application" for the job, as the whole family would be involved if he did get the assignment.

I had still been having some health problems. Though I had lost quite a bit of weight in that sick spell of early 1963, I had gained some of it back by now. One of the medications I took for my joint pain, Chloroquin, had bleached my hair out in a spotty sort of way. For the portrait, I had my hair done, and my beautician dyed my eyebrows, which were practically white and made me look very pale. But she got a little carried away and overdid it. When I got home I scrubbed and scrubbed on them and was able to lighten them up a
~~~

little bit; but they still looked pretty dark. We used those pictures on our Christmas cards for 1964; and I thought we looked like the All-American Family. But when Mother and Daddy got their card, Mother thought I looked like death warmed over and called me up crying about how bad I looked.

The Hamiltons at the USAF Academy, fall 1964
Dave, 9; Ann, 4

So I'll never know whether Ike got the job at Maxwell <u>because of</u> that picture or <u>in spite of</u> it. We did learn in the spring, though, that he would be assigned as an instructor at Squadron Officer School, reporting in July of 1965. It was to be a three-year assignment; so that let him off the hook for at least three more years as far as a combat tour was concerned. Since we had decided that, come what may, he would retire from the Air Force as soon as he reached the twenty-year point, we were hoping that he could escape without another combat tour.

Something somewhat funny happened in the spring of 1965. Ike had been doing fill-in preaching at the (black) Prospect Street church of Christ for several months, because they had lost their preacher. Several men had come and tried out for the position. One Sunday afternoon while Mother and Daddy were visiting us, Ike and I were taking a nap when the doorbell rang. Daddy went to the door, and there stood two nicely dressed black couples. Now, you have to remember that Mother and Daddy were from Baton Rouge, Louisiana, one of the most racist cities in the South. My folks were not as rabid on the subject as some in Baton Rouge, including my uncle; and they knew how Ike and I felt about racial discrimination and that we wouldn't tolerate their saying anything derogatory about the blacks. Daddy didn't blink an eye. He invited them in and sent Mother to wake us up and tell us we had visitors. By the time Ike and I got dressed and made it into the living room, Mother was already serving them cake and coffee. We had a nice visit, meeting the new man whom the congregation later decided to hire as their pulpit minister.

That night Mother and Daddy took us out to dinner at a restaurant in Colorado Springs. Daddy finally spoke up and said,

"I just have one thing to say: Do you realize that Colorado Springs, Colorado, and Montgomery, Alabama, are two different places?"

"Yes, we know," was our answer. And nothing else was ever said about it again.

~~~

We knew that Mom Hamilton would not be up to making the long, hard drive with us from Colorado to Alabama when the time came for us to go. So Ike took some leave and flew to Montgomery with her, placing her in a nursing home he had scouted out when on a TDY to Montgomery some time before. Although getting progressively weaker and fuzzier in her thinking, Mom had been continent up to the time of that trip. But since she was a dead weight and practically had to be carried everywhere, we decided that Ike
~~~

wouldn't be able to get her to the rest room; so we made the decision to put adult diapers on her for that trip. It turned out to have been a bad decision, because she became incontinent for the rest of her life after that. We could have probably gotten the stewardesses to take her to the bathroom but didn't think of that in time. In addition, Ike should have gotten help getting her in and out of the wheel chair because he did permanent damage to his already weak back on that trip.

~~~

When Ike got back, it was just a matter of my finishing up the teaching and year-end wrap-up chores at school, getting packed up, and then making the final move to Alabama. It had been decided that Martha, Ike's niece, would come and visit us for several weeks; so her folks flew her up to Denver and Ike went to get her. He was already through with all his duties and was on leave; while I was still hard at it at my school. Martha proved to be a Godsend, as she, at age fifteen, already had developed good organizational skills. She and Ike together directed the packers, helping them allocate certain things to go with the household goods, the other things being carried by us in the travel trailer. All went well except for one minor SNAFU—one drawer-full of my unmentionables that I was going to need for the next few weeks until we got into housing and our household goods were delivered, got sent instead of being left for me to take. I could definitely not get by with just the one set of underwear I had on; so Ike was dispatched to the BX to buy me some new ones. When he got there, he couldn't remember the size I'd told him; so he guessed at the size. I suppose I should have been flattered that he got the size he did—one size smaller than the one I was used to! But they really got uncomfortable after a day or two; so I was forced to go and invest in a few more pairs in the right size.

~~~

Martha was now the proud possessor of a no-restrictions driver's license; so we were counting on her to fill in with the driving chores on the long trip South. The only problem was that she had learned to drive in a car with an automatic gearshift, and both of our cars had standard shifts. In addition, Ike would be pulling the trailer with the Mercedes; so Martha needed to learn how to drive the Volkswagen, famous for it's four-on-the-floor, a difficult reverse gear, and, of course, a clutch. We wanted to take the time to give her a few lessons in driving it before we left; but the time never presented itself because of my working and the packing that they were doing. So each night at the dinner table Ike would give her oral instructions in how to drive the VW. He always did love to go into excruciating details on anything mechanical like that; so he would wax eloquent in giving her the nitty-gritty on how to drive the VW.

Finally our caravan struck out—Ike and Dave in front, pulling the trailer with the Mercedes, and Martha, Ann and I bringing up the rear in the VW. It soon became apparent that there was not going to be a good time to give Martha any further instructions in driving the VW. So, after about 100 miles, I pulled over and got out, putting Martha in the driver's seat. After a few false starts, she finally got it going and things went along fairly smoothly—until, that is, we came to a town. Towns, of course, have stoplights and stop signs. Martha would pull up to a light, stop the car and, not being used to having to deal with a clutch, kill the engine. A pattern developed—kill the engine, start it up, not give it enough gas, choke it, kill the engine again. It took her sometimes three or four times to get it going and actually begin moving again. Meanwhile, the cars behind us were growing impatient; but I wouldn't budge. This was Cold Turkey. Sink or Swim. Four-year-old Ann got so used to hearing me give Martha the same instruction, that when Martha would kill the engine, Ann started beating me to the draw and yelling, "Keep that foot on that 'celerater!"

Martha finally got it down pat and became a great driver, taking it all the way from Colorado to Memphis. After those problems, it had become clear to us that it would be better for Ike to drive behind us with the trailer, which we could always easily spot, so that he could keep an eye on us in case anything went wrong with the VW.

We spent our first night on the road in a campground in Kansas, through which a tornado had just passed the night before, leveling most of the trees in the area. That was scary. If we had been there in our trailer, we'd have been pretty vulnerable. The Lord was certainly looking after us. After sightseeing in Dodge City, we headed on down through the Ozark Mountains, camping on the beautiful Buffalo River in North Arkansas. There was an ice-cold babbling brook running right beside our camping spot. I had remembered those wonderful watermelons, chilled in the icy mountain creeks, that my family used to buy when traveling through those mountains. So we went out and found a watermelon and chilled it there in the brook, bringing back some precious memories of my Arkansas childhood.

Our itinerary took us through Searcy, Arkansas, the Home of Harding College, a four-year institution operated by the churches of Christ. When Martha and I saw a sign pointing to the college, we wanted to catch a quick glimpse of the campus there because we had heard a lot about the school. When we turned off of the highway that went through the heart of town, Ike kept going. But we were determined we were going to have our way in this. We went one block, turned left on Center Street, drove two blocks, and turned back onto the highway. Just a brief detour but we fell in love with the lovely campus, with its old brick buildings and picturesque white swings spotting the quadrangle.

Everything went fine until we got to Memphis. From there we just had one more short leg of our journey before arriving in Starkville, Mississippi, where Lydia Blanche and Earl Terrell lived. I guess Ike got antsy; and when we stopped at one light, he pulled on up ahead of us and struck out. Wouldn't you know the VW would pick that time to start acting up? I got in the driver's seat but could not get it to start. We were now blocking traffic in a large city. A policeman came over to see whether he could help. Instead of sending him ahead to stop Ike—as I should have done—I asked him to help us get the VW over to a service station. Well, for the rest of the trip to Starkville, we kept having problems losing power, but Ike Hamilton was long gone. Someone would get us on the road again, only to have the VW lose power again within minutes. It not only was getting annoying but was beginning to reach the frightening stage, as it was starting to get dark on us.

Once again we lost power and had to pull to the side of the road. Dusk was definitely setting in. Then a couple of guys pulling a motorboat stopped beside us. Two scruffier looking characters never existed. I was actually afraid, because we were at their mercy. But they asked what our problem was, then pulled over and proceeded to work on the points with my emery board, enough to get us going again. These two Good Samaritans went to the top of my Sweet List, while Ike Hamilton, who had deserted us in Memphis, went to the top of my Black List. One of our problems was that I didn't know the address of Ike's sister or how to get to their house. But as we came into town, we saw the Terrells' teenage son, Wayne, sitting on the hood of their car on the side of the road, watching for us. The next day, when Ike took the VW to be repaired, he learned that the problem had been a faulty gasket and none of the fifteen-or-so different things that people had worked on whenever the car had lost power.

Chapter 31 – Squadron Officer School – Part 2

After a nice visit with the Earl Terrells, which, as always, included some of Earl's good old homemade peach ice cream, we headed out for Montgomery, Alabama, for our third assignment at that base, this time PCS.

Learning upon arrival that we would not be able to get right into our apartment in base housing because it was undergoing renovations, we parked in a trailer park right off the base—the very one where we had made reservations twelve years earlier thinking we had gotten SOS before going to Tallahassee. It was convenient enough until Ike reported in and started having to look sharp in his uniform every day. The one tiny closet in the trailer was simply not adequate for the active military and social life we now were leading. Getting the two of us showered and dressed for formal occasions—me in an evening dress and Ike in his dress blues—was no mean feat in the small space we had, and especially in Alabama's sub-human summer heat.

To make matters worse, about a week after our arrival there, the toilet in the trailer broke. No part was available to repair it in Montgomery; so the part had to be ordered from California, which might as well have been the moon for all the speed that was involved. We made use of the Little Blue Potty that we always carried for the kids in the car under the seat, but had to resort to the Shell Station on the corner for more serious business.

We had been able to look inside our apartment once and had driven by it several times to let the kids see where they'd be living. We were around the corner from the Elementary School; and there was a huge playground right across the street from us. When Dave saw it he exclaimed,

"Oh, good! A playground! Ann can play over there while I'm playing with my friends—my friends I'm going to make."

It always made me feel good to remember that statement whenever I was wondering if the vagabond life of a Military Brat was doing the kids any harm. Dave had always been very outgoing. So, though he knew he would miss his friends when we left one base, he had no fear that he'd not have friends when he got to his new home. In later years when I asked him whether he felt that he had been short-changed in not being able to settle in one place for very long, he didn't hesitate a minute, but replied,

"No. Money couldn't buy the education you gave me in taking me to so many different places in the world." I guess that's why he wanted to make a life in the Air Force for his own family when that time came.

~~~

Martha wound up staying with us five weeks in all. She turned out to be the family *chauffeuse* the entire time she was there, even getting up early and taking Dave and Ann to the O Club for the long-awaiting swimming lessons. Yes, the third time was the charm: Dave finally learned how to swim, and Ann even learned the rudiments of swimming, although she didn't turn five until August. Floyd and James came to get Martha and to visit Mom Hamilton, who had settled nicely into one of the local nursing homes. Then they left, taking Martha, whom we had come to look upon as a fifth member of our family.

~~~

We placed membership at the West End congregation, the same one we had attended way back in 1953, where everyone had been so nice to us. The building was just two blocks from the East gate of Maxwell and couldn't have been handier. Some people remembered us and were glad to get to know our kids. The elders put Ike and me right to work teaching classes. So it didn't take us long to get settled in there.

~~~
~~~

Chippie was now almost eleven years old and was getting pretty decrepit and very sot in her ways. With the exception of when Ike would come home from work in the afternoons and she would go wild with happiness at seeing him, and then go into an asthmatic coughing spell, she spent all of her time in her "room," the bottom of the closet in the bathroom. She now had cataracts and was arthritic and practically deaf. We knew that it would not be long before we would have to have her put to sleep; but we dreaded that moment.

Shortly after we arrived in Montgomery, we made a sentimental journey over to Selma, where we looked up the veterinarian from whom we had bought cute little Monk fourteen years before. He was still there and still raising those adorable little Toy Manchester-Terrier dogs. He used his own dog, Pete, for stud purposes; so he took us by his house to see Pete. We fell for him right away. While we were there, he was busy catching flies. We put in our order for the next little male puppy that Pete produced. When the litter was born, we rode over to Selma again to pick out our puppy. We wanted one with markings as close to our original Monk's as possible: black and tan with little white "spats" on all four paws, and a white "shirt" on his chest, which made him look as though he were wearing a tuxedo. The timing worked out in such a way that, on our return from a Christmas trip to Louisiana, we were able to pick him up.

We named him Monkey Doodle after Monk but called him "Dood." And he turned out to be a real <u>dude</u>. He had inherited the fly-catching gene from Pete. Dave immediately latched on to him and made him his very own dog, keeping him at first, on our insistence, in his closet. But each morning when we would get up, there would be Dood in bed with Dave; so we eventually gave up and let him keep him there. Our kid had definitely "gone to the dogs."

Dood made a hit with everybody except Chippie. She would put him in his place in a hurry when he would try to play with her. She was interested in only two things, eating and sleeping. We had had to start pouring hot water over her Purina Dog Chow to soften it because of her scarcity of teeth. When we would feed the two dogs, she would scarf down her soft food in about two seconds and then growl, run Dood away, and begin on his dry food. We really had to watch her carefully and grab it away from her, as she would swallow it practically whole.

~~~

Dave was now in the fifth grade, and Ann was starting kindergarten. Both schools were within walking distance of our apartment, which made it nice. Ann had already taught herself to read from billboards and cereal boxes; so she was ready to move on with her education. She had developed a lisp that we had not really noticed, I guess because we just thought of it as part of her being a baby. But when I took her to the pediatrician once for one of her many earaches, he asked me,

"How long has she had that lisp?"

I almost said, "What lisp?" But he went on:

"Children can be very cruel about that sort of thing. You should get it taken care of before she starts school. We have an excellent Speech Therapist here at the Base Hospital; so I'm going to refer her to him."

I guess he knew whereof he spoke, because he himself had one of the worst lisps I have ever heard in a grown-up. He had probably experienced first hand some of the cruelty he had mentioned.

So I took her once to the therapist. He won her over in that one visit, to the point where she never wanted me to go with her again, but always walked there by herself. She actually went only about a half dozen more times because the lisp cleared up almost immediately. The doctor had her make a scrapbook with pictures of items starting with the S and Z sounds, the two sounds that gave her problems. We sat down and cut pictures out of magazines and pasted them in her scrapbook. She was to go through it twice a day saying the sounds the correct way. Ann has always been a ham; so she loved being in
~~~

the spotlight this way. Just let anyone walk in our door, and she would go drag out her scrapbook. The visitors couldn't do another thing until she had gone all the way through that booklet with them. She was so proud of herself. In no time at all her lisp was history.

Dave had done well at Douglas Valley Elementary at the Academy in the second through fourth grades. He did well at Maxwell Elementary in everything except for one subject: Math. He had gotten left behind when the "New Math" came out; because Alabama had started teaching it the previous year, in Dave's fourth grade; but Colorado didn't start it until the year we left. So he had a struggle with math from then on, although he was doing well in all of his other subjects.

~~~

Ike threw himself headlong into his work as Instructor at Squadron Officer School. As such he was to wear at least two hats at a time: one as Lecturer to the entire class, and one as Section Leader of one of the many sections of junior officers attending the 3-1/2 month school. He was to become manager of the Leadership area of the curriculum, one of the five major ones. This involved his completely rewriting and updating two major seminar instructional manuals, Leadership and Establishing a Training Program. Another lecture of his was on the Code of Conduct. I helped him work up his own version of the lectures that had been given by the previous person who had covered those subjects. The delivery had to be right down to within thirty seconds of the allotted time, which meant that he had to go over and over his lectures, actually memorizing them. His personal style of leadership was to keep as low a profile as possible, letting the others in the group think that they had come up with the plan they were to use, when actually he had unobtrusively influenced them in that direction by throwing in skillfully worded questions at strategic times. In defining Leadership, he used the personality traits that had made Jesus the leader that He was, making many references to his own Christian beliefs. In the Code of Conduct lecture, also, he always managed to work his faith into the picture. When talking of the necessity for a POW to have a strong faith in
~~~

something that he could look forward to in order to survive the ordeal, he always brought out that his faith in God was what would have allowed him to keep on, had he ever been in that position. He spoke of God's knowing the actual number of hairs on each person's head, always getting a laugh when he would run his hand over his own rapidly thinning hair.

One of Ike's Additional Duties was to host visiting celebrities who would come to lecture in the thrice-yearly classes. He would meet them on the flight line, see to their needs, and escort them to the auditorium for their lectures. He met some very nice, high-ranking officers that way and always got good write-ups for his hosting duties.

~~~

I had been under the impression that all Section Commanders had lecturing duties, or that all Lecturers were also Section Commanders. But in reading back over an OER covering this early period, I found this:

During his first class as a faculty member he not only was a section commander, which is a full-time job, but also successfully delivered three lectures of the high quality that this school demands. This is a task that, to my knowledge, has never been performed before. Although Maj Hamilton has been in a learning status during most of this period, he has developed rapidly and has indicated such potential that I intend to appoint him as my assistant division chief. He strives for perfection and is a meticulous and thorough planner, making extensive preparation prior to giving the dry runs of his lectures. A portion of one of his Leadership lectures concerns the attribute of integrity, a quality he personally projects in his bearing and behavior both from the platform and in his everyday work. Although he has been somewhat hampered by injury and illness, regardless of the state of his health, he has never missed a lecture or an important duty. On three occasions I asked him to deliver lectures to other AU schools, which he did in an outstanding manner. With no
~~~

supervision, he set up and managed the Zero Defects program for the division.

~~~

The wives of the faculty members at SOS played a larger role in their husbands' jobs than in any other assignment Ike ever had. Since the student officers were kept extremely busy, ways had to be found to keep the student wives busy and happy so that they wouldn't make too many demands on their husbands. That's where the Section Leaders' wives came in. In addition to the regularly scheduled introductory teas and coffees given by the wife of the General who headed up SOS, we had to hostess such events on a smaller scale for our sections. That meant that three times a year I had to have some sort of welcoming event for the wives of the students in Ike's section. I could have had it at the O Club, making it a formal type of thing, or a poolside party, or whatever I could come up with. But since I've always been an informal type of gal, I usually had them over to my home for an icebreaker—coffee or cokes or something of the sort. Many of the student wives were new to this sort of thing; so it always seemed to make them relax and feel more at home if I kept it very informal.

The section wives would have to decide how much they wanted to do and what sort of activities they'd like to do to keep themselves and their children busy. I was fortunate in that most of the ones I drew were reasonable and didn't insist on doing a lot of things during the class besides "required" ones. About the most that my ladies ever wanted to do was to get together informally, maybe have a picnic, play a little bridge, go to a movie, eat out, or something of the sort. One class took one of the OWC-sponsored tours to the towel factories in a nearby Georgia city, but I didn't go along. Remembering the disastrous occasion during Ike's pilot training days, I'm glad none of them ever wanted to go deep-sea fishing down off the coast.

The families always became the cheering squad for the section in their sports events, which were the same old ones from Ike's 1957 student days: soccer, volleyball and flicker-ball. You would have
~~~

thought this was professional or college ball the way some of the sections threw themselves into this. Never having been much of a sporty person myself, I dreaded these events, but went through with it as if I loved it. I always feared getting a bunch of wives, as some did, who were fanatical and would want to wear outlandish costumes. About the most complicated uniforms that any of my groups ever chose were for all of the women to wear identical black stretch stirrup pants (something that could be worn anywhere) and matching shirts in our section's colors.

~~~

Ike had continued to have problems with his back over the years, at the same time trying to keep his fitness up. Jogging was the first thing that had to go, because it involved jarring movements on the vertebrae, with the attendant squeezed disc material. While he was on the faculty there, the faculty members played the sports right along with their students. This started taking its toll on Ike's back, especially soccer. The jerking movements caused by the running and sudden turns necessary to play soccer sent him to the doctor more than once. Finally the doctor banned soccer for him, letting him referee it only. But that still required running and jerking back around; so that, too, had to go. Ditto with playing flicker-ball. Ditto with refereeing flicker-ball. Ditto with playing volleyball. By the end of his first class on the faculty of SOS, the only participation he was allowed was refereeing volleyball, which could be accomplished while sitting up on a high perch and following the game with his eyes. He was now thirty-seven years old and no longer a young man so had to face up to the fact that he couldn't do a lot of the things he had always done.

~~~

At the end of each class, the faculty and some of their wives always put on a program for the students the night before their graduation. This had been a very intense period for them and they needed a little levity in their lives at this point. It was always a fun time for everybody. Some of the faculty members had worked up what they called The Beetle Bottle Band, the brainchild of Major Emile Boado, a multi-talented guy if ever there was one. Emo had gotten together bottles and jars of all sizes, putting the amount of water in them needed to get the right musical sounds from them when they were blown into. About eight of the guys would blow into those twenty or thirty bottles, making actual musical sounds. You could even recognize some of the songs they played. That was always the highlight of that faculty program.

After one of the first graduating classes of our assignment at Maxwell, a young Captain came up to me and said,

"Mrs. Hamilton, you probably don't remember me, but I was in your USAFI English class back at Phalsbourg Air Base, France, in 1960. If it hadn't been for you, I wouldn't have been able to pass the GED test, get my High School Equivalency, or go to OCS. I just wanted to thank you."

Was that ever music to my ears?! Teaching is so often a thankless task, and positive feedback like that is scarce. But one testimonial such as that is enough to thrill one's soul and make it all worthwhile.

~~~

In the summer of 1966, I got sick once while Ike was (where else?) away on TDY. I got progressively more nauseated as the day wore on and finally began vomiting uncontrollably. Dave went to get the next-door neighbor lady, who wasn't home; but her husband, a Major, was. He took one look at me and called the Base Hospital, managing to talk them into sending an ambulance for me. That wasn't really being done in the Air Force; but he refused to take the responsibility for getting me to the hospital; so they sent an ambulance for me. After a shot to break the cycle of vomiting, they had to send me home because there were no empty beds left. It seems that the Medical OD that day had already seen six cases like mine, something he termed an Inner Ear Virus. The next-door neighbors took Dave and Ann in and a friend from church came and got me; and I spent the night with her.
~~~

I was sick off and on all summer that way, but never as bad as that day. The least little thing nauseated me, especially the smell of food cooking. That was disastrous, as I had a family to feed. But bless Dave's heart! That was the summer he earned his Cooking Merit Badge at Boy Scout Camp; so he took over most of the cooking for me that summer. He learned how to make several dishes, one of them being meat loaf. He'd come into my bedroom, listen to the next step or two, go back in the kitchen and carry out my instructions; then come back for more. At the age of ten, he was literally Chief Cook and Bottle Washer.

In later years, that condition of mine got worse and worse and was finally diagnosed as Menière's Disease, an imbalance of the inner ear. I've decided to spare my readers the tedious details of each trip to the Emergency Room to bring my condition under control. Suffice it to say, that such a condition is a serious deterrent to most of the things inherent in the active, mobile life of an Air Force Wife.

~~~

Shortly after arriving in Montgomery, we had scouted out a new violin teacher for Dave; and he began taking lessons from Mrs. Helen Carter. She lived quite a distance across town, which meant that I had to taxi him there each week. Sometimes I would run errands during his lesson and sometimes just sit in her L-shaped den off the living room, where I could hear the lesson but not be seen. Mrs. Carter was an excellent teacher but a real slave driver. Poor Dave had to un-learn practically everything Ike and Sgt. Greenhouse had taught him in Colorado. Mrs. Carter had a way of rapping his knuckles with a ruler or barking at him, "Why did you do that?" It wasn't long before he was dreading going to his lessons. Playing in a Christmas concert she had with all of her students and, later, in a recital, did help him to have more confidence in himself.

~~~

One weekend in the summer of 1966, we towed our travel trailer down to Maxwell's Recreation Area on the North shore of Okaloosa Bay, right off the Gulf of Mexico, intending to park our trailer there. On the way out there, when passing through the little town of Niceville, Florida, we noticed the building where the Pine Lake church of Christ met. We learned when we got to the Recreation Area that we couldn't park our trailer there, since they rented out trailers; but we could use all of their other facilities. So we parked across the road at a State Park, and went and used the beach at the Maxwell place. When Sunday rolled around, we went back to that church we had seen coming into town. Cliff Thompson, a boy Dave's age, immediately latched onto him, taking him to Bible class and inviting him to sit with his family during worship. After services, he invited Dave home to spend the afternoon with him. So Dave already had made fast friends with somebody at that church.

That night, the whole family was invited over for dessert to the home of the preacher, Terry Hanna, who was also one of the elders. He and his wife Billie and the other couple there heard our life story and we heard theirs, as well as the plans the church had for sending missionaries on the field in a few years. We were already starting to think about that "full-time work for the Lord" Ike had been planning ever since 1962 when he had the cancer surgery and almost got out of the Air Force. Now retirement was right around the corner, and decision-time would not be far off. We had been thinking of staying in Montgomery and working with the West End church after retirement and had even looked at some property in the area. So we told them about those tentative plans. Brother Hanna said,

"Well, just keep us in mind in case you change your mind. We might be ready to take on another minister by then (we were looking at 1970, after twenty years of AF time for Ike). So after making some friends that were to turn out to be life-long ones, we returned to Maxwell with plenty of food for thought.

~~~
~~~

During that summer we had also taken our trailer out for some "primitive" camping in one of Alabama's beautiful National Forests. Camping was allowed in certain non-improved areas, meaning there was no campground and no electrical or water hookups. That was about as "next to nature" as we ever wanted to get; but our cozy little trailer was completely self-contained; so we could exist for a while like that.

On our way back home on a Sunday morning, we had planned to stop off in Centerville, Alabama, not too far south of Birmingham, look up the church of Christ, and worship with them. But, to our surprise, this part of the so-called "Bible Belt" didn't have a congregation of the church. Someone told us there was one meeting a few miles North in a little town called West Blocton. We were on the fence as to whether to go up there or just head on back home and catch the evening worship at West End. But we had gone to the trouble of putting on our Sunday-Go-to-Meeting clothes that morning; so we turned north and headed up to West Blocton.

Sure enough, there was a small church building with a handful of enthusiastic Christians, who sang at the top of their lungs, almost on key. Afterwards, they invited us over to the home of one of the "pillars," where they were having a potluck dinner. We tried to say "No," but they coerced us; so we stayed. In the course of the visit, we learned that they had no regular preacher but had to be supplied with preachers from different congregations in the Birmingham area, some of whom did not show up on their designated Sundays to preach. Besides the inconvenience of that arrangement, it meant that the preaching they got was a hodge-podge, nothing coordinated or edifying to the church over the long haul. When they learned that Ike was in the habit of doing fill-in preaching, and had already done some in the Montgomery area, nothing would do but he must promise to come back and preach for them the next Sunday.

We all piled in and drove the 85 miles to West Blocton the next Sunday. They were impressed and prevailed upon Ike to be their regular Sunday-morning preacher. And thus began a yearlong association with a group of wonderful people, some of whom we've maintained contact with for these many years. It was quite a chore for us to make that four-hour round trip every Sunday, getting back to Montgomery just in time to grab a quick hot dog at the Dairy Queen on Bell Street and go screeching in for the evening services at West End. We were both still teaching Wednesday night classes and were involved in every way with West End. I began teaching the "children's" Sunday School class at West Blocton, which consisted of about twelve kids from Ann's age, six, all the way up to a boy eighteen who had recently obeyed the gospel but had very little over-all Bible knowledge. David and Sue Pickett, the couple who had originally invited us over for the potluck, fed us a wonderful meal every Sunday and allowed us to have a small rest before heading back to Montgomery.

~~~

Still flying the T-Bird at every opportunity, Ike always heaved a sigh of relief whenever he made it through another "purge" of high-ranking officers who were still on flight status but whose flying was not considered essential to the mission of the Air Force. It costs a tremendous amount of money to keep a pilot proficient, but it is essential to maintain a large pool of proficient pilots in case of war or other emergencies. But, more and more, they were grounding those higher-ranking officers who were not in front-line flying. That's why he was so glad when, on 15 September 1966, he had racked up the 2,800 flight hours to qualify him as a Command Pilot, adding a laurel wreath around the Senior Pilot star on his wings.

~~~

On 21 November 1966, Ike made Lt Colonel. We had been to many a Promotion Party before but had never been "required" to give one. But since three men in the organization were promoted at the same time, it was decided that the three would go in together and have one party. We weren't very enthusiastic about it for two reasons: Ike was not the most gregarious person in the world and usually avoided large parties if he could. And then there was the drinking thing. Everyone knew we didn't drink; but who had ever heard of a

Promotion Party with no drinks? We knew it would be a losing battle to propose such a thing. But we couldn't conscientiously provide drinks for people. Finally, someone came up with a compromise: we would split the cost three ways, Ike and I providing the *hors d'oeuvres*, and the other two men paying for the drinks. Probably, no one ever knew about that arrangement; but it did make us feel better about the whole thing. Everything went very well, if I do say so myself; and I even got a new "Little Black Dress" out of that occasion!

~~~

There were officers from various countries that were attending SOS; so we decided to sign up to "sponsor" a couple of them in the fall of 1966. We were assigned a Philippino and an Ecuadorian. I'm ashamed to say that we didn't get to know the Philippine officer very well, as we were able to manage having them over for a meal only once that fall. But since the Ecuadorian officer was there a total of nine months, attending various schools, we got to know him quite a bit better.

His name was José "Pepe" Torres. He was single when he came there but went home during the Christmas holidays and got married. Pepe was thirty-two years old, his bride being only 19; but those May and December marriages are quite common in Latin American countries. We had determined that we would leave them alone for a few weeks and give them time to get adjusted. But in January, about the third day into Pepe's SOS class 67-A, Ike came home from work and said,

"You'd better get over to see that Mrs. Torres soon. She's threatening to go back home to Ecuador."

So I went by to see her right away, armed with my Spanish-English, English-Spanish dictionary, since my Spanish was pretty rusty; and Ike had told me that she didn't speak English. Pepe had not chosen to get an apartment where most of the other student families were living because he wanted to get a nicer place, a house, more
~~~

commensurate with the style of living Isabel was accustomed to. So she was stuck off clear across Montgomery from everybody else and was extremely homesick. When I found the house, I went up and knocked on the door, where instead of a screen door, there were jalousies. She finally came, opening only the inner door, and, in a faint little voice, said,

"*¿Sí?*"

So I told her in Spanish who I was and that I had just come to meet her and have a short visit. When she heard a woman's voice speaking to her in Spanish, she quickly opened the door and almost threw herself into my arms, she was so glad to see me. She had been afraid to open the door because she had heard about the state of race relations in Montgomery and didn't know but that it might be a black man coming to do her some harm.

We hit it off real well, and I learned that my Spanish hadn't gone to pot quite as much as I had suspected. I really felt sorry for her because she was having Culture Shock big-time. The daughter of a prominent dentist in Guayaquil, Isabel was a beautiful, pampered girl who had never lifted a finger, her family having had several servants. Here she was with a big house and didn't know the first thing about shopping, cooking or cleaning.

I felt sorry for Pepe also because Isabel was not mingling with the other student wives and lived just for the minute he would walk in the door in the evening. But he had hours of studying to do after he got home, and in a second language at that, making him at more of a disadvantage than the other overworked students. To make matters worse, Isabel had gotten pregnant right away and was having full-blown morning sickness every day.

So I took Isabel under my wing, and she became my shadow from then on. Pepe would bring her with him when he'd come to work at seven a.m., dropping her off at our quarters. Since Ann was getting up and getting ready for school about that time, Isabel would go to bed in Ann's room and sleep until almost noon. Then I'd prepare *café con leche* and toast for her. And she would then go through my schedule with me the rest of the day. It turned out that she did speak a little English but had been afraid to say so for fear that she wouldn't understand what others were saying and would be embarrassed and unable to answer them. Little by little, she got to feeling better, I got her plugged in with the wives of Pepe's section, and she began taking part in some of their activities.

Then about March of that year, her mother, Violeta Vanegas came for a visit. She was a charming lady, not much older than I. She really didn't speak a word of English; so I got to practice my Spanish every day with her. She took over the Torres household and whipped it into shape, cooking some marvelous meals which Ike and I were frequently invited to share.

About that same time, I had made contact with some missionaries, sent to Quito, Ecuador, by the Gadsden Street church of Christ in Tallahassee, Florida, where we had been living when Dave was born. I was trying my hand at doing some translating for Ed Sewell and his wife Sybil. I got Isabel to help me with some grammatical points; and, although she didn't have a Biblical vocabulary at all, together we put out a pretty good product.

Pepe attended the 6-week Academic Instructor Course at Maxwell after finishing SOS in April; so he was at Maxwell about nine months in all. We had become very close to him and Isabel and really hated to see them go when they left. They kept insisting that whenever we were in Guayaquil, we should look them up, and we assured them that we would. Little did any of us know!

~~~

Dave was still "hanging in there" with Mrs. Carter and learning a lot from her, although he and Denise, the girl who rode with us from the base, would sometimes come away from the lessons in tears. We had told Dave back in Colorado when he first started playing the violin that if he found he didn't like it, he didn't have to go on with it and could drop the lessons. At one point, he called our bluff on that,
~~~

saying that he was ready to give it up. What could we do but say, "O.K., if that's what you want"? But when we told Mrs. Carter, she nearly had a fit, exclaiming,

"Oh, no! He can't give it up. He has a real talent and is doing so well."

When Dave saw her the next time, she prevailed upon him to keep on with his lessons until after the recital she was getting ready to give. So he reluctantly stayed on; and when the recital was over, decided to keep up his lessons.

Ann had been wanting to start violin lessons, too; and Mrs. Carter had been periodically measuring the angle in her arm to see whether she was big enough to begin. Although we owned a ¾-sized violin that had been given to Ike as a child, it appeared that Ann would have to begin with a ½-sized one. In the summer of 1967, before Ann was even seven years old, Mrs. Carter declared her big enough and began having lessons with her, too. I think Mrs. Carter must have let up somewhat on her Drill Sergeant tactics, because both kids got along fine with her from then on.

~~~

One Sunday morning in late May of 1967, as we arrived in West Blocton for Ike to preach, we were greeted with the message that Ike was to return a telephone call from his sister, Floyd Williams. Ike's mother had been living in a nursing home in Lake Charles ever since Medicare had gone into effect and it had become unnecessary for her to be Ike's dependent. She had been in remarkably good health in her later years, but was now 77 and had Hardening of the Arteries to the brain and had gradually been slipping away from us mentally. This call was to tell Ike that, if he wanted to see her alive again, he had better come on to Lake Charles.

He went ahead and preached his sermon that morning, giving very little sign that anything was different about that day. The congregation had planned a Dinner on the Ground, because Ike was to
~~~

give his first sermon that day on what was to be a weekly 15-minute radio program, sponsored by the West Blocton congregation. Sue Pickett wrote weekly articles for the Centerville newspaper and had contacts in that town; so she had engineered it with the local radio station for a weekly fifteen-minute program of preaching, with the congregational singers adding their special touch.

Ike was holding up well; but I had been getting more and more nauseated during the worship service in the boiling hot church building in West Blocton. When I began eating, I started vomiting—as only I can do!—and couldn't stop. So as soon as the radio program was over, I had to be taken to the ER and given a shot to break the cycle of nausea. I remained there while Ike went home to Montgomery, Mother and Daddy made a quick trip from Baton Rouge to "hold down the fort," and Ike headed for Louisiana. He stayed several days; but Mom lingered; so he had to return. About a week later, on June 1st, they called to tell us that she had died. Ike and the kids went to Lake Charles for the funeral; but since I was still wobbly from my hospital stay and couldn't handle that extra motion, I remained in Montgomery.

~~~

We usually took about thirty days' leave in August and took the trailer on a long trip. Coming from swampy Louisiana, Ike loved the mountains; and we had thoroughly explored the Rockies while living in Colorado. Now we were close to the Great Smoky Mountains; so that's the direction we headed in this time. The only bad part about August vacations was that Ann's birthdays, on the 22nd, always fell while we were off in the Boondocks somewhere. We had to have ingenuity to come up with something entertaining to do on her birthday. And, of course, it was hard to keep anything a secret from her. That year in the Smokies, in North Carolina, I think it was, we took a day off and went into town. Ann knew that we were planning to eat out at a restaurant that night; but we surprised her all along the way by stopping at various tourist places and allowing her to pick out one gift at each of the places we went. At a candle factory she got a nice big candle; at the lapidarist's she got a big, pretty, polished
~~~

rock—nothing really very exciting for a seven-year-old, though. We all went out to dinner as we had planned, eating at the restaurant in an old hotel with lots of rockers on the front porch. Ann liked that but figured that it wasn't going to get much more exciting than that. When after dinner we took her to an old theater, she had no idea that we had made reservations there to see an old-fashioned Melodrama. We all loved booing and hissing at the Villain and cheering on the Hero, as he rescued the Damsel in Distress. Ann went back to the campground a happy 7-year-old that night.

Another important event that took place on that camping trip was our visit to nearby Brevard Music Camp. We were there long enough to make reservations for a concert that would be held during our stay. We all enjoyed it immensely, and Brevard was to play a big role in Ann's music career downstream a few years.

~~~

At the end of that summer, Ike quit preaching for the church in West Blocton. It was just getting to be too much of a drain on all of us. After all, he did have his Air Force duties and was given more and more responsibility as a Lt. Col. Plus, all that driving every week wasn't helping my motion sickness problem any. But he still did occasional fill-in preaching in Montgomery at the various congregations there. When West End's preacher, Vernon Chastain and his wife Evelyn, went on vacation, he asked Ike to fill in for him with the preaching for Sunday morning and evening services; and Ike accepted. He was to be gone only two weeks; but it entailed three Sundays. Little did any of us know what was going to take place during that short period of time. There were, not one, not two, but three deaths in the congregation during that time! We had both sung in small groups for funerals; and I, of course, had done my part in providing food for the bereaved families. However, Ike had never preached a funeral before.

He was soon to learn how, though. He got a book from his mentor, Tom Estes, another local preacher, who also owned a Bible Bookstore and had been helping Ike systematically build up his
~~~

religious library. Ike felt the need to spend time with the families in order to know what to say at the funeral; so he was up several nights into the wee hours, getting only a few hours sleep before reporting to work the next day. He also felt that he should print his funeral remarks so that the family could have them for later. Since I always typed his sermons anyway, I was elected to type them up on a mimeograph stencil and run them off. I sang at all three of the funerals, was also preparing dishes to take to the homes; and twice, I sat up all night with a lady who was dying of cancer. I'm ashamed to say that I was praying that she wouldn't die on my watch; and the Lord answered that prayer.

In all, Ike preached two of the funerals and sang in two of them, including one of the ones he preached. It was for the cancer victim and was a graveside service out in the country. It was a rainy, dreary day; and we had had trouble getting singers. In the end, no men showed up to help with the singing. So Ike would sing bass with the group of lady singers standing at the head of the casket, then step forward a few paces to read scripture, pray or give the sermon, then come back to sing another song with us.

When Vernon Chastain got back home he was bowled over to learn of everything that had happened in the congregation while he was gone. (One of the deaths had been that of a 12-year-old boy accidentally shot by a neighbor boy.) I was proud of Ike for having been able to do everything he did and still—mostly—take care of his Air Force duties. I had been scheduled to pour tea for the General's wife at one of her welcoming teas for new student wives; but because of needing to sing in one of the funerals, I called her an <u>hour</u> before the tea and begged off. That was a major social *faux pas* on my part; but she was very gracious about it.

One of Ike's later OERs from Maxwell, under the heading of Civic Responsibilities, said this:

"Lt Col Hamilton is very active in the affairs of his church where he teaches and preaches."

Under the same heading in an earlier OER, his reviewing officer had this to say:

"Maj Hamilton is very active in the affairs of his church, where he preaches and teaches, and for which he organized and supervised a youth meeting of 1,000 teenagers."

Ike was fortunate that his COs viewed it that way.

~~~

The Viet Nam War was still raging, with no end in sight. Ike received orders in 1968 to go overseas to Udorn AB, Thailand, for a one-year tour. Since he was now a high-ranking, rated officer, it was expected that he would fly while there; and he was made the offer to up-grade into the RF-4 Phantom. The F-4 was one of the hottest aircraft being used in Viet Nam then; and since he had been a recce pilot before, he could fly the RF version of it there if he wanted to. The "Hot Jet Jockey" in Ike wanted nothing more than to accept that offer. Another attractive part of it was that he could virtually be assured that if he asked for a European assignment after Viet Nam, he would probably get it. It was very tempting to do that and finish up his career in Europe, where he could retire, and we could work with some church in that "mission" area. Uncle Sam would move our household goods anywhere in the world for up to one year after his retirement. But to accept that deal, Ike would automatically pick up an additional four-year commitment, three more years than we had planned to stay in. Part of his reasoning went this way: If he up-graded, he'd have to stay in the Air Force until 1973. In the normal course of events, he could probably expect to be promoted to full Colonel during the three years in Europe. But in order to retire in a certain rank, he'd have to have held that rank for at least two years. If the timing weren't just right, that could add on to the time he'd have to stay in. If he extended his overseas tour, the regulation against more than one PCS tour in a fiscal year could prolong the time he'd have to stay. That could mean staying in until as long as 1975. In other words, it could turn into a vicious cycle. Getting out after the combat tour with 20 years of AF service, Ike would already be forty-
~~~

two. Since he wanted to begin his new career in the ministry, after much consideration and prayer on our part, we made the decision for him not to up-grade into the RF-4.

He thought for a while that they would take him off flying status, since he would not be flying a front-line aircraft. But because of the many hours he had racked up over the years, and his Command Pilot status, he managed to stay on flying status right up until the end. The galling part of it for him was that he was to fly the C-47 Gooney Bird, a twin-engine cargo plane. All of the derogatory remarks he and other fighter jocks had made about Multis, and especially cargo birds, came back to him; and he was now going to have to Eat Crow. But at least he was to remain on flight status until he finished out his career, and that was worth everything to him.

~~~

We had made many more trips down to Niceville, Florida, and finally decided to take the Pine Lake church up on their offer for Ike to come there after his combat tour and share the pulpit and other ministerial duties with Terry Hanna. They were looking forward toward the day they would send missionaries out on the field somewhere; and we were wanting to be those missionaries. So it was "a match made in heaven." We even began looking for suitable housing to buy so the kids and I could be settling in there while Ike was overseas. We found one house, not far from the church building, that we really liked. The couple was selling it because they were getting a divorce; so the details were up in the air. But we had to leave, as we were taking our last Air Force-financed August vacation. But we were to place a call to the Real Estate dealer on a certain date from wherever we were to learn whether the people were really going to sell the house or not.

~~~

1968 was to be no exception in our vacation routine. This time we headed out for the Ozark Mountains, taking Martha Williams with us. She was now 18, had graduated from High School in Lake

Charles, was In Love, and just a delight to be with. She had given our itinerary to Jimmy Sigmund, her boy friend; and we were to check for letters from him in General Delivery at the Post Offices along the way. Jimmy must have been smitten, too, because he never missed getting a letter to Martha at any of the Post Offices we had given him. We found my native state to be beautiful in every way and made the most of its National and State Parks.

Martha Lynn Williams, High School Grad, 1968

While we were up in the mountains, away from "civilization" waiting to call the Real Estate agent, I was so excited about that house that I could hardly sleep at night. In my mind I had all of our furniture moved into it; and was really enjoying decorating it. I just had one problem—I couldn't get our king-size headboard around the corner at the top of the stairs and into the master bedroom! You can see that I was obsessing about that house. Then the day finally came when we could call the Real Estate agent and learn whether we would be able to get it or not. Would you believe that it had already been sold?! What a scald! We were now back to the drawing board on house hunting.

~~~
~~~

On our way up to the campground at Magazine Mountain, we had stopped off and stocked up on groceries at an A & P store. Unbeknownst to Ann, we had bought a plain Angel Food cake for her birthday, which was coming up the next week. On the way up the mountain, we also stopped and cased the restaurant at the lodge, with its terrace overlooking a breath-taking scene of the Ozarks. Ike managed to sneak into the kitchen without Ann's realizing it and talk the kitchen staff into doing their best to decorate the Angel Food cake and have it ready on the 22nd, when we would come back to the lodge and eat dinner. They said they had no cake-decorating equipment but would do their best.

On the 22nd, we all piled into the car and headed for the lodge. But we had built it all up for Ann so that she had no idea where we were going. We blindfolded her, and Ike drove all around the campground area, screeching in and out of various driveways, slamming on the breaks, etc. If Ann had only put those gray cells to work she would have realized that there were very limited roads going to and from the campground. But Ike had her completely fooled; she was happy when, after getting out of the car and walking her blindfolded 360 degrees around the lodge, we entered the front door and removed the blindfold.

She probably thought that was to be the only surprise of the evening; so I think dinner was rather an anti-climax for her. As soon as she finished eating, she asked to go out on the terrace and look out from the overlook. When we refused her that permission (She was, after all, a grown-up eight-year-old now!), she was bent out of shape and sat there pouting. But when the waitress came out bringing the decorated birthday cake—complete with "ANN" spelled out in jelly beans, little flags of all nations and several other ingenious touches— and the rest of the patrons in the dining room started singing Happy Birthday with us—she was genuinely surprised and happy.

~~~

We had programmed a week into our schedule to attend some workshops being held in Searcy, Arkansas, at Harding College, that
~~~

beautiful school Martha, Ann and I had seen briefly three years before *en route* from Colorado to Alabama. We thoroughly enjoyed the workshops, the campus, and the College church of Christ, and were glad that Martha and Jimmy had decided to go there in a few short weeks for their college studies.

~~~

Back in Alabama, Dave was beginning the Eighth Grade in Junior High, and Ann was starting the Second. Dave was running track; Ike was always out there for the meets if he could possibly make it, and I went as often as I could, too. Ann was ahead of her classmates; and her teacher was letting her tutor some of the slower kids. When we had first arrived at Maxwell and Ann was in Kindergarten, we had subscribed in Dave's name to a set of books called *The Happy Hollisters.* Two books arrived each month, and both kids loved them. But Dave got a little bent out of shape because, since Ann got home at noon, she had usually opened the box, finished reading the first one, and started on the second before he got home from school.

~~~

Both kids were getting better and better at the violin and kept me hopping carting them all over town to various lessons, rehearsals and performances. We were naturally very proud of them. Ike dug out some of his old violin music and played with them occasionally. There were even one or two easy trios they could play together. Those occasions provided wonderful memories that I still cherish.

That summer, 1968, Dave got a two-week tuition-free scholarship to a music camp outside Columbus, Georgia. He did so well while there that he was offered another free week of music camp at Jekyll Island. About the same time, Mrs. Carter had signed both Dave and Ann up for statewide competition in Birmingham. So I had to drive over to Jekyll Island and pick Dave up in order for him to be able to perform in his time slot. He did well in that, also. Ann, who had now been taking lessons only one year, was told by the man they auditioned for that when she was Dave's age, she should be at least as good as he was. That wasn't too surprising since she had started lessons a good two years younger than he had been when he began playing.

~~~

We now had to get serious with the house hunting in Florida. Niceville was one of two small towns near Eglin AFB that were called the "Twin Cities." You really couldn't tell where one stopped and the other began, and the distance from one end of one of them to the far end of the other was probably not over ten miles. We looked at many houses in both places and finally settled on one in Valparaiso, Niceville's "twin," of the Doolittle Raiders fame. We had been dealing with a builder named Rupert Miller and were about to have him build us a house. But we were sobered to learn how much it was going to cost us for a house with a very small amount of floor space. Then Mr. Miller took us to see a house he had built three years before for the Barrys, a couple from New Hampshire who were returning to their home state. When we first saw it, we thought there was no way we could afford it. It was huge compared to the ones Mr. Miller was currently building, and even the one near the church building that I had obsessed over while in the Ozarks. This house had been their Dream House, a labor of love for them; and they had not spared the checkbook. Counting the double garage and three huge storage areas, it had 3,300 square feet of floor space, four bedrooms, three baths, formal living and dining rooms, a foyer and a <u>huge</u> family room with a fireplace. It was definitely overbuilt for the neighborhood, being the largest house for miles around.

Our first thought was "No Way." But then, novices that we were at buying houses, we learned an important lesson: the interest rate on loans had gone up drastically since this house had been built just a few years before. So, in spite of the size of the house, by assuming the Barry's loan, we were able to get that wonderful house for <u>less</u> than we would have had to pay for a new, much smaller house. The Lord was certainly looking after us this time. We jumped at it, and were never sorry.
~~~

The Hamiltons' House in Valparaiso, Florida

~~~

Events were now moving inexorably toward the time when Ike would have to go to Thailand. We closed on the house in Valparaiso and started making payments on the first of November; but Ike wasn't released from duty at Maxwell until the first of December. Then he would have to leave on the 12th for Thailand.

~~~

We had been wondering how Chippie was going to make the transition to a new house and yard. She was totally blind and deaf now; and sometimes she would get disoriented 180 degrees in the house and bump into walls and doors. Most of the time when she scratched on her door in our bathroom to be let out, she could find her way to her food bowl in the kitchen, and then to the front door to be let out into the yard. She knew just where to go in the yard, and we could trust her alone out there because she would always come right back to the door and scratch. If we were not Johnny-on-the-Spot to let her back in immediately, she would go trotting down the sidewalk to one of the other apartments in the building and scratch on their door. We think she did it out of spite because we weren't right there to let her back in. Once we had gotten busy and hadn't brought her in soon enough, and a neighbor called us to let us know she was scratching on their door.

At any rate, one Wednesday night about a week before our move, we were running late and scurrying around trying to get ready to leave for Bible Study. Chippie wanted out; so I let her out—and then forgot about her! When we got back home from church and went to her room to let her out, she wasn't there. Then I remembered having let her out before church! We all four went out looking for her on bicycles all over the neighborhood, screaming and yelling for her. But it was dark, and she was a tiny black dog who couldn't hear or see us. We gave up after about forty-five minutes, asking the Air Police to keep an eye out for her.

The next morning the APs called us. Chippie had been hit by a car a full block away, down by the Elementary School—a direction in which she had never gone before. They said that probably she had never known what hit her. We felt awful about it; but then we determined that it had probably been for the best. She was, after all, fourteen years old and in poor health. Now, she would not have to make that transition to Florida; and we wouldn't have to make the difficult decision to have her put to sleep.

~~~

One of Ike's final OERs had this to say about his performance while at Maxwell:

DUTIES: Operations Staff Officer, Command and Staff Division. Manages the Leadership area of the curriculum. Prepares seminar instructional manuals on Leadership, Problems of Military Justice, and Establishing a Training Program. Researches, develops, and presents lectures on The Air Force Leader, Code of Conduct, Fundamentals of the Air Force
~~~

Organization, and Training in Air Force Organizations. Develops curriculum plans, examination items, and textbooks for both resident and Extension Course Institute use. Arranges for guest lecturers, monitors their presentations, and acts as host officer for their visits. Monitors and critiques the lectures of other instructors...Lt Col Hamilton's performance of duty has been outstanding in every respect...Because of his knowledge of education on leadership, he was selected to represent Squadron Officer School at the annual National Conference on Higher Education whose theme this year was Leadership...Outstanding teaching and speaking abilities and strong moral character...Three times during the year he has organized and directed a one hour skit on Leadership and Command. This humorous skit, involving 19 faculty members, has been highly successful in teaching the application of leadership principles.

In May of 1968, Col Mish wrote this about Ike:

Mild mannered, unobtrusive, and somewhat gentle in his approach to matters; but he gets outstanding results...Best suited for staff duties, because of his analytical approach and his attention to the details of a job.

Col. Blank's endorsement read: Performs duties efficiently, dependably and without fanfare. Has an acute sense of moral responsibility and fairness. I am pleased to have him in the school.

Chapter 32 - Valparaiso, FL, and Udorn AB, Thailand

The move to Florida on December 2nd went smoothly, partly because we had already become acquainted with practically everyone in the Pine Lake church during the two and one-half years we had been going down there for visits. We loved our new home, the first one we had ever owned. Ann's elementary school was within walking distance; and Dave had only a short walk down to the bus stop for Ruckel Junior High School.

Ike was to leave on the12th for Thailand. We put up a Christmas tree early in December and celebrated Christmas with Ike on the 11th. Since the tree was in the large den by the picture window, it could be seen easily from the side street, which curved around in a loop off Charles Drive. One morning when Dave was on his way to school, one of the neighborhood boys walking with him spied our tree and said,

"Boy! Look at those crazy people! They already have their Christmas tree up!"

Maybe we were crazy; but we had always felt that "home" was where the family was; and Christmas, or Easter, or a birthday, was when it was convenient for us to celebrate it together. We were happy that both Ike's mother and my folks had shared that same feeling, not minding our splitting holidays between them. Whenever we showed up, that was Christmas. It's really the only way it could have been with our living such a vagabond life. Both my brother and my Daddy, being construction men, knew all about that kind of living; so we had all learned to be flexible about such occasions.

~~~

Ike was assigned to the 432ND Tac Recon Wing, Det 1, 7th AF PACAF at Udorn AB, Thailand. He was one of three who pulled
~~~

eight-hour shifts as Senior Operations Duty Officer at the Control Center there, which controlled all of the flying in Thailand and Western Viet Nam.   He made frequent flights in the C-47 to coordinate things in Viet Nam. Whenever he flew into Da Nang AB, Viet Nam, he would look up our dear friend, Sgt. Don Patterson, who had been stationed at Eglin and was a member of the Pine Lake church while in Niceville. Ike was also able to get a lot of flying time in around Thailand, going frequently into Bangkok and, while there, looking up missionaries Jesse Fonville and Parker Henderson. He arranged to fly them around to the different US bases where there were churches of Christ so they could encourage and minister to the men there.

~~~

The church that met at Udorn was very active, the membership consisting of about twenty to 25 men and one lady, the wife of a civilian Air America pilot who was over there on some hush-hush mission. She lived On the Economy would attend whenever she could with her two children; and at least once, she and her husband had the whole church over to their home for a cookout.

Udorn AB, Thailand, church of Christ, 1969
(Ike Front and Center)
~~~

Ike immersed himself in the affairs of the church as soon as he got there and was a welcome addition to the group. All of the men shared the preaching and teaching responsibilities; but he had had quite a bit more experience at preaching than most of them had; so he preached quite regularly. While he was there, he worked up a very good study on "The Christian Man," which he later taught in Bible classes at Niceville, and years later we were to publish in book form.

The guys who were overseas were very vulnerable, many of them being away from their families for the first time. Ike became almost the "official" counselor for the church there because he was so respected by all of the men. At the same time, it took his mind off of how slowly the year's assignment was passing and how much he missed his own family. The men were all very supportive of each other and did everything they could to encourage each other. It was not uncommon at all for two or three of the brothers to be waiting for Ike when his shift would be over at 2 a.m. and to say something like,

"We couldn't sleep; so we thought we'd come and have prayer with you before you went home." This was one of the things that helped Ike to get through that time.

~~~

His family was missing him, too. He was absent at a very crucial time in both children's lives, Dave being in the Eighth Grade and reaching puberty during 1969, and Ann being nine years old. We all wrote frequently and sent him "Care" packages, which he enjoyed in his off-base quarters with a Thai family. He bought a bicycle and rode it the twelve miles back and forth from the base, losing many of the 200+ pounds that he had been carrying when he left us.
~~~

Ike on the Porch of His Thai Home

Ike would occasionally call us through the MARS station. Since he was many hours ahead of us in time, it was usually early in the morning. On one such occasion, Dave answered the telephone before I could get to it, and Ike didn't even recognize his voice! It's true his voice was getting deeper almost daily. That plus the early-morning graveliness had made him sound like a grown man. I accused Dave of trying to get me in trouble with his Dad because of that!

Besides writing many letters back and forth, we exchanged mailing tapes. Ike had always been very much into electronics, getting State-of-the-Art hi-fi equipment while we were in France and later buying one of the first home reel-to-reel recorders when they came out, a small Uher machine. Before he left for Thailand, we bought a larger one as well. Then he got a Sony reel-to-reel when he got to Thailand. It made it much better to be able to hear each other's voices through tapes. Besides talking, the kids could play their violins for him so that he wasn't missing out entirely on their progress. We had also begun a type of round-robin tape communication with my parents and brother and Ike's sisters and brother. We kept that up while he was gone; so everyone was able to hear from him frequently.

~~~

Getting to know Jesse Fonville and Parker Henderson better, Ike proposed that they start having a Thailand Lectureship similar to the Lectureships that had been held for years at our brotherhood colleges in the States and overseas in Europe and Latin America. Flying to Bangkok frequently, he helped them coordinate the program, even inviting Terry Hanna, our Niceville minister, to fly over and be the keynote speaker. Another teacher for the occasion was Richard Rogers, one of the faculty members at Sunset School of Preaching in Lubbock, Texas. Richard taught some of the best lessons I've ever heard on the book of Revelation; and when Ike got back home we listened to those on tape.
~~~

Ike and Missionary Jesse Fonville, Bankok, Thailand, 1969

~~~

One funny thing happened in the Control Room where Ike worked. There was a refrigerator where people kept their drinks and snacks cold. Ike would buy and chill six-packs of his favorite drink "Like." That was the name of the diet version of 7-Up at that time. Someone on another shift was pilfering drinks from Ike's stache. He let it go—until the time that this thief took his <u>last</u> drink and left him the empty carton! That was too much. So Ike had a brainstorm: he tore open the carton and placed it back in the fridge with this message on it:

<div style="text-align:center">

I like Like.
You like Like.
I like that you like
your own Like.
Ike.

</div>
~~~

When he reported in for his next shift, there was a full carton of Like waiting for him in his spot in the fridge. The purloiner did have a conscience after all.

~~~

Ike had also flown up to Cheng Mai, Thailand, to visit Darsey Traw and the other missionaries there. That was a beautiful area of Thailand, famous for its wood carvings. While he was there he ordered a specially designed teakwood cabinet. I had sent him measurements for the cabinet which had to be a certain width, depth and height to fit into the available space in the foyer of our home. It was to have shelves on one side and drawers on the other. While in Thailand, the home of teakwood, he bought many teakwood items such as lamps, salad bowls and candlesticks, which were to blend in beautifully with the teakwood furniture we had bought in Europe. His favorite was the teak wall-hanging of Command Pilot wings

Teak Command Pilot Wings
~~~

~~~

Back in Florida, we were coping as best we could. I was teaching a 3rd Grade Bible class and doing some personal evangelism, and the kids had made good friends. The class of Eighth Grade students at church had a great teacher, Donny Kesler, who seemed to be just an overgrown kid himself and enjoyed planning outings with the kids. So they had lots of parties, and with Fort Walton Beach and Destin so near, many of those were beach parties. Dave especially loved anything to do with the water. Although we had moved from pillar to post, he has always considered himself a Floridian, having been born in Tallahassee, although he didn't remember anything about living there.

~~~

That summer when the elders asked me to be in charge of the Vacation Bible School, I was flattered—but also scared to death. I had never done anything like that before. Sure, I had taught Bible classes for kids for years, including in VBS, and had even fed thirty hungry cadets at a time; but putting it all together and keeping it going for five days was something else. But I had not taken into consideration all of the great, serving people who were going to make up my team. They were always willing to do whatever I asked them to do and bring whatever I asked them to bring. I don't even remember now what the theme of the VBS was or one Bible lesson that was taught, I'm ashamed to say. But I do remember that it went off smoothly, and people were saying that it was one of the best ones they had ever had. I had been told that Cliff Thompson, the young man who had befriended Dave on our first stop at that congregation three years before, had attended a VBS some years earlier and had brought his parents to the closing ceremonies. I knew, too, that his parents had subsequently been converted and his father later became an elder. So I knew that with God's power, many good things could come from that VBS.

~~~
~~~

Ike was having continued back pain and even spent a while in the hospital on base while the doctors vainly tried to diagnose the problem. Nothing came of it.

~~~

We had scouted out a violin teacher for the kids; so I was now driving all the way to Fort Walton Beach to take them to their lessons. Pat Chaffin, their teacher, had formed a Youth Orchestra, which gave some very good concerts. We were proud of their progress with the violin. The lessons, rehearsals, and concerts all took place in Fort Walton Beach, about 25 miles away through horrendous traffic; but I gamely played taxi driver, knowing that it would all pay off some day. I also knew that both kids were growing up and that we'd have them with us only a very few more years.

~~~

In February, Dave's Eighth Grade Bible class had a Valentine's Day party at our house. Though he naturally wanted the dress and food to be casual, I thought it was time these kids learned how to act on more polite occasions. I knew they all had nice clothes because they wore them on Sunday mornings to worship. I set my foot down (as only I can do!) and the party was "formal"—meaning that the girls wore dresses and the boys wore slacks, shirts, ties and jackets. We used the Rosenthal china, my wedding crystal, and the beautiful rosewood and bronze dinner service that Ike had sent from Thailand, as well as candles in the teakwood candlesticks. The camellias in our yard were just starting to bloom, when an unseasonable cold snap came along and stopped it. I was still able to garner enough to put a flower by each girl's plate. Fortunately, there was an equal number of girls and boys, about twelve or fourteen in all; so we alternated the seating, with Dave hosting at the head of the formal dining room table, a dinner bell placed by his plate to ring for service from the parents who had been pressed into service for the occasion. We parents ate in the huge family room, while we closed the doors into the dining room and gave the kids privacy. Some of them were a little stiff at first; but I think Dave was actually enjoying playing host; and the others loosened up after a while. Afterwards, they played parlor games in the den and all seemed to be having a good time. I think it was a time to remember for them. I know I enjoyed it, whether they did or not.

~~~

That June, Dave turned fourteen and was getting bigger and better looking every day; and the girls were starting to take an interest in him. But he had eyes for only one of them: Suzette. So did his two best friends. There was no dating going on yet; but they all hung around her at church and at every youth event. Donny Kesler encouraged all of the Eighth Graders to sit together with him down in the front of the auditorium at every Sunday Morning worship service. We liked that as we could keep an eye on Dave, and we knew that Donny wasn't going to let them get into too much trouble. Suzette would be one of the first to arrive in the auditorium after class and would sit in the very middle of the pew. Then others would fill in most of the pew on either side of her. Whichever two of those three Lotharios to arrive first would climb over everyone else on the pew to get to Suzette in the middle. Dave usually saw to it that he got one of the sides, and the other two boys had to battle it out over the other side. It was hilarious to watch them.

~~~

That summer nineteen-year-old Martha came to spend some time with the kids and me. We ordered up two exciting events for her: a moon shot and a hurricane.

Everyone knows about NASA's putting the first man on the moon on July 20th, 1969. We didn't have a very big TV set; but we had a pretty big crowd in our big den to watch that awe-inspiring event. It was hard to believe that we were watching history being made right before our eyes. I was sorry that Ike wasn't there to experience it with us.

~~~

Equally as exciting, but in a different way, was the arrival of the hurricane season. There is nothing unusual about the Florida coast's receiving numerous hurricane warnings, and we were sitting ducks for those whimsical phenomena of nature. But Hurricane Camille was really serious. All indications were that this one was headed right for Fort Walton Beach, just across Choctawhatchee Bay from Niceville and Val'P. We were down on the beach at Destin in the early stages of it. I'm here to tell you that those high waves and the rain and wind made a believer out of me; so we didn't stay long.

What a time for the Man of the House to be gone! But Ike had always called me a "Big Girl," and expected me to handle anything that came my way. He trusted that I would see to the welfare of the family and our property; and I wasn't going to let him down if I could help it.

It seemed that everything was happening at once in our household. Ann had her ninth birthday on August 22nd and celebrated with a "slumber" party with a few of her closest girlfriends. It goes without saying that I didn't get much sleep that night. The next morning I took some of the girls home, one of them being the Prisock girl. She lived with her mother, Edna, and four siblings in a trailer park while their father was in Viet Nam. Since Camille was continuing to brew up pretty strongly, I told Edna,

"If this hurricane gets worse, bring your kids and come over to my house. You shouldn't stay here in this trailer; it's dangerous."

"No, we'll be all right; but thanks anyway," she replied.

So we went on back home and started making all of the preparations that the media had been suggesting for the impending hurricane.

Also present in the house at that particular time were John and Kathy Parsons and his parents and teen-aged sister. John was a young
~~~

Airman, stationed at Eglin AFB, who was getting ready to be transferred to Udorn AB, Thailand, where Ike was. He and Kathy had been married over the Christmas holidays just eight months before and were a lovely couple. They had met in a chorus at college, both of them having fantastic voices. When we coerced them, they would sing popular songs for us, harmonizing beautifully. They spent a lot of time at our house and had stayed with Dave and Ann if I had to be away overnight. They had moved out of their apartment and his parents had come down to help them move. John took over the responsibilities of Man of the House and was directing the whole hurricane-preparation operation.

We filled as many G.I. cans as possible with water, in addition to the two bathtubs. We taped over the windows with masking tape. We brought in extra food, flashlight bulbs and anything else we thought we would need if stranded for several days. I actually cleared out the junk from the garage so that two cars could be parked there. (That turned out to be a mistake, as we were unable to open the door to the freezer we had out there.)

As the blowing and the media threats became worse, Edna Prisock called and said that maybe she'd better take me up on my offer. So she and her five children came over and joined the *menagérie*. That made a total of fifteen people on the bottom floor of the house (John had gotten it into his head that we shouldn't use the two bedrooms and bath on the upper floor). When bedtime came, Martha, Ann and I slept in my king-sized bed, with Dave and the Prisock boy in sleeping bags on the floor in the same room. Edna and one of her daughters slept on the double Hide-a-Bed in the living room with her other two girls on the floor. Between the five of them, the Parson clan slept on the double bed in the guest room and the Hide-a-Bed in the den, with possibly a sleeping bag for the girl; I can't remember.

As we turned in for the night, the winds were getting stronger and stronger; and the media were still promising that Camille would pay us a visit. Not that we got very much sleep, but when we awoke in the morning, it was to learn that, instead of coming to Florida, capricious Camille had decided to hit on the Mississippi Gulf coast, between Biloxi and Gulfport. A tremendous amount of damage was done, with much loss of life, including a lot of people who had laughed in Camille's face by deciding to hold a "Hurricane Party" in one of the beachside hotels and not evacuate as they were warned to do. The entire hotel had been demolished, as well as many of the stately old beachside homes I had always admired when driving along the coast. Plenty of wind and water damage occurred in our area (nothing major to our premises, thank Goodness); so I thought I could imagine what it was like in Mississippi.

When the time came for me to drive West to Louisiana and return Martha to her parents in Lake Charles, I couldn't drive along the coastal route, US 90 "The Old Spanish Trail," as I'd always done before, but had to go quite a bit farther North, through the middle of the state, because the roads were not passable along the coast. Even so, I was astonished at the damage I saw sporadically along the highway I traveled. Many trees were down, some still on the tops of houses and cars; while others remained almost bent double pointing northward, the direction the wind had taken. Southwestern Louisiana had gone through a similar experience with hurricane Audrey in 1956, with many lives having been lost; but the damage didn't cover nearly so wide an area as this. It was a long time before Mississippi recovered from the devastation; and I'm sure that those who lost family members and property never did completely recover.

~~~~

Ike was beginning to ship things home piecemeal from Thailand. He had bought the lovely carved teakwood chest and other items in Cheng Mai. I had just heard about them via letters and tapes, but was really enjoying having them show up. It was like Christmas almost every day there for a while.

December was not far away. I was wanting to surprise Ike with a recliner that was on sale. Not only did it recline, rock and swivel, but it had a massage unit for the lumbar region of the back, the very place Ike had always had problems. However, our finances were very tight, and we were keeping very close tabs on each other's use of the
~~~~

checkbook. So the question was: How do I get the recliner and have it ready for him by Christmas without his knowing about the expenditure? Solution: Go to work. So I applied for substitute teaching at Ruckle Junior High, Dave's school. Soon I began to be called with some frequency to teach English there. Fortunately, I never was called to teach Dave's English class. He was already embarrassed enough by my presence there. He came home from school my first day of teaching there, asking,

"Mom, is it true that you sent some kids to the office for being tardy?

"Why, yes," I answered. "Why?"

"Well, people are coming to me and telling me what a bear you are. Not only are you sending them to the office for being tardy, but you're also making them do English work. Everyone knows that when a substitute teacher comes, it's a holiday for the class."

How true it was! When I had taught before, I had become resigned to having no work turned in when I would leave lesson plans for a substitute to follow. Well, I had standards and wasn't going to change them just so my son wouldn't be embarrassed.

I continued substituting until I made enough money to buy the recliner, and then I quit. We had it delivered the day before Ike was to come home; and we hid it in one of the large storage rooms on either side of the bedrooms upstairs.

~~~

Ike flew commercial to Pensacola, fifty miles away. I got the kids out of school and we drove over there to meet him. Boy, was he a sight for sore eyes! He had barely been able to squeeze into his dress blues when he left a year before. Now, partly because of the long bicycle commute to work, he was tanned and slim and handsome—for a forty-one-year-old guy. I had laboriously lost several pounds myself and was wearing a beautiful cream-colored suit Mother had
~~~

tailored for me from some shantung Ike had sent home from Thailand. I guess, for a forty-year-old gal, I didn't look so bad myself. At least I had Ike fooled.

The official end of his military service took place at Eglin Air Force Base, right at our doorstep. We felt as though we lived right on base, since Charles Drive was right in the pattern for the planes landing there. (It had taken us only about two days' living there to learn to tune out the sound of aircraft.)

All of the formalities of his retirement having been taken care of, and just awaiting midnight of January 1, 1970, for it to be completely official, we took leave and traveled to Louisiana for the long-awaited reunion with our families.

Back in Florida, everyone at church was happy to see Ike and anxious for him to take on his new duties as Associate Minister of the congregation. We threw a huge retirement party for Ike on New Year's Eve, and nearly everyone in the congregation was able to be present. We were thankful we had bought a house with such a nice big room so that everyone could be in the same room at midnight.

Ike's Retirement Party – Midnight, January 1, 1970

~~~

This was a rather bittersweet occasion for us. We felt blessed to be among so many loved ones who had become so close to us during our 3-1/2 year acquaintance with them. At the same time, we were going to miss the Air Force. It was an organization that had taken us in and given us a large family. We had made friends literally all over the world, some of whom I am still in touch with today. We always felt secure, no matter how well or how poor the economy was doing, and even when hostilities were going on all over the world. We were in a better position than some to know that because of the United States' military might, people could lay their heads on their pillows at night and not have to worry about whether they would still have a pillow, or even a life, the next day. There were countries spanning the globe that were safe because the United States had come to their defense when they were threatened by totalitarianism.
~~~

For twenty years, six months and one day, Ike had been paid for doing what he loved to do most in the world—fly. His last flight record listed him as having flown 3,220.5 hours. Although by his own choice he hadn't flown his beloved fighter planes during that last assignment, he had even learned to respect and love the Gooney Bird he flew in Southeast Asia. It's true that, over the years, he had put himself at risk to help preserve peace all over the world; but he never looked at it that way. He always felt that the Air Force had taken good care of him and his family and would continue to do so. We used the slang expression, "It all goes toward twenty," as did everyone else in the Air Force when wanting to slough off. But in reality, that was never his attitude. Ike Hamilton gave the Air Force everything he had and felt that he had been well repaid and blessed.

1978 – Anne, 18; Anita, 49; Dave, 23; Ike, 50

Ike – Director of Housing, Harding University, 1979

Epilogue

1970-1972 – Ike serves Pine Lake Church of Christ, Niceville, FL, as Associate Minister

1971 – Lydia Blanche Hamilton Terrell, Ike's sister, dies in Jackson, MS

1972 – Martha Lynn Williams and James Batey Sigmund graduate from Harding College, Searcy, AR; marry in Lake Charles, LA

1972 – 1975 – Hamiltons serve as missionaries to Quito, Ecuador

1973 – Dave graduates from Alliance Academy High School, Quito; begins studies in Spanish and Bible at Harding College, Searcy, AR

1974 – Ike has orthopedic back surgery at Gorgas (US Dept. of Defense) Hospital, Panamá, Panamá; Hamiltons take furlough to US

1975 – Hamiltons return Stateside; move to Searcy, AR; Ann (now Anne) enrolls in Harding Academy, Searcy; is appointed Concert Mistress of Harding College Orchestra

1975-1981 – Anita works as Textbook Specialist, Harding College Bookstore

1976-1990 – Ike serves Harding University as Director of Housing

1976 – Dave Hamilton marries Jacquie Purdom in Searcy

1977 – Dave enlists in USAF; Ike has neuro-surgery on his back at VA Hospital, Little Rock, AR;; Dave and Jacquie graduate from Harding; Anne attends Brevard (NC) Summer Music Camp; Ike becomes co-coordinator of College church's student summer campaigns to USSR and Warsaw Pact countries

1978 – Ike makes first of ten evangelistic trips to USSR and Warsaw Pact countries; Milburn Lane Rivers, Anita's father, dies at age 77 in Baton Rouge, LA; Anne graduates from Harding Academy; marries Larry Bean in Searcy

1979 – Rachel Leigh Hamilton is born to Dave and Jacquie in Berlin, West Germany

1980 – Anita receives MEd degree in Spanish; Larry receives bachelor's in Bible and Biblical Studies from Harding University; Ike swears Dave in as 2nd Lt, USAF, San Antonio,

TX; Robert Allan Sigmund born to Martha & Jimmy Sigmund in Sherman, TX

1980-1992 – Anita teaches Spanish, French, Exploratory Languages and Cultures, and English as a Second Language at Harding Academy, Searcy

1981 – Jonathan Lane Hamilton born to Dave and Jacquie at Langley AFB, VA; Anita makes summer evangelistic trip to Honduras

1982 – Larry Everette Bean, Jr., born to Anne and Larry in Clinton, SC; Ike and Anita revisit Ecuador and Chile

1983 – Anita makes evangelistic trip to Barquisimeto, Venezuela; makes first of 12 evangelistic trips to USSR and Warsaw Pact countries; Adam David Bean born to Anne and Larry in Richmond, KY

1984 – Nicholas Lee Hamilton born to Dave and Jacquie at Fort Ord, CA

1985 – Ike expelled from USSR for "massive influence in teaching Soviet citizens about Jesus Christ"

1986 – Chernobyl, Ukraine, nuclear accident; Ike and Anita take Harding students on evangelistic trip to Nairobi, Kenya; Dave receives Master's degree in Soviet Studies from Naval Post Graduate School, Monterey, CA; Anita teaches adjunct French class at ASU-Beebe

1987 – Ike diagnosed with Failed Back Syndrome and Bi-Polar Disease; Ike and Anita make return trip to Ecuador, Chile, Honduras; James Cone Williams, Martha's father, dies in Lake Charles, LA

1988 – Anita makes evangelistic trips to San José, CR, and Caracas, Venezuela; Randall Hewitt Hamilton, Ike's brother, dies in Port Arthur, TX

1989 – Ike works in World Bible School follow-up campaign to South Africa; Anita in evangelistic campaign to Geneva, Switzerland. Both revisit Budapest, Hungary.

1990 – Ike retires from Harding University; Hamiltons and Harding students able to return to Russia and Estonia; Dave and Jacquie divorce; Dave marries Amy Parks

1990-1993 – Ike and Anita lead Harding campaigners in English Bible Schools in Pyatigorsk, Russia; Budapest, Szolnok, Miskolc and Debrecen, Hungary

1992 – Chloé Alexandra Hamilton born to Dave and Amy at Ft. Belvoir, VA; Dave separates from USAF; moves to Searcy; Anita retires from Harding Academy; William Lane Rivers, Anita's brother, dies in Houston, TX, at age 70

1993 - Alexander David Hamilton born to Dave and Amy in Searcy, AR

1994 – Ike has morphine pump implanted to control back pain; Jettie Opal Hickerson Rivers, Anita's mother, dies at age 89 in Searcy, AR

1996 – Trevor Michael Hamilton born to Dave and Amy in Searcy, AR

1996-1997 – Anita teaches Spanish as adjunct at Lyon College, Batesville, AR

1997 – Ike and Anita celebrate 49th anniversary on January 31st; Ike dies in Searcy, AR on February 1st—six days before his 69th birthday

1997 – Katelyn Veronica Díaz born to Rachel Hamilton and David Díaz in Cassville, MO

1997-1999 – Anita teaches Spanish and French as adjunct at Searcy High School

1997-2000 – Anita teaches Spanish as adjunct at Harding University, Searcy

1997-2001 – Anita makes four evangelistic trips to Ciego de Avila, Cuba

1998 – Madeline Floyd Hamilton Williams, Ike's sister and Martha's mother, dies in Dallas, TX; Anne graduates Summa Cum Laude with degree in Music Education from Arkansas Technical University, Russellville, AR

1999 – Jonathan Lane Hamilton graduates from Searcy High School

2000 – Anita makes evangelistic trip to Toluca, Mexico

2000 – Larry Bean, Jr., graduates from Paris, AR, High School, enters Harding University in Searcy

2001 – Twins Taylor David Lane Hamilton and Logan Isaac Madison Hamilton born to Dave and Amy in Fairfax, VA; Chloé

Hamilton illustrates Anita's book *Quaint Quatrains*; Jonathan Lane Hamilton married Cristina Joanna Talley in Searcy

2002 – Nick Hamilton graduates from Purdy, MO, High School; Adam Bean graduates from Clarksville, AR, High School, enters Arkansas Tech with full music scholarship; Dave and Amy adopt Olla, a 24-year-old Israeli woman; Dave and family move to Osan AB, Korea, with Department of Defense Schools; Anita makes evangelistic trip to Debrecen, Hungary

2002-2003 - Anita visits Dave and family at Osan AB, Korea

Ike Hamilton in His Sixties

Appendix

Air Force Abbreviations and Slang

ABGp - Air Base Group
AIC – Academic Instructor Course
ASAP – As Soon as Possible
Benelux Countries – Belgium/Netherlands/Luxembourg
Bird – Aircraft; plane
BOQ – Bachelor Officer Quarters
BX – Base Exchange (Department store on an AF base)
CO – Commanding Officer
COLA – Cost of Living Allowance
COMMISSARY – Military grocery store
DEROS – Rotation date
Det – Detachment
DFC – Distinguished Flying Cross
DOD – Department of Defense
ECI – Extension Course Institute
ETO – European Theater of Operations
Exec – Executive Officer; second in command
FBS/FBSq – Fighter Bomber Squadron
FBW/FBWg – Fighter Bomber Wing
FEAF – Far East Air Force
Flt – Flight (4 planes)
FSU – Florida State University, at Tallahassee
G – Gravity Force
GED – General Education Development
GI – General Issue, term coined in WWII that later came to be
    associated with soldiers/sailors/airmen
GI Bill – Bill passed by congress at end of WWII to help veterans go
    to college
Ground-Pounder – Non-rated (non pilot) Officer
Gung Ho – Avid; eager
Hold Baggage – Small amt of household belongings sent overseas to
    tide over until rest of household goods arrive
Hop – Space-Available flight on an AF plane

Hq – Headquarters
IP – Instructor Pilot
Jets – Jet-propelled aircraft
K ("Click") – Kilometer
LSU – Louisiana State University, at Baton Rouge
MAC – Military Air Cargo Command (cargo multis)
MARS – Military Air Radio Service
Mothballs – Permanent storage of obsolete aircraft
Multis – Multi-Engine planes
NATO – North Atlantic Treaty Organization
NCO – Non-commissioned Officer
OD – Olive Drab (Army uniform color)
OER – Officer Effectiveness Report
On the Economy – Not in AF provided quarters
Ops - Operations
OWC – Officers Wives Club
PAS – Professor of Air Science
PAST – Professor of Air Science and Tactics, former name of PAS
PCS – Permanent Change of Station
Pinks – Beige-colored army uniform pants or skirts
PIO – Public Information Officer
Port Call – Travel orders to go overseas
PTO – Pacific Theater of Operations
PX – Post Exchange – Department store on an Army post
Quad – Main part of the campus at the Air Force Academy
R&R – Rest and Recuperation
RAF – Royal Air Force
Rated – On flying status
Recips – Reciprocating-engine planes ("Prop jobs")
Recce – Reconnaissance
RF – Reconnaissance Fighter
Rotate – Return to the US from overseas
ROTC – Reserve Officer Training Corps
SAC – Strategic Air Command (Multis)
SLI – Southwestern Louisiana University, later U. of SW La, now
     Louisiana University-Lafayette
SNAFU – WWII acrostic for "Situation Normal, All Fouled-Up"
Socked in – Weathered in; weather too bad for flying

SODO – Senior Operations Duty Officer
SOP – Standard Operating Procedure
Sortie – Individual flight mission
SOS – Squadron Officer School; formerly Squadron Officer Course (SOC)
SQ – Squadron (several flights make a squadron)
Stand Down – Stop flying
T – Trainer
TAC – Tactical Air Command (fighters)
T-Bird – T-33, two-seated jet aircraft used for training purposes
TDY – Temporary Duty
TNG – Training
TO – Take-off
USAF – United States Air Force (formerly US Army Air Corps)
USAFE – United States Allied Forces-Europe
USAFI – United States Armed Forces Institute
VFR – Visual Flight Regulations
VOQ – Visiting Officer Quarters
WG – Wing (made up of several squadrons)
WWII – World War II
ZI – Zone of Interior

Ike and Anita Hamilton, 1993

8 of the 11 Hamilton Grandchildren, 1996
Adam Bean, Nick Hamilton
Rachel and Trevor Hamilton; Larry Bean and Chloé Hamilton; Lane
and Alex Hamilton

About the Author

A retired language teacher, Anita Hamilton lives in Searcy, Arkansas. Her late pilot husband spent two decades in the Air Force, serving in two wars.

In between visits to her two children, Anita serves on her church's missions, Spanish and jail ministries.

She has published three other books: *Quaint Quatrains: Childhood As Seen Through the Eyes of One Much Older and Now More Wise*, a book of poems; *Flexibility, Flexibility, Flexibility*, a tongue in cheek look at mission work; and *Entre Hermanas*, a Bible study for Spanish-speaking Christians – also translated into English.

Among Anita's interests are writing children's stories and puppet scripts, researching her geneology, reading and watching mysteries, working crossword puzzles and knitting for her eleven grandchildren and her great-granddaughter.

www.ingramcontent.com/pod-product-compliance
Lightning Source LLC
Chambersburg PA
CBHW032058050726
47590CB00001B/324